TEACHING TO DIVERSITY

The Three-Block Model of Universal Design for Learning

Jennifer Katz

Foreword by Faye Brownlie

PORTAGE & MAIN PRESS

Portage & Main Press gratefully acknowledges the financial support of the Province of Manitoba through the Department of Sport, Culture and Heritage and the Manitoba Book Publishing Tax Credit, and the Government of Canada through the Canada Book Fund (CBF) for our publishing activities.

Printed and bound in Canada by Friesens
Cover and interior design by Relish New Brand Experience Inc.

Permission Acknowledgment
The publisher has made every effort to acknowledge all sources that have been used in this book and would be grateful if any errors or omissions were pointed out so they may be corrected in subsequent editions.

Credits for screen shots on pages 60–61—Manitoba Education, Citizenship and Youth. *Grade 7 Social Studies: People and Places in the World: A Foundation for Implementation.* Winnipeg, MB: Manitoba Education, Citizenship and Youth, 2006. Reproduced with permission.

Library and Archives Canada Cataloguing in Publication

Katz, Jennifer

    Teaching to diversity : the three-block model of universal design for learning / Jennifer Katz.

Includes bibliographical references.
Issued also in electronic format.
ISBN 978-1-55379-353-3

    1. Inclusive education. 2. Social learning. I. Title.

LC1200.K38 2012   371.9'046   C2012-903936-5

23 22 21 20   5 6 7 8 9

 **PORTAGE & MAIN PRESS**

1-800-667-9673
www.portageandmainpress.com
Winnipeg, Manitoba
Treaty 1 Territory and homeland of the Métis Nation

FSC
www.fsc.org
MIX
Paper from responsible sources
FSC® C016245

Dedication

To Jorel, whose journey has shown more wisdom, insight, and resilience than we will ever know, and to all the children—past, present, and future—who have taught me more than I can ever teach them, thank you for your many gifts, with a prayer for a more peaceful and loving world for you to grow up in.

Table of Contents

Portage & Main Press, 2012, *Teaching to Diversity*, ISBN: 978-1-55379-353-3

Foreword

For many years I have believed that, as teachers, we each need to have a mental model for learning, a model that we can articulate and apply to our everyday work of teaching and learning in classrooms, a model that we can use when collaborating with our colleagues to improve learning opportunities for all our students. Without this personal model, we can too easily be swayed by slick packaging, charismatic speakers, teacher-proof programs, out-of-school directives, and the proclamation "evidence-based." We are working in challenging times: teachers have never had more choices; at the same time, we have never had more diverse students in our classrooms; nor have we or our students ever had such easy and rapid access to information. How do we balance the demands on our time and attention? How do we make the wise choices that best inspire student learning?

Enter the voice of Dr. Jennifer Katz. She is a passionate educator. She cares deeply about making a difference in the lives of her students, which is clear from the outset in her book, *Teaching to Diversity*. She presents her model of what counts in learning, and describes what she as a teacher does in order to cultivate this learning—for all students—in inclusive classrooms. Peppered throughout the text are vignettes of complex students who have pushed her thinking. We can all identify with these students—we have met them and others in our own classrooms. And thus we begin our journey to discover the "three-block model" of "universal design for learning" (UDL), a model based on accessibility and choice, on discovering students' talents and needs, and on linking them explicitly to key curriculum goals.

In my model of learning, UDL and "backwards design" are the organizing frameworks. To this model, Jen adds the lens of "multiple intelligences" (MI) and MI centres. Block One is the backbone of her UDL model. Naming it "social and emotional learning," she centres it on building community. Who can argue with the premise that all learners learn better when they know themselves, respect themselves, are resilient, and embrace an inclusive classroom that values diversity? In her classroom, each school year opens with her "respecting diversity" (RD) program, a sequence of nine easy-to-follow lessons to develop self-awareness and other-awareness in students. The RD program uses MI not only to help teachers teach or students learn more effectively, but also to build community in the classroom, creating a bond among students that moves that community forward, not just the individuals within it. The implications of this are considerable. Curriculum is designed to connect to the lives and interests of the students. Also in Block One is curriculum design, following a "backwards design" model.

Portage & Main Press, 2012, *Teaching to Diversity*, ISBN: 978-1-55379-353-3

Knowledge of the curriculum is critical; planning is key; learning is organized in large chunks—term-by-term, built from integrated curricula, grouped learning outcomes, essential questions, and inquiry. Lessons move from modelling, through guided practice in centres, to individual performance. While the approach may initially seem daunting, it is based on the premise that teachers are professionals, and as professionals, they are prepared to personally and collectively design the work they will do with their students.

Block Two, Inclusive Instructional Practice, is presented in two chapters, including a sampling of specific lessons to teach collaboration. If all students are to belong and learn in the classroom, then all participants in the classroom must actively work on including others, by helping others be the best they can be at all times. In Block Three, Systems and Structures, the focus is outside the classroom itself, and considers how we can better work together to improve learning for all students. Specific examples of what administrators have done in schools to support teacher collaboration and inclusive education are presented.

I believe that all students can learn. I also believe that we, collaboratively, have the skill and the knowledge to teach all students—and the responsibility to do so. This belief resonates throughout *Teaching to Diversity*. Repeatedly, reference is made to creating and maintaining a compassionate classroom, a classroom where students learn that they are stronger and smarter together, and that all voices count. Special attention is called to First Nations learners and to our responsibility to improve learning for them.

Jen has a clear vision of her mental model. She offers it to us, to continue to add to our own models and to make a greater difference in the learning and the lives of all our students. You may not agree with all that Jen says, but she is sure to cause you to ponder and reflect upon your teaching—and isn't that what professionalism and learning are all about?

—*Faye Brownlie*

Acknowledgments

I would like to thank Faye Brownlie, a friend and mentor, who, after co-teaching in my classroom, urged me to make the move to the university and to write this book, helped me find a publisher, and took time out of a hectic schedule to write the Foreword. I am grateful for her time, her wisdom, and her support. To Myra Laramee, who spent beautiful summer afternoons cloistered with me in her living room, sharing her experiences and her expertise, *Megwetch*. To all the Portage & Main staff—Annalee, Catherine, Marcela—and my editor Jean, thanks for supporting my passion and perfectionism, and for persevering!

Thank you to the Faculty at the University of Manitoba, in particular, Zana, Charlotte, Rick, John, and Bob, who both formally and personally have supported this work. To Alan Schroeder, John Van Walleghem, Karen Priestly, Ron Sugden, Joan Zaretsky, Terry Price, Bobbi Ethier, my graduate students, and all the members of the Manitoba Alliance for Universal Design for Learning, the Manitoba First Nations Education Resource Centre, and the Canadian Research Centre for Inclusive Education, who have taken on this work and helped disseminate it—thank you.

I am profoundly grateful to all my colleagues who opened their doors and shared their classrooms and students with me. Your dedication to the well-being of "our kids" is inspiring. I hope this book brings support, inspiration, and joy to your teaching.

To all the family, friends, mentors, and spiritual teachers who have guided my spirit, nurtured my heart, and enlightened my soul, my heartfelt thanks. A special thank you to Reb Zalman, Reb Nadya, Reb Shefa, and Reb Victor for helping me to connect my past with my present, and my spiritual life with my profession, I am eternally grateful. I have been blessed with a sisterhood of incredible women who have mentored, nurtured, and prodded me to grow and learn. To Gina Rae, Ida Ollenberger, Kathyrn D'Angelo, Marion Porath, and Pat Mirenda, my thanks for your love, your support, and your ability to extend my thinking and pose the right questions. To my sister, Vivi, my soul mate, David, and to my soul sisters Lisa, Andi, and Dafna, there are no words for what your friendship and support mean to me. This work would not exist but for you.

This project, as with all of what I do and how I live, is dedicated to the two guiding women in my life: my aunt Sheila, who introduced me to my love for special children and gave me the confidence to believe I could make a difference, and my mother who for forty-five years has dried my tears, listened to my stories, and shown me how to live life with love, integrity, compassion, service, and spirit. I do my best to share your legacy.

Introduction
Student/Teacher Vignettes

T.

In December of 1996, in my first year as a learning assistance teacher, my principal walked into my office, plunked a thick file on my desk, and said, "He'll be here in January. Do something." That night, with a cup of tea in hand, I read the contents of the file, a biography of another lost child. His file, I would realize years later, told an all too common story, but at the time, I had no idea how far along my own professional journey this child would move me.

From the file, I could see that T. was officially in grade 6, and was by heritage half African-American, half Caucasian. The early records noted that he was verbally precocious and mechanically adept, and he had challenged adults immediately, even in his kindergarten year. His teachers, confused by his ability to express advanced ideas and concepts articulately, mistook his difficulties with short-term memory as a negative attitude when he would reply to questions with a shrug and say, "I don't know."

Although he could take apart and put back together any electronic device, he could not do the same with words. By grade 3, he was on a modified educational program. Dressed as a rapper with a hood pulled low over his head, he covered his challenges with a fast retort, verbal inflections down pat. And yet, his grade 4 teacher had noted that he was deeply sensitive, that he would offer insightful and empathetic responses to stories in which a child struggled with discrimination, loss, or other emotional stress. No formal testing had been done; however, T. had attended many small-group intervention programs, all with little success.

Behavioural goals around anger management began to appear in his IEP, and by grade 5, could be summarized by the idea that as long as he didn't hurt anyone, he could choose to go, and do, where and what he wanted. He had spent his time with an educational assistant playing educational games on a computer, shooting hoops in the gym, and drawing cartoons. He had neither participated in, nor received a mark for math in two years.

Cole

T.'s file reminded me of Cole, another student I had been puzzling over that year. Cole's test results showed him to be in the 92nd percentile of performance IQ and in the 34th percentile for verbal ability. Although he was unable to retell a story in sequence, he could easily state the main idea of the passage and was able to give sophisticated abstract and inferential answers to comprehension questions. He could tell you that the theme of a book was about discrimination, but could not describe the main events.

Portage & Main Press, 2012, *Teaching to Diversity*, ISBN: 978-1-55379-353-3

Cole struggled with the concept of sequencing — of the beginning, middle, and end of events or of stories. For instance, in one of his stories, he ended each page with "and they lived happily ever after," confusing the end of the page with the end of the story. He could tell you that the character was suffering from depression, but could not use ordinary details to describe the character.

Cole's spatial skills were phenomenal. He could solve every manner of visual puzzle (e.g., Rubik's cube, the 3-D game of pentominoes), but his drawings looked like those of a 3-year-old. He built amazing replicas of buildings and ancient wonders out of scraps, but could not write a factual report. Cole could spout poetry off the top of his head, only shrugging when asked where the ideas came from, but when he wrote a poem down, it was illegible even to him. He knew enormous amounts of trivia, especially about spiders and sorcerers, but he could not remember how to spell basic sight words.

Emotionally, Cole had great difficulty controlling his moods: sometimes, he could be excited and overly silly; at other times, when he was frustrated or upset, he referred to his evil twin, Ole, as "taking him over." Cole said, "Ole lives in a mental institution; you know, that place where crazy people go." When asked whether he felt that he was crazy, he said, "Oh, yes. Crazy just means different from normal." On bad days, he would descend into crying and sometimes escalate into withdrawal and depressive or suicidal statements like "I wish I was dead" or "God is mean. He made school." He would mumble under his breath about hating school, hating "my life," and wishing God never invented him or school. Cole showed high anxiety when presented with social or written tasks. He would often begin crying and pull his shirt over his head, telling familiar adults that he was "just nervous."

Author's Note

The stories of T. and Cole were the reason for beginning my journey into universal design for learning (UDL). Soon, my interactions with diverse students became the impetus behind the development of my Three-Block Model of UDL. As my readers explore the chapters of this book that set out the rationale and criteria for the model, they will encounter more student/teacher vignettes, bearing the pseudonyms of students whose stories illustrate the value of developing compassionate learning communities and incorporating the principles of UDL in their classrooms, schools, and education systems.

Portage & Main Press, 2012, *Teaching to Diversity*, ISBN: 978-1-55379-353-3

Chapter 1
Diversity in Education

T. and Cole faced severe challenges in literacy skills, but had unusual strengths in areas not emphasized in school curricula. Like many students in our schools today, they had talents that are valued in the real world but, in school, they were made to feel like failures. Their families had been told their children had severe learning disabilities, were not at grade level, and had behaviour problems. Both had tried to fit in, but failed. One had externalized and become a behaviour problem. The other had internalized and become withdrawn. The oldest was 11 years old, the other 8, yet they were already casualties of the system.

When I taught in a Jewish private school, my class was about as homogeneous as it is possible to find: the children all came from one ethnic group, were all Caucasian, all middle-class or above, and they all had English as their first language. Nevertheless, some students learned best when they could see the teacher model a process first, while others had to work out the process for themselves in order to understand. Some students could remember the words to a song, but not to a poem. A few students needed quiet time in order to learn; some had to talk aloud with other students in order to clarify their thinking. The students' background knowledge about any topic introduced also varied—some had travelled there, seen that, had a parent who worked in the field; others hadn't a clue. There were children whose families were in distress, children who weren't getting enough sleep, children who were depressed. No matter where you teach, no matter what age group you teach, diversity will exist in the classroom.

Diversity Defined

It is important that we all recognize that *diversity* does not refer only to children with exceptional needs, nor does it refer only to ethnic, racial, or linguistic diversity. Diversity encompasses all children—their diverse personalities, ethnicities, languages, family structures, and learning styles all contribute to the makeup of a diverse classroom. Even a group of so-called typical learners from Caucasian, middle-class families are diverse in how they learn best.

Diversity is neurological. Diversity is societal. Diversity is human. Teaching to diversity requires that teachers create a learning climate in the classroom and devise activities that allow all children to feel safe, respected, and valued for what they have to contribute. Poet Carl Sandburg, when asked what he thought was the ugliest word in the English language, answered *exclude*, adding "Everyone wants to belong."

Portage & Main Press. 2012. *Teaching to Diversity*, ISBN: 978-1-55379-353-3

Diversity and Social and Emotional Learning

In recent years, education systems in both Canada and the United States have undergone significant reforms, one of which is the movement toward inclusive education which places children of diverse racial, cultural, and linguistic backgrounds, socioeconomic status, and learning abilities together in regular classrooms. To teach such a range of individual students in one classroom, we must build a compassionate learning community that recognizes the deeper needs of all people, including a sense of safety, a sense of belonging, and the feeling of being part of something meaningful. Such a learning community leads participants to lifelong understanding of who they are, why they are here, and what they have to contribute (Palmer 2007).

Learning cannot be separated from living. The human mind cannot learn when overcome with a sense of anxiety, alienation, and stress (Grover, Ginsburg, and Ialongo 2007). To build a less violent and more compassionate world, we need to nurture a deeper sense of self in our children while expanding their ability to empathize with and value diverse others (Miller 1998/99). Parker Palmer describes a "system of education so fearful of things spiritual that it fails to address the real issues of our lives—dispensing facts at the expense of meaning, information at the expense of wisdom. The price is a school system that alienates and dulls us" (1998/99, 6).

Spotlight

The Collaborative for Academic, Social & Emotional Learning (CASEL) has many valuable resources related to social and emotional learning on their website — http://casel.org/

At the same time, the demand to prepare students to be "knowledge workers in a globalized world" apparently means expanded curricula, technological knowledge and skills, and higher literacy rates than ever before. Teachers struggle to balance the demands on time and energy, both their own and that of their students. To combat alienation and the increasing rates of depression, substance abuse, and suicide (Modrcin-McCarthy and Dalton 1996) and at the same time meet academic and curricular demands, schools must explore instructional frameworks that integrate a spiritual paradigm within academic learning.

By *spiritual*, I do not mean *religious*. Rather, I use it to mean teaching to the heart as well as to the mind, exploring the deeper meanings of what we learn, connecting with the community we learn and live with, and coming to know ourselves. In his book *The Courage to Teach* (2007), Parker Palmer describes such spiritual questions as "Does my life have meaning and purpose?" "Do I have gifts that the world wants and needs?" and contrasts them with such discipline-specific questions as: "Why does a historian care about the dead past?" and "Why does a biologist care about mute nature?" The answers always lie within our relationships to ourselves, our community, and our world. It is within this wide-ranging form of inquiry learning that compassionate classrooms evolve.

Education Defined

In the Merriam-Webster Dictionary online, *education* is described as deriving from the Latin root *educare* which means *to rear* or *to lead forth*. *To teach*, however, is

Portage & Main Press, 2012, *Teaching to Diversity*, ISBN: 978-1-55379-353-3

defined as *to cause to know, to know how; to show how; to guide; to make to know the consequences of*. It appears that *education* includes more than instruction in academic subjects; and *teaching* includes more than just content delivery. Education must develop the whole child and cultivate all the skills, attitudes, and knowledge necessary for a person's successful integration into society. Inclusive practices that aim to educate students in the full sense of that word must promote their social, emotional, and physical development in addition to their academic achievement.

In recent years we have witnessed a growing proportion of school-age children demonstrating social-emotional behavioural problems that interfere with their relationships, their academic achievement, and their potential to be contributing members of their community (Greenberg, Domitrovich, and Bumbarger 2000). This and other recent findings indicate that schools are among the most effective socialization institutions in our culture, and among the most influential in guiding the social and emotional learning of elementary school children (Schonert-Reichl, Smith, Zaidman-Zait, and Hertzman 2011).

Schools provide a unique opportunity for encouraging the development of social competence because many of the students' interpersonal interactions occur in a setting in which adults can intervene and, thus, foster positive growth and development. A growing number of studies suggest that children's social and emotional learning can be fostered by intervention efforts in classrooms and schools (Graczyk et al. 2000; Greenberg et al. 2001). Given the data indicating the rising rate of children at risk (Greenberg et al. 2001), school-based programs and instructional paradigms that develop all children's social and emotional learning must be a priority for educational researchers and teachers.

Social Inclusion and Social Exclusion

Social inclusion or exclusion has become a rising concern around the world. Organizations like Ontario's Laidlaw Foundation advocate for and conduct research on marginalized populations in Canada, in particular recently, on children and youth at risk. Research studies they have conducted note the rising number of Canadian children living in poverty, suffering from hunger, and excluded from opportunities to fully realize their potential.

Spotlight

For more information, visit www.laidlawfdn.org/working-paper-series-social-inclusion

Social inclusion recognizes the need that all people have for belonging, for acceptance, and for opportunities to participate fully and equally in economic, social, cultural, and political institutions. Inclusion also means recognizing and valuing diversity, engendering feelings of belonging that lead to social equality through the participation of diverse populations, including the disadvantaged. In education, at all levels, the terms *inclusion* and *inclusive* are used increasingly to mean that all students have the opportunity to learn and grow in learning communities alongside their peers.

The United Nations, through the *Universal Declaration of Human Rights*, and Canada, through the *Canadian Charter of Rights and Freedoms*, make *equality* a constitutional right—yet, in practice, schools on Aboriginal reserves are terribly underfunded (Wotherspoon 2002), which makes it difficult to hire qualified teachers, to purchase resources such as computers and multi-levelled books, and to provide specialized services to children with exceptional needs. Despite the policies of inclusiveness in every province and territory, more than half of the children with disabilities spend more than half of their learning time outside of the regular classroom (Canadian Council on Learning 2007).

UN: www.un.org/en/documents/udhr
CDN: http:laws-lois.justice.gc.ca/eng/charter

Schools have a key role to play in ensuring that all students receive the education that will enable them to become thoughtful, caring, and productive citizens, where they have the opportunity to explore the gifts of diversity and learn to relate with diverse others while reflecting on the gifts they have been given. Inclusive schools offer students the experience and enrichment of learning first-hand about other cultures, races, and languages. It is a powerful experience to see how a student with disabilities perseveres through challenges to overcome them and contribute to the world. In human history, segregation has never been a positive—for anyone. So how do we create truly inclusive schools? According to the Laidlaw Foundation, there are five criteria for successful social inclusion (Wotherspoon 2002).

1. **Valued Recognition:** Conferring recognition and respect on individuals and groups.

2. **Human Development:** Nurturing the talents, skills, capacities, and choices of children and adults to live a life they value and to make a contribution that both they and others find worthwhile.

3. **Involvement and Engagement:** Having the right and the necessary support to make, or be involved in, the decisions affecting oneself, one's family and one's community, and to be engaged in community life.

4. **Proximity:** Sharing physical and social spaces to provide opportunities for interactions, if desired, and to reduce social distances between people.

5. **Material Well-Being:** Having the material resources to allow children and their parents to participate fully in community life.

Let's briefly explore each of these from a teacher's point of view. When we consider the first criterion, we must ask ourselves how we can help students to value themselves as well as others; that entails having roles that are valued—socially and academically. In chapter 3, we discuss the "respecting diversity" (RD) program for ways of addressing the issue of equality in roles.

When we examine the second criterion, human development, in a school setting, we need to recognize that all students are diverse in the ways in which and the rates at which they learn—emotionally, physically, and intellectually.

In my opinion, the third category, involvement and engagement, is the key to identifying the ways in which teachers can support student learning in school settings. All students must become involved and engaged in both the social and the academic life of the classroom. Being included in the classroom, but being asked to sit at the back of the room with an educational assistant is not real inclusion, neither is being enrolled in a separate classroom or learning assistance centre and just visiting a regular classroom, or working on a modified program in a regular classroom.

The fourth criterion is proximity. When some students are in a separate room down the hall or in the basement, they cannot learn and grow together—and here we are making the most progress. Many schools have begun to place students with disabilities, students who are learning English, and other marginalized populations in classrooms together, if only physically—however, it's a beginning.

The fifth and final criterion, material resources, is the most difficult one for teachers to resolve because the lack of resources is grounded in issues of poverty and marginalization. Students who come to school having not slept or eaten struggle to learn. Students who are witness to or victims of violence have levels of stress and trauma that affect their brains and their capacity to learn. Students who don't have school supplies or access to books or computers at home are at a disadvantage relative to students who may come from literary and intellectual environments. Such disadvantages affect their literacy, background knowledge, and general cognitive development. Even amid funding cuts, many schools do what they can to address such needs: hot breakfast and lunch programs, head-start and early literacy programs, adult literacy programs, and homework clubs are just a few of the community-based services that schools try to provide.

Teachers can also bridge the gap by relying on the concept of "cultural capital." Cultural capital is what parents hand down to their children—experiences with literature, language, field trips, travel, and intellectual discussion of beliefs and values, languages, and relationships. We can become more inclusive by valuing what our students do bring—their languages, experiences, talents, and cultural richness. More and more children's books are written in a variety of voices, featuring characters who come from a wide range of cultural backgrounds. We have both fiction and nonfiction literature that honours a variety of cultures, celebrations, and nations. Many teachers who have a significant proportion of Aboriginal students in their class seek out such literature—all of us could do so and enrich everyone's classroom. The more we share what the diversity in our classroom and society offers us, the more we bring people together.

We can also intervene early, consistently, and intensively with children who lack such cultural capital. Programs for the Early Years should immerse children in language, literacy, and community experiences—we cannot assume that they have ever been to a museum, to the seashore, to a play in a theatre, or even on a trip outside the place where they live. In the Early Years (ages 3, 4, and 5), direct teaching of pre-reading skills, social register, and voice is crucial. And reading many, many books to children while teaching them what a book is—that it holds a story, that the words of the story are in the black squiggly lines that we read going from left to right—can help deprived children catch up to those children who have been read to since they were babies. It is very difficult for a young child, upon entering grade one, to be asked questions about a story when the child has never before heard the language and syntax of a story.

In the Middle Years, students still need to learn about voice and social register. We can teach them usage labels such as "school language" and "social language" without devaluing how they communicate with their friends, family, and community. Children need to learn how to switch back and forth, just as they do when they switch from talking to a buddy to talking to their mom or dad. Even in secondary school, students from disadvantaged populations do not have the networks that many other students do to help them find that first job, explore career possibilities, and so on. Schools can play a role in helping the kids who do not have similar connections by providing career fairs, work experience courses, visits, and mentorships with educators in postsecondary settings and professionals in the field.

Social inclusion involves sharing the wealth, which does not mean taking from one group to give to another. I believe all children have the right to feel good about themselves and about what they contribute, to experience a sense of belonging as well as the joy of learning and connecting with others, and to have many doors opened through which they might choose to walk. We are a wealthy country, and there is enough for everyone. It can be done.

Diversity and Academic Complexity

When I speak to teachers, I ask them what the hardest part of their job is. Inevitably they say, "Teaching to the range of students." By that they mean "delivering a complex curriculum to a group of students with diverse academic abilities." The education system used to offer a simple answer—we streamed kids and, gradually, we excluded them. In the early years, kids learned together but as their talents became evident, we quickly placed them into ability groups, sometimes as early as grade one (reading groups, for instance). In later decades, we kept kids in school, but sent them to streamed classes, vocational training, and learning assistance centres, based on our beliefs about intelligence and learning. We modified their programs so that they worked on math when the other kids did, but theirs was a separate math curriculum, usually practice activities on worksheets under the supervision of an educational assistant. This meant that the neediest learners were being taught by the least trained people and involved in the most rote pencil-and-paper styles of learning.

The learners who were advanced in some way were also streamed or excluded, that is, sent to advanced placement and international baccalaureate programs, or gifted classes and other enriched opportunities. Such classes might be intellectually stimulating, but they are also socially isolating and frequently less culturally diverse. As a result, recently, the move toward inclusive education has grown beyond its roots in social justice into an awareness of the need for inclusion at all academic levels.

Portage & Main Press, 2012, *Teaching to Diversity*, ISBN: 978-1-55379-353-3

Academic Inclusion and Academic Exclusion

Academic inclusion in education is an approach to educating all students together. Under the inclusion model, all students are placed in their home schools, and services are delivered in the classrooms and in the school. The classroom teacher takes primary responsibility for all students enrolled in the class. Inclusive education differs from previous models of integration or mainstreaming, which were concerned principally with disability and the needs of special education students. But *inclusion* is not just about children with special needs; it is concerned with all students accessing their right to the very best education regardless of race, religion, language, socioeconomic status, sexual orientation, or disability.

Earlier models presumed that students "earned" an education, when they were "ready" to be given the privilege of entering the school and their classroom. We kept them in separate settings, ostensibly to get them ready, which few ever did. In contrast, *inclusion* is based on the assumption that all children have the right to be a part of the life of the classroom—socially and academically, and that schools need to create programs that accommodate and celebrate this diversity. In other words, we fit the program to the kids, not the kids to the program.

Academic *exclusion* refers to denying the opportunity for an education, in the fullest sense of the word, to some individuals or groups of students:

1. the denial of enrolment in neighbourhood schools
2. the lack of exposure to curriculum and instructional activities
3. the absence of interactions with qualified teaching personnel and services
4. the separation from peers during learning activities

For many years, some students were denied enrolment in their neighbourhood school. If a brother or sister could attend that school but the disabled child could not, that was discrimination, pure and simple. Imagine how it felt for them to see their siblings off to the neighbourhood school, while they had to be bussed to another school.

As regards lack of exposure to curriculum content, I worked in a room with eight students who each had one of the autism spectrum disorders (ASD). For their lessons, we did not include Shakespeare, or world events, or chemistry experiments; instead, we spent a lot of time on vocational training, functional math, and basic literacy. One of the students from that class, an adult now, is attending the university in which I teach—in spite of us, not because of us. When he found me and walked into my office 16 years later, he told me the day of my birthday (in that earlier class, he had memorized everybody's birthday), and sat down to chat. Perry, as I will call him, was always capable of far more than we bothered to teach him, but we were too busy managing behaviour and focusing on life skills to see it.

Time and time again as I have worked in inclusive systems, I think back to those kids in special education and wonder "What if?" I hear teachers who work in segregated classrooms say, "Well, my kids are too low for ... that (whatever that is)" and I shudder because I would have said the same thing some years ago,

Portage & Main Press, 2012, *Teaching to Diversity*, ISBN: 978-1-55379-353-3

but I was wrong and so are they. In that class, we had students who entered the program at age 6; some were nonverbal and some not toilet-trained, so the belief was that they were "low functioning." In contrast, I more recently had a student named Peter with a similar profile in my first school in a "full inclusion" district. Peter had entered kindergarten as nonverbal, not toilet-trained, and rocking and flipping his hands. By the time he was in grade 7, he was the lead in the school play. Was he cured? Of course not, but he could read and write, he had an excellent memory, he loved video games, and he could communicate with his parents and his friends—a demonstration of the power of peer modelling, which has been greatly underestimated in special education.

A downside to inclusive educational programs is that, in the transition, we have sent children into inclusive classrooms without having provided enough professional training for the classroom teachers and resource teachers, but with educational assistants for children with special needs. The lack of training meant that many teachers believed that the EAs knew their assigned child best so they handed over responsibility for their program—to staff who are not trained teachers. We must get better at building capacity in our classroom teachers, and we must make clear their job is to teach all the students in their classroom, and I do mean all. Not only are students with disabilities often being taught by untrained personnel, they are also segregated from interacting with, and learning from, their typical peers—a situation that has serious outcomes, for all involved.

In the early days of the inclusion movement, arguments for it were often made on the basis of social justice, which has led some to believe, unfortunately, that children with special needs are in school just to be socialized and that, as long as they're happy and maybe even have a friend, we've done our job. All children should be happy and have friends, but they can do that at home or in the community. All kids come to school in order to learn. Recent research shows us that many children, previously deemed unable to learn, greatly exceed our expectations when given appropriate educational opportunities and peer models (Crisman 2008). Individuals and groups have often been academically excluded when they were assumed to be, and then deemed to be, incapable of learning at a chosen standard.

Philosophically, most teachers agree that inclusion is the right thing to do. However, saying so does not eliminate the challenges that inclusion poses. How do you teach reading in a classroom where some students are reading complex novels while others still can't decode fluently and still others don't even speak English adequately well? How do you teach math when some students have had after-school tutoring and can compute faster than the classroom desktop, and others don't know what division is? How do you teach about ecosystems when some students have travelled around the world with their biologist parents and others have never seen snow, planted a garden, or been to the seashore? And how do you deliver an increasingly complex and varied curriculum while supporting students' social and emotional well-being? How can we set up our classrooms in such a way that all students learn, play, and grow together—in celebration of their diversity, not in spite of it?

Portage & Main Press, 2012, *Teaching to Diversity*, ISBN: 978-1-55379-353-3

There is a way, although not to solve all of society's ills. It's not a perfect panacea, but it is do-able, it is efficient, and it won't have you on stress leave by October. One way to educate (in the full sense of the word) diverse children is in one classroom together. It can be done, and this book pulls together, in an organized way, the key pieces of what I have learned and implemented over the past fifteen years on my journey to explore and implement a "universal design for learning" framework that includes all students in compassionate learning communities. I hope it helps you.

Portage & Main Press, 2012, *Teaching to Diversity*, ISBN: 978-1-55379-353-3

Chapter 2
A Framework for Teaching to Diversity

The concept of universal design comes from the field of architecture. In the late 1980s and early 1990s, architects were exploring the concept of accessibility to accommodate people with physical disabilities. Retrofitting buildings with ramps or elevators was not cost-effective, nor was there the space or time to do it effectively. Because building entrances are an important feature of the design, architects want to provide a specific experience for those entering the building. They design entrances to evoke a particular emotional experience, or to have people learn something upon entry about the purpose of the building—for instance, the grandeur of a hotel lobby or the stark efficiency of a bank. When people in wheelchairs have to enter from a side entrance or the back door, as often happens with retrofitting, they are denied the intended experience.

Architects began to push for buildings to be designed so that all people could enter a structure at the same point, if not in the same way. The term *universal design* was coined by Ronald Mace, an architect who challenged traditional architects to better attend to the needs of all people rather than design for only the able-bodied. As architects began to do so, they discovered that many people benefited from the additional options. In the Vancouver airport, for example, people can enter the building using an elevator, an escalator, a ramp, or stairs. All points of entry converge in the same place.

Although a ramp was originally meant for people with disabilities to use, it also serves parents with strollers, travellers with rollerboard suitcases, and many others who, at times, cannot negotiate a flight of steps. Ramped curbs are another excellent example of access initially designed to allow people in wheelchairs a degree of independence in travelling around the city. But many unintended populations benefited—parents with strollers, kids on skateboards, the elderly. All enjoyed the advantages of the new design, and the experience of those capable of stepping up onto the curb was not diminished. This concept is key to the transfer of universal design to education.

Universal Design for Learning (UDL)

Universal design is, I believe, the concept that can help make inclusive education work. The question is: "How do we provide accessibility to the learning, the curriculum,

Portage & Main Press, 2012, *Teaching to Diversity*. ISBN: 978-1-55379-353-3

and the social life of the classroom for diverse learners without taking away from the experience of those who can step up onto the curb?" In other words, how do we diversify our curriculum, instruction, and assessment in such a way that students who have previously not been able to participate can be actively involved—without dumbing down the curriculum? What are the ramps we can use in education?

Ronald Mace along with Molly Story and James Mueller in *A Brief History of Universal Design* (1998) define the concept as "the design of products and environments to be usable to the greatest extent possible by people of all ages and abilities" (Burgstahler 2009, 1) They outline seven principles for the universal design of products and environments:

1. **Equitable use:** The design is useful and marketable to people with diverse abilities. In education, this means the instruction is planned to involve all students.

2. **Flexibility in use:** The design accommodates a wide range of individual preferences and abilities, background knowledge, and attention span.

3. **Simple and intuitive use:** Use of the design is easy to understand, regardless of the user's experience, knowledge, language skills, or current ability to concentrate.

4. **Perceptible information:** The design communicates necessary information effectively, regardless of environmental conditions or the user's sensory abilities. In education, for instance, visual, written, and kinesthetic models of instruction reach a range of students.

5. **Tolerance for error:** The design minimizes hazards and the adverse consequences of accidental or unintended actions. In education, this means both instruction and assessment recognize differences in student comprehension, pace of learning, and need for repetition of the instructions along with the actions.

6. **Low physical effort:** The design can be used efficiently and comfortably and with a minimum of fatigue. In education, the instructional design for presenting the curriculum reduces busy work that wastes time and mental energy, and focuses instead on the big ideas.

7. **Size and space for approach and use:** Appropriate size and space is provided for approach, reach, manipulation, and use—regardless of the user's body size, posture, or mobility.

Educators have adopted these principles to design universally accessible curriculum for diverse students with a wide range of abilities, ethnicities, language skills, and learning styles by using multiple means of representation, expression, and engagement.

However, we also recognize that what works for architecture cannot perfectly fit an educational model. Thus, educators have developed a different set of criteria for evaluating universal design for learning beyond those of universal design in architecture (Burgstahler 2009). In doing so, they have identified eight important factors to consider when planning instruction and activities for students.

Portage & Main Press, 2012, *Teaching to Diversity*, ISBN: 978-1-55379-353-3

1. **Class climate:** Adopt practices that reflect high values with respect to both diversity and inclusiveness.

2. **Interaction:** Encourage regular and effective interactions among students, and between students and the instructor. Ensure that communication methods are accessible to all participants.

   Dr. Burgstahler at the University of Washington elaborates on these factors in her "Do It" series: www.washington.edu/doit/Brochures/Academics/instruction.html

3. **Physical environments and products:** Ensure that facilities, activities, materials, and equipment are physically accessible to and usable by all students, and that all potential student characteristics are addressed in the safety considerations.

4. **Instructional standards:** Maintain high expectations for all learners, and provide supports to help them reach these standards.

5. **Delivery methods:** Use multiple instructional methods that are accessible to all learners.

6. **Information resources and technology:** Ensure that course materials, notes, and other information resources are engaging, flexible, and accessible for all students.

7. **Feedback:** Provide specific feedback on a regular basis.

8. **Assessment:** Assess student progress regularly, using multiple accessible methods and tools, and adjust instruction accordingly.

Not since John Dewey urged educators in 1916 to teach "the whole child" has there been such a promising call to action, and now through universal design for learning, teachers have the challenge but also the tools to create classrooms that focus on students' social, ethical, and intellectual development (Silver 2005, 163).

Insights through Brain Research

Research has shown that teaching and learning activities have the capacity to change brain function and, indeed, brain structure by producing adaptive responses in social and intellectual functioning (Davidson 2008; Goleman 2006). The brain is like a muscle; when asked to do a particular task or function repeatedly, it gets stronger and lays down wiring to handle that task faster the next time. Imagine the brain as a new-built house: in the early stages (to age 4), only the outer walls have been built. It is like one big room—for any task you ask of it, the whole brain gets involved. As children grow through the elementary years (ages 5 to 12) and into adolescence (the teens), the brain's inner walls begin to rise, separating into rooms for specific functions.

Dr. Davidson's videos on the Edutopia website are fascinating. Watch www.edutopia.org/richard-davidson-sel-brain-video

Thus, there is an area for language processing, another for numerical reasoning, a third for processing musical tones, and so on. The brain, like a contractor or architect, makes decisions about how to use space and function. The more you cook, the larger the kitchen needs to be. The more a child is exposed to a particular stimulus (music, for instance), the more wiring the brain lays down to efficiently process and use that stimulus. While the brain can build new rooms and lay new wiring throughout a person's lifespan, it is much harder to do once the walls have been raised. That is why it is easier for a young child to learn a new language than for an adult to accomplish the same task.

It is vital, then, that children be exposed to a wide variety of stimuli when the brain's walls and wiring are being formed so that they have all of these options available to them later in life, and that they learn to live in diverse communities and relate to diverse others through their childhood and adolescence, as they will do as adults. Worldwide, it has become imperative to develop truly inclusive learning communities (Katz, Porath, Bendu, and Epp 2012).

For more information, visit the CAST website at www.cast.org/udl/

The brain has three significant neural networks: recognition networks, strategic networks, and affective networks (Center for Applied Special Technology, CAST 2011).

1. **Recognition networks** are responsible for the acquisition of factual knowledge and information processing, and because we gather information through all of our senses, we have multiple recognition networks. Providing students with multiple means of representing information in visual, auditory, tactile, and multi-sensory formats is crucially important in the development of these networks.

2. **Strategic networks** are developed when we are learning how to learn. Giving students specific instruction in different modes of learning gives them options for ways of representing their understanding of what they have learned, and provides them with strategies for overcoming challenges.

3. **Affective networks** are responsible for motivation, attention, and perseverance. To activate affective networks, students must be empowered to make choices and be provided with opportunities to challenge themselves and discover new ideas.

In short, then, we must teach in a variety of ways, give students choice within their learning, and give them opportunities to show what they know in a variety of ways.

Seven Ramps for Brain-Based Instruction

There are seven significant ramps that facilitate an inclusive classroom, all of which are drawn from brain research. More detailed information, instructions, and resources are given in subsequent chapters, but brief descriptions of these ramps follow:

1. **Technology:** The original application of universal design for learning placed great emphasis on the use of technology to allow access to the learning for students who found traditional text-based learning rather challenging. Students could use computers to assist them in reading and writing tasks, audiobooks, and other forms of technology that allowed them to be included in the daily activities of the classroom. The staff of CAST developed a website and resources dedicated to assistive technology

and strategies in education, especially for those with disabilities. There is no question that technology can be a powerful tool for allowing multiple means of processing and demonstrating knowledge. However, it is one tool, albeit a powerful one, in a box with many tools.

When the technology is not available within the regular classroom and students have to leave and go to the computer lab or a resource room, it no longer facilitates inclusion. Sending a student to another room to use technology, separated from their peers, is like sending people in wheelchairs to a separate building—it is not creating access, it is segregating. UDL is not about "special education"; it is about "full education." Consequently, I have scattered "spotlights" on the uses of technology throughout this book as I believe they should be scattered throughout the curriculum of all learners and throughout the day—used when appropriate as part of varied methods of teaching and learning.

2. **Gradual release:** Research on best practices for all learners indicates that students learn best when given independence gradually. This concept leads to the "three-part lesson" or "gradual release" of responsibility for learning. Think about how a parent teaches a child to ride a bike. First, the child watches while the parent does it. Second, the parent runs alongside holding onto the bike while the child pedals and steers. Finally, the parent lets go and allows the child to carry on independently. This process can be described as the "I do, and you watch. Then we all do together. Then you do, and I watch." sequence. Too often, teachers forget the vital second stage. They model a sample question and response on the board, then set students to work independently, missing the "we do" phase in which students work together, with teacher facilitation, to familiarize themselves with the process. This is where cooperative learning and other small-group approaches find their place. Within a unit and within a lesson, it is best to begin with some teacher modelling and move to cooperative discovery before asking students to independently apply their learning. There are times for constructive inquiry learning that reverses these two stages. Based on students' needs and goals, support can be provided to some while others work more independently.

In inquiry models, teachers might present a problem or scenario and let their students discover the information, concepts, and skills they need to resolve it. See also chapter 4, pages 72, 78, 85, and 111 for more on inquiry

3. **Flexible groupings:** Activities for different student groupings—whole-group, small-group, partner, and individual projects—provide opportunities to include and support all learners. When we differentiate instruction and place students in learning teams, students who have language challenges, or problems in writing out their ideas, or other types of learning difficulties can still participate in the learning process when they have peer support for using appropriate vocabulary and in recording ideas. They can thus be seen as contributing group members when their strengths are called on—for instance, in building a model or representing a concept visually.

Portage & Main Press, 2012, *Teaching to Diversity*, ISBN: 978-1-55379-353-3

The classroom peers of students who have more significant behavioural and cognitive challenges can help these students develop such group interaction skills as turn-taking and teamwork based on the strengths of each member of the team (e.g., "I'll do the writing and you draw the pictures."), and appropriate methods of disagreeing.

For students who are developing higher order thinking skills, being exposed to diverse points of view helps them develop critical thinking and analysis skills. In teamwork, they have more opportunities to recognize that their own interpretation may differ from another's, which prompts them to determine whether that other person's viewpoint changes their thinking, or whether they can defend their own opinion if they still hold it. Such exchanges of opinions and ideas help students analyze their own thinking critically. Of course, they also need time alone to reflect on and process their thinking (metacognition), and independently develop conceptual schemata and evaluate ideas.

4. **Integrated curriculum:** Research has revealed that the brain is like a parallel processor in that it operates like the hard drive on a computer (Caine and Caine 1990). When new information is presented, the brain looks for where this new information fits in with what it already knows, or with other new information coming in, and decides where to file it or delete it from memory. Nothing stays in memory if it's not connected to prior knowledge or current life experience, unless attached to novel and clearly critical ideas or emotions. So, if we want students to pay attention and remember what we are teaching, we have to find ways to connect their learning to their lives by activating students' prior knowledge and experience, and imbuing it with a level of emotional interest that engages the student. Similarly, teachers who make connections between subjects help their students see how what they are learning in science is connected to what they are learning in social studies, or how reading skills support them in learning about both content areas. We want students to generalize their developing skills and knowledge across disciplines, so we need an integrated curriculum. The brain is programmed to be alert to relevance: if it's not relevant to students' lives and interests, they're not interested.

5. **Choice, risk-taking, and safety:** The brain has an emotional threshold: too much emotion or too little, and it cannot process. If students are too anxious or too bored, they tune out. To get around such obstacles, give students choice. When they are involved in the decision making, they are likely to choose topics or formats that are within their realm of experience, which gives them some confidence—when interested, they are not overly anxious. To build student choice into your planning, devise a unit assessment that allows them to choose their preferred format for presenting their understanding of the topic. When teaching a particular skill or format (e.g., essay writing), give students choice in the topic.

Portage & Main Press, 2012, *Teaching to Diversity*, ISBN: 978-1-55379-353-3

The social and emotional climate of a classroom is a key factor affecting brain development in children. Multiple areas of the frontal and prefrontal lobes of the brain are involved both in processing social and emotional information and in decision making. Because these same areas are also involved in the development of critical and analytical thinking, children's academic learning is affected when they are overwhelmed, according to Brian Dwyer (2002). He points out that training in the related social and emotional learning (SEL) skills has been shown to regulate brain response, such as reducing the reactive response of the amygdala and lowering the release of cortisol, a stress hormone that limits our ability to process, pay attention, and remember. Students who are trained in SEL can recover more quickly neurologically from a negative stimulus such as an incident of bullying or test anxiety, which allows them to regulate their thinking, to problem solve, and to respond more appropriately (Davidson 2008).

Focusing only on academic instruction to help students improve performance is therefore unlikely to lead to success (Adelman and Taylor 1984; Noddings 1995). Addressing students' social and emotional development should not be an add-on to the curriculum but rather an integral and necessary process for helping all students succeed.

6. **Authentic assessment:** The purpose of assessment is to determine the level of student mastery of a given concept or skill—either to guide further instruction as in assessment *for* learning, or to guide evaluation as in assessment *of* learning. When we want to know what level of mastery a student has achieved, it is best to assess a child through their strengths. For instance, if I want to know what a student has learned in a study unit on Ancient Egypt, it doesn't matter whether they demonstrate their learning through a written report, an oral presentation, or a role-play. I am not assessing their writing skills; I am assessing their knowledge. If I assess achievement only through a written test, I am biasing the assessment toward verbal-linguistic learners; a student who may have in-depth knowledge of ancient Egypt but has difficulty with written output will be penalized. The use of rubrics that allow for multimodal assessment is key when teaching diverse learners.

7. **Differentiated instruction:** As I began my master's program in special education, I came upon the theory of multiple intelligences. Psychologist Howard Gardner at Harvard, in his now well-known book *Frames of Mind: The Theory of Multiple Intelligences* (1983), detailed the multiple ways in which the brain processes information, solves problems, and creates products. Although I had been focused on educational pedagogies that facilitated the inclusion of students with exceptional needs in regular classrooms, his concept fit with my own beliefs.

Spotlight

Gardner's Project Zero research group continues to conduct research and training for professionals in mental health, education, and medicine. For more information, visit www.pz.harvard.edu/

Portage & Main Press, 2012, *Teaching to Diversity*, ISBN: 978-1-55379-353-3

The phrase "multiple intelligences (MI)" recognizes the different ways in which the human brain processes information. Gardner's proposition of multiple intelligences explores the types of information processed by the brain, and the ways in which people acquire knowledge, solve problems, and represent their knowledge and understandings. Gardner, who worked with patients who had had brain injuries, wanted to determine their processing pathways, and map them within the brain. He identified the following eight different intelligences, that is, eight different ways in which the brain processes a specific type of information and uses it to solve problems and demonstrate understandings.

Multiple Intelligences

Verbal-Linguistic

Verbal-linguistic intelligence is the capacity to develop verbal skills and sensitivity to the sounds, meanings, and rhythms of words. People with this capacity demonstrate strength in the language arts—listening, speaking, reading, and writing. In traditional classrooms, students who demonstrate verbal-linguistic abilities have always been successful because traditional teaching has used methods and materials focused on these abilities.

Visual-Spatial

Visual-spatial intelligence is the ability to visualize in detail, the capacity to think in images and pictures, accurately and abstractly. People who demonstrate visual-spatial intelligence learn best visually and by organizing things spatially. They like to see what they are asked to deal with in order to understand. They enjoy charts, graphs, maps, tables, illustrations, art, puzzles, and costumes—anything eye-catching.

Logical-Mathematical

Logical-mathematical intelligence is the ability to think conceptually and abstractly, and the capacity to discern logical or numerical patterns. People who display an aptitude for numbers, reasoning, and problem solving are deemed to have logical-mathematical intelligence. In traditional classrooms, children with this ability typically do well where teaching is logically sequenced and students are asked to conform to very convergent, repetitive types of tasks such as math drills or spelling tests.

Bodily-Kinesthetic

Bodily-kinesthetic intelligence is the ability to control one's body movements and to handle objects skillfully. Bodily-kinesthetic students experience learning best through activity: games, movement, hands-on tasks, and building.

Portage & Main Press, 2012, *Teaching to Diversity*, ISBN: 978-1-55379-353-3

Musical-Rhythmic

Musical-rhythmic intelligence is applied to the ability to produce and appreciate rhythm, pitch, and timbre. Many people learn well through songs, patterns, rhythms, instruments, and musical expression. People who can remember the words to a song better than a poem know what this kind of learning is like.

Interpersonal

Interpersonal intelligence is the capacity to detect and respond appropriately to the moods, motivations, and desires of others. Learners with this capacity are noticeably people-oriented and outgoing, and they do their learning best cooperatively in groups or with a partner.

Intrapersonal

Intrapersonal intelligence is the capacity to be self-aware and in tune with inner feelings, values, beliefs, and thinking processes. People with highly developed intrapersonal intelligence are reflective, metacognitive learners who are especially in touch with their own feelings, values, and ideas. They may tend to be more reserved, but they are actually quite intuitive about what they learn and how it relates to them.

Naturalistic

Naturalistic intelligence is the ability to recognize and categorize plants, animals, and other objects in nature. Naturalists love the outdoors, animals, and field trips. They notice details such as characteristics and behaviours in the natural world. More than this, though, these students' detailed minds love to pick up on subtle differences in meanings across the curriculum.

The following ninth intelligence has been proposed.

Existential

Existential intelligence describes the sensitivity and capacity of a person to probe the deep questions about human existence, such as how we got here, why we die, and the meaning of life. These people ask "Why are we here?" and "What is our role in the world?" They want to know why what they are studying is important in the bigger picture, and what the philosophy is behind ideas and expectations.

MI Framework for Differentiating Instruction

Cultures differ in the value they assign to these different areas of intelligence. For instance, whether a hunter's kinesthetic prowess or an author's linguistic prowess is held in higher esteem is a cultural value, not a neurological one. Both involve the brain's ability to process information, coordinate it with the environment, and produce an outcome or product of use to the individual. Both can be creative and unusually well-developed—or damaged by brain injury.

A teacher who uses an instructional framework that respects multiple intelligences and accommodates multimodal learning and assessment will stimulate all the brain's major areas and methods of processing, allowing students more career options as they grow up. To someday become an architect, a child needs visual stimulation, the opportunity to work with 2-D and 3-D images and models, the experience of rotating images in their mind, instruction to pay attention to visual detail, and the understanding that emotions, information, and function can all be expressed visually. Such a child might be successful in a text-based learning program, but might not develop all his or her potential abilities, thus missing options that might have opened up if the child had learned about the concept of visual-spatial intelligence. Not only are struggling learners able to benefit from differentiated instruction, but the students who are successful in the current, verbal-linguistic style of teaching and learning also expand their thinking and skill sets.

Differentiating instruction, whether through differentiated content, process, or product, allows diverse learners to work through their strengths, develop skills in areas of challenge, and learn at their unique developmental pace. Gardner's proponents argued that all intelligences were of equal value for, after all, what society could survive with only verbal-linguistic prowess?

Education systems have traditionally placed greater emphasis on verbal-linguistic intelligence and logical-mathematical abilities over all other forms. Both T. and Cole, the students I described in the Introduction, had become victims of this imbalance in their experience of education. I determined to change that, and I couldn't do that in someone else's classroom. I wanted to see if I could shift the classroom balance by valuing and emphasizing all of the intelligences. So I left my position as a resource teacher and went back into the classroom. Thus began my journey to UDL.

Bringing It All Together

Twenty-five years of research describes what works in inclusive practice. So why has it not been fully implemented? The answer seems to be the narrow focus often taken by government ministries, school districts, researchers, and administrators who have all tried to choose one ramp to focus on in an effort to not overwhelm teachers. Key strategies such as "differentiating instruction" "understanding by design" and "assessment for learning" are mentioned in policy and practice internationally. Many teachers have discovered, however, that application of one piece of inclusive practice rarely has the desired impact. It is like performing surgery without the anaesthetic—painful.

Teachers seeking the big picture end up at professional development workshops that explore only one piece of the puzzle, so they don't see how all the pieces fit together. It can seem overwhelming to consider implementing all of these pieces at once—for instance, understanding by design, differentiating instruction, inquiry, assessment for learning, and so on. But it is possible to provide a comprehensive framework for K to 12 in a practical, research-grounded, efficient manner.

In proposing a three-block model for UDL, I have tried to synthesize decades of research on inclusive educational practice. I did not invent the pieces of this framework, with the exception of the Respecting Diversity program described in chapter 3. As a classroom teacher, I attended professional development workshops on the many strategies designed to support diverse learners: differentiating instruction, inquiry, assessment for learning, literature circles, performance assessment, student self-assessment, democratic classrooms, class meetings, positive behaviour support—all of which had their resident gurus and inspired me to believe they would lead to positive change, but I always left wondering: How do they all fit together? How does one teacher do them all?

As I proceeded into my PhD, my questions expanded to: How do I make inclusion work? What are the foundational best practices of a truly inclusive learning community? How does one create such a community? In this book, I try to synthesize the research to provide the answers to these questions. I describe a three-block model of universal design and suggest a step-by-step approach to implementing it. This framework includes:

1. building compassionate learning communities, that is, ensuring social and emotional learning influences the climate of school and classroom;

2. inclusive instructional practice; and

3. systems and structures that support inclusive learning communities.

My Three-Block Model meets all the criteria set out by Burgstahler (2009) as well as those found to be effective in the literature on inclusive learning.

Block One: Social and Emotional Learning

Social and emotional learning involves developing schools that are compassionate learning communities in which all students feel safe and valued, and which give them a sense of belonging; such learning communities are socially inclusive classrooms. I created the Respecting Diversity program for the beginning of the school year to establish an inclusive classroom climate. The program falls within the guidelines of a universal design for learning framework in that the program not only promotes social and emotional learning but also promotes respect for diversity by providing opportunities for students to understand their learning profiles and by supporting multiple modes of presenting curriculum.

Block Two: Inclusive Instructional Practice

The second block of the Three-Block Model is the "inclusive instructional practice" section in which physical environments are designed so that all students have access to all the activities presented in the classroom. We use an assortment of differentiated instructional methods to address multiple intelligences and different learning modalities. We develop course materials to address the needs of all students in the classroom. Teachers devise assessment rubrics that reflect multiple developmental levels of understanding, and that can be used to assess multimodal expressions of understandings. Teachers provide regular feedback and assess individual learning progress as and when needed. Students benefit from this

Portage & Main Press, 2012, *Teaching to Diversity*, ISBN: 978-1-55379-353-3

feedback because knowing what is expected of them means that everyone has the opportunity to work to their academic potential. We embed accommodations in the program so that learning supports are always available for students without their being singled out negatively. Our goal is to create academically inclusive classrooms.

Block Three: Systems and Structures

We have to make significant changes in some of the policies and practices in our current school systems. Creating inclusive learning communities requires changes to educational policy, budgeting, staffing, training, and interactions with communities—indeed, a major reworking of the whole system. Across the country, the process has begun and is being implemented to varying degrees of success. Inclusive policies already exist in every province and territory across Canada. School boards and divisions as well as individual schools and staff members are aware of the expectations, and have the goal of working toward it. However, such support services as teacher training, staffing practices, and reallocations of budgets have not yet been comprehensively revamped.

In chapter 3, I focus on Block One, Social and Emotional Learning, which includes building compassionate learning communities. The next chapters focus on Block Two, Inclusive Instructional Practice, that is, first planning and adapting the curriculum (Chapter 4), and then the practice of teaching, assessing, and reporting (Chapter 5). Chapter 6 is focused on Block Three, Systems and Structures.

Portage & Main Press, 2012, *Teaching to Diversity*, ISBN: 978-1-55379-353-3

Figure 2.1 Universal Design for Learning: The Three-Block Model

BLOCK THREE CHAPTER 6
Systems and Structures
- Inclusive policy — no "except"
- Hiring administrators with expertise and vision; learning community
- Distributed leadership
- Professional development (PLCs)
- Staffing to support collaborative practice:
  - collaborative decision making
  - team planning time; scheduling in cohorts and teams
  - resource allocations (e.g., of EAs) to classrooms and cohorts, not individuals
  - co-planning, co-teaching, co-assessing
  - consistent, authentic assessment across classes and with co-developed rubrics
- Budgeting
  - change from segregated practices and allocations of funding resources
  - assistive technology
  - multi-levelled resources

BLOCK TWO CHAPTERS 4 AND 5
Inclusive Instructional Practice
- Integrated curriculum
- Student choice
- Flexible groupings and cooperative learning
- Differentiated instruction
- Differentiated assessment
- Assessment for learning; class profiles; strategic teaching
- Technology
- Discipline-based inquiry
- Metacognition, assessment as learning
- Understanding by design; essential understandings
- Social and academic inclusion of students with exceptionalities

BLOCK ONE CHAPTER 3
Social and Emotional Learning: Developing Compassionate Learning Communities
- Respecting Diversity (RD) Program
- Developing self-concept
  - awareness of, and pride in, strengths and challenges
  - sense of belonging
  - goal-setting and -planning; building a vision for the future; self-efficacy; hope
  - leadership skills; opportunities to lead
- Valuing diversity
  - awareness of the strengths and challenges of others
  - valuing of diverse contributions to community
  - sense of collective responsibility for well-being, achievement of all
  - empathy, perspective-taking, compassion
- Democratic classroom management
  - collective problem solving; recognition of rights and responsibilities
  - promotion of independent learning; student choice and empowerment; leadership
  - increase in student engagement and ownership

Portage & Main Press, 2012, *Teaching to Diversity*, ISBN: 978-1-55379-353-3

Chapter 3
Creating a Community—Block One: Social and Emotional Learning

Ideally, all children would learn to be compassionate, kind, and responsible citizens of their communities, and the schools would have a role to play in this process. However, debate continues over the extent to which schools can, or should, devote time to social and emotional learning (SEL) while their primary responsibility is for academic learning. What is not recognized in this debate is the link between social and emotional development and academic success. As research shows, strengthening students' sense of self in their school community actually increases their motivation to learn and their aspirations for greater knowledge and academic achievement (Zins, Bloodworth, Weissberg, and Walberg 2004).

Students' social and emotional learning improves their attitude, their behaviour, and their performance in school, including their performance on standardized tests (Malecki and Elliott 2002; Porath 2003). If students are stressed out, unhappy, and thinking about what's going to happen at recess, they're not learning. If they think they are going to be made fun of, they won't ask the questions in class that show they do not understand.

Students' sense of belonging also impacts their attendance, and they cannot learn if they're not in class. Teachers cannot fix all the issues that their students face or that their neighbourhoods face. However, we can create a safe haven. Schools should be the place where students feel safe and cared for, valued and respected. When they feel that way, students will come to school because it's a better place to be than hanging out on the street corner or, sometimes, at their home.

Link between Emotion and Academic Achievement

Stress causes the release of a hormone called cortisol. Cortisol helps us function in times of crisis, such as when a car sideswipes ours and we have to brake suddenly to avoid an accident. That shaky feeling we have afterwards is the effect of cortisol activated in our bloodstream in face of a crisis. When stress becomes chronic, cortisol remains in the bloodstream affecting our ability to concentrate, to remember, and to feel joy or connection. We become irritable, unfocused, and even obese—yes, cortisol has been directly linked to abdominal fat (Moyer, Rodin, Grilo, Cummings, Larson, Rebuffé-Scrive 1994).

Portage & Main Press, 2012, *Teaching to Diversity*, ISBN: 978-1-55379-353-3

Students whose life circumstances are constantly stressful become physically damaged. But the hormone does leave the bloodstream quickly when the stressor is no longer present. Half an hour after the car incident, the shakiness will pass. When our schools offer a safe haven for students under stress, their cortisol levels will reduce after they arrive at school, their stress will subside, and they will be better able to pay attention, to remember, and to enjoy their learning.

At the beginning of the school year, teachers work hard to establish routines, teach organizational structures, and articulate expectations for students' behaviour. Their efforts help establish a classroom climate in which students develop their understanding of the rules of the game and they begin to form friendships. The beginning of the school year is a crucial moment in time, a moment in which we can create a spiritual, compassionate space, a magical moment in which students can discover that the new school year might be different, that they themselves might be different. Such a moment is all too easily lost amid the organizational paperwork and the frenzied activity that often accompanies the first weeks of school.

Setting the stage for the magical moments may sound idealistic, but it is not unrealistic. Coaches do it all the time. They tell the students: "Being a star quarterback is great, but if there's no receiver to catch the ball, you can't win the championship." Coaches point out that every member of the team contributes something different: "You can't expect a wide receiver to do what a linebacker does, but both are necessary." They convince even adolescents that they are a team, and that they need to support each other if they want to succeed. Why can't learning, too, be a team sport? Our students do not have to compete for the only three A's available. Why not work together as a team to win the championship—being the class with the best scores on the exams, the best marks, even the deepest learning?

The old excuse of "boys will be boys" does not have to be true. We do not have to accept bullying as a fact of life. Teachers, like coaches, must help both children and adolescents recognize that every member of a team contributes something different to the team, and that the members need to support each other if they want to succeed—learning can be a team sport. Students can be taught that every member of their learning community brings different skills, perspectives, and background knowledge to the community, and all members can help the team reach the goal of mastering the concepts and skills through the problem solving required by the content that teachers present to them.

Teaching to the Heart and Mind

Steven Glazer's book *The Heart of Learning* (1997) is a collection of presentations made at a conference on "spirituality in education" in which His Holiness the 14th Dalai Lama is quoted as saying, "What we call love and compassion are not necessarily a religious matter. Love and compassion are basic necessities of life—not only for the individual but also for society." He connected self-actualization to a life of meaning and service when he said, "With the realization of one's own potential and [with] self-confidence in one's ability, one can build a

Portage & Main Press, 2012, *Teaching to Diversity*, ISBN: 978-1-55379-353-3

better world." In addition, he noted that negative emotions can create illness, both physically and psychologically, but that a loving community and support network can protect both children and adults from the negative effects of crises and illness.

We make the mistake sometimes of thinking only children from disadvantaged populations experience high levels of stress and alienation. However, many children living in poverty have loving families and a welcoming school experience, and just as many children from economically successful, seemingly healthy families struggle with high anxiety, a strong sense of alienation, and low self-concept. In fact, students who are gifted are one such population that we might have thought would have less stress than other students. Gifted students make up one subgroup of the population—between 2 and 5 per cent, yet they constitute up to 33 per cent of adolescent suicides (Delisle 1986; Dixon and Scheckel 1996). Studies vary, but the rate is disproportional.

Recent neurological research shows that the brains in gifted people have a structure different from that of the average person (O'Boyle 2008). Typically, the brain develops specialized areas for different functions, as a positron emission tomography (PET) scan reveals. When the person is involved in math activities, for instance, areas of the left hemisphere of the brain are activated. When the person walks, a different area, the motor cortex, is activated.

In contrast, the brain of a gifted person remains more like that of a young child. When that person's brain is scanned while they are involved in math, multiple areas of the brain light up (including both the right and left hemispheres). This activity is considered evidence of divergent or lateral thinking, an oft-noted strength of the gifted learner, who is very good at making connections and seeing multiple perspectives because of the involvement of multiple areas of the brain. However, when asked to do a step-by-step, logical, sequential task, the same person might struggle, having become distracted by the other connections and tangential ideas flooding in.

On a social and emotional level, the tendency to involve multiple brain functions activates the limbic system, which is responsible for emotions and which releases hormones into the bloodstream. As a result, gifted students tend to be highly sensitive and intense perfectionists who may be coping with high levels of anxiety. Gifted students face difficulty making friends. While their intensity, sensitivity, and divergent thinking may make them seem much older, their physical and social skills may still be age-appropriate. This discrepancy may leave them in a social void at school, especially in their younger years.

Their sensitivity may also be misunderstood by their parents. The response of parents and teachers, while benevolent, is often invalidating: "You need to get a thicker skin," "Don't be so sensitive," "You're making too big a deal about this." These comments send the message to such children that they shouldn't be feeling what they are feeling—yet they are. Although the stress hormone is coursing through their bloodstream and their feelings are real, they may think, "There is something wrong with me. I don't fit in. No one understands. No one cares." Such a thought process can become a deadly one.

Portage & Main Press, 2012, *Teaching to Diversity*, ISBN: 978-1-55379-353-3

Michael

As the resource teacher in my new school, I sent a note to other teachers, describing the characteristics of gifted students and asking for the names of students who might fit the criteria. Michael, one of those named and the son of two high-powered corporate executives, was a globally gifted student. Art, music, athletics, academics — he excelled at them all, and he ended every day by turning to his teacher and saying "Thank you for teaching me today."

I started a small group, including Michael, T., and Cole and a few others, who came down to my room in the morning twice a week to engage in independent projects and social and emotional demystification. Michael always sat quietly, worked diligently, and remained ever the perfect student.

One morning when I entered the room, Michael was tearing around, throwing things back and forth with T. Although I was shocked, I didn't want to shut him down, so I humorously asked, "What did you eat for breakfast this morning?" Smiling, he turned to me and said, "I've decided I can take the chains off in here." I was stunned. After he left, I phoned his mother, the CFO of a major corporation, to tell her what Michael had said. I asked her permission to talk to him about the nature of the chains. She, too, was concerned and agreed.

So I brought Michael down to my room, took two blank pieces of paper, wrote School in the middle of one and Home in the middle of the other and said, "I want to know what the chains are." He looked at me and asked, "Is anyone going to see this?" When I said, "No, not without your permission," he filled both pages. Some issues were small ones, but some were serious and dark, things no one would have suspected were going on inside this "perfect" child.

When Michael's parents later came in without him for a meeting on an individualized education plan (IEP), his mother began the conversation by saying, "He is going to have to get a thicker skin, or he is never going to make it in the corporate world." I suggested that, given what I knew about him, Michael was not likely to ever enter the corporate world. He had a poet's heart and a philosopher's mind, and there were many, many ways in which he could be successful in the world, but becoming a CEO was not likely one of them. It had never occurred to her that Michael could not just become less sensitive, that it was not even desirable for him to do so, and that the corporate world was not a safe one for him. She loved her son deeply and only wanted to protect him, but he felt that she did not understand or value who he really was. It took five years of working with Michael and his family to begin to unlock the chains, to free Michael to be whoever he chose to be, and to help his parents find ways of relating to him.

A few years after that first meeting, I got a call from Michael's mother. She was concerned because he wasn't sleeping, and she didn't know what was bothering him. When I asked Michael whether he wanted to talk, he told me he was up at night praying that the weather wouldn't get cold. I asked him why. He proceeded to pour out a convoluted story about a tree by the family's driveway. Apparently, it was dripping sap and leaves on their car, and Michael had overheard his parents saying that when it got colder, they would have the tree cut down. Michael did not believe they should "kill a living thing" over some leaves and sap, so he was praying for the weather to stay warm. I asked him whether he had talked to his family about his feelings, and he shook his head, saying that they would never listen or understand. I encouraged him to find a way to communicate how he was feeling.

Portage & Main Press, 2012, *Teaching to Diversity*, ISBN: 978-1-55379-353-3

The next morning, Michael's mother came in and, with a sly smile, said, "You spoke to Michael, didn't you?" I said yes, and asked what had happened. She laughed and said, "We awoke this morning to find a banner around our tree with the words 'Please don't kill me.'" Michael had found a way to communicate his feelings. That Christmas, I got a card from them:

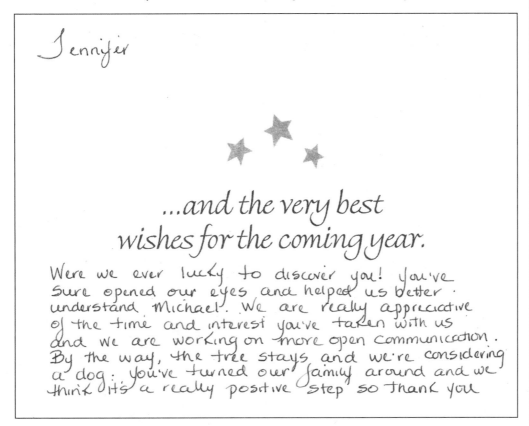

Jennifer

...and the very best wishes for the coming year.

Were we ever lucky to discover you! You've sure opened our eyes and helped us better understand Michael. We are really appreciative of the time and interest you've taken with us and we are working on more open communication. By the way, the tree stays and we're considering a dog. You've turned our family around and we think it's a really positive step so thank you

Figure 3.1 Card from Michael's family

Multiple Intelligences and Social and Emotional Learning

Even a child who seems to be happy and healthy can feel alienated and alone, and we must be vigilant about the possibility of developing the wrong perception of individual students. We need to help all students develop a positive self-concept, and to establish a compassionate classroom climate in the midst of the hectic beginning of each academic year.

Some ten years ago in my classroom, I developed a program called Respecting Diversity (RD). After much discussion and collaboration during the intervening time, the program has been implemented in many classrooms and schools from kindergarten to grade 12. The program's objective is to develop four interrelated constructs that lay the foundation for students' social and emotional learning—self-awareness, self-respect, awareness of others, and respect for others. As children learn to know and understand their strengths and challenges, they

Portage & Main Press, 2012, *Teaching to Diversity*, ISBN: 978-1-55379-353-3

begin to develop confidence in their abilities; they learn to set goals and persevere through difficult times; and they develop the emotional coping skills necessary to stay healthy through the adolescent years.

Self-awareness and self-respect allow children to answer broad spiritual questions with a resounding "Yes, my life has meaning. Yes, I have gifts that the world wants and needs. Yes, I matter." As children develop their awareness of and respect for others, they gain perspective, develop social skills, build positive relationships, and work cooperatively with diverse others. These abilities are necessary not only for personal well-being throughout one's life but also in seeking and maintaining employment. They help children develop the sense of being part of something bigger than themselves, of their connection to a living community and a living planet.

Social awareness and self-awareness

Howard Gardner's description of eight categories of intelligence (Gardner 1999) includes two social and emotional constructs (Gardner 2009).

Interpersonal intelligence ...

allows us to develop a genuine sense of caring and empathy for each other. Through interpersonal intelligence we 'stand in another person's shoes,' so to speak. It is a person-to-person way of knowing, through which we maintain our individuality but also become more than ourselves as we identify with and become a part of others. (Lazear 1992, 17)

Intrapersonal intelligence ...

involves an awareness of the internal aspects of self — feelings, thinking processes, intuition, or spirituality. Both self-identity and the ability to transcend self are a part of intrapersonal intelligence. When we experience a sense of unity ... feel the lure of the future, or dream of heretofore unrealized potentials in our lives, it is the result of our intrapersonal way of knowing. (Lazear 1992, 18)

Interpersonal intelligence is related to social awareness and respect for others. Intrapersonal intelligence incorporates self-awareness and self-respect. We must introduce the distinction in ways that facilitate students' attempts to understand themselves and appreciate others.

The Respecting Diversity Program

The Respecting Diversity (RD) program has the goals of developing specific components of self-awareness, social awareness, and respect: self-efficacy, goal-setting, emotional resiliency, perspective-taking, empathy, valuing diversity, and creating a positive, inclusive classroom climate. Research (Katz and Porath 2011) indicates that the RD program significantly increases students' self-respect and their respect for others. Helping all students understand their strengths as well as their challenges improves the classroom climate. Helping students understand the advantages of having diverse learners in a classroom community helps them develop emotional resiliency and acceptance of others.

Traditional curricula and instruction focus on a narrow range of techniques, primarily text-based, for teaching and learning. They therefore create an

Portage & Main Press, 2012, *Teaching to Diversity*, ISBN: 978-1-55379-353-3

educational disadvantage by favouring the students who are verbal-linguistic over other students (Gardner 1995; Hearne and Stone 1995). Students who do not learn best through text (who are not verbal-linguistic) face a struggle to learn in ways that do not best fit with their learning strengths. For instance, a student whose strength is visual-spatial and who might one day become a great architect might feel incapable because he or she cannot write as well as others—art, after all, is generally considered of secondary importance in the curriculum. Introducing students to the concept of multiple intelligences, which recognizes all intelligence categories as equally valid and valuable, helps create a climate for student self-acceptance and acceptance of others. As Elias (2004) eloquently states, "Working through multiple intelligences is more than just pedagogy. It represents finding windows into the souls of children and ways to reach them in powerful and meaningful ways" (58).

Introducing Multiple Intelligences to Students

Demystification is the process followed in the Respecting Diversity program. Introducing students to the concept of multiple intelligences allows students to explore their own interests, the different levels of interests and talents, different abilities, different feelings, different strengths that describe their current learning profile. As well, they begin to experience the diversity of intelligences in the learning profiles of fellow students who make up their school community.

Helping children understand their strengths and challenges leads to more accurate personal insight (Levine 2002). As they begin to appreciate the advantages of having diverse learners in a classroom community, they develop emotional resiliency and acceptance of others (Shepard 2004). The goals of demystification through the RD program are to develop students' respect for self and for others. The program has been used in inclusive classrooms from kindergarten to grade 12, in resource room settings, and in one-to-one counselling situations, with some adaptations.

Teachers in secondary schools face the dilemma that students might repeat the same lessons several times if all their teachers (in each discipline) were to undertake the program, but some secondary schools I worked with found one of these solutions helpful:

Solution 1: For the first few days in September, they postpone implementing the planned regular class schedule; instead, they place the students in homerooms—if necessary, ones created for the purpose of the RD program—and work through the lessons in those few days. Then, when they start the regular class schedule, all their students have the vocabulary and thinking with which to approach study units designed for universal learning.

Solution 2: They create a homeroom period at the beginning or end of each school day, and work through the RD program over a more extended period of time in these homerooms.

Portage & Main Press, 2012, *Teaching to Diversity*, ISBN: 978-1-55379-353-3

Script for Respecting Diversity Program

The RD program offers the following nine lessons for teachers to introduce the vocabulary and concepts of multiple intelligences (introduced in chapter 2) to students and to explore and discuss how they apply to teaching and learning under the umbrella of universal design for learning. The lessons are designed to help students become aware of their own and others' learning profiles, and to help build a positive learning climate in the classroom. The lessons do not have to be spread over nine days, depending on the age and level of the students. Teachers should work through them at a pace that their students find comfortable.

Working with young students

The lessons that follow for the RD program can be used by teachers at all grade levels, with personal adaptations appropriate to their students and their grade. The amount of scaffolding provided and the language level used will differ for younger students. For instance, when asking students to make predictions (lesson 1), older students could do this in written form; however, teachers might have children in kindergarten and grade one turn to a partner and talk, or place a sticker with their name on it on the chart next to their strength. Teachers might choose to do the surveys (lesson 2) for children in the Early Years as an activity for a parent night, or with older students as buddies, or in small groups with teacher facilitation. When discussing careers (lesson 4), focus on "community helpers" familiar to the children—firemen, police officers, doctors, librarians, and so on. For lessons 5 and 6, some pre-teaching of group work (chapter 5) could be helpful, particularly when working with one group at a time.

Lesson 1 — Introducing Multiple Intelligences

Rationale

This lesson introduces the language to describe "intelligence," to discuss different levels of intelligence, different interests, different abilities, different feelings, different strengths, needs, and values. As students begin to expand their ideas of what "smart" means, they may begin to understand that there are many ways to acquire and demonstrate one's knowledge and abilities, and that each way is equally valuable in contributing to one's overall intelligence. The ways (or modalities) may overlap, but it is helpful to distinguish among them.

Depending on the age/level of your students, introduce the terms "learning profile" and "learning style" as synonyms for "intelligence" in some situations and descriptions.

Materials

Ensure students have their journals for these lessons. Have chart paper stands and pads of chart paper, as well as coloured markers, at hand.

Process

- Brainstorm: Ask: *"What does 'smart' mean to you?"* As students give their answers, record them on chart paper as a web. Use coloured markers on chart paper instead of chalk on the board, because you will come back to this summary later. As you write, begin to group the responses into the MI categories (e.g., *Can read well, Knows lots of words, Can spell accurately* would be grouped together because they are all part of "verbal-linguistic" intelligence). When possible, use different coloured markers for each intelligence to make them stand out visually.

- Ask questions when the students run out of ideas: *"What other ways can people be smart?" "What things are you good at?"* (If a student says 'hockey,' group it with other sports, eventually to identify "bodily-kinesthetic" intelligence.) *"How do you learn best?"*

- Continue to prompt until you have listed examples of all 8 or 9 intelligences, filling in as necessary (*e.g., "Does anyone here play piano?" "I have a friend who…"*).

- Introduce the areas of cognitive abilities that Howard Gardner called "multiple intelligences." Discuss each category separately. Circle the phrases from the students' brainstorming session related to that intelligence, and discuss what activities or skills help define this group of people. Name the intelligence. (e.g., *"You're right, some people are word smart, they are good at _____, which we call* "verbal-linguistic intelligence.")

- Journal response: Have students discuss, draw, or write their thoughts in their journal in response to your question *"What strengths do you think you have?"*

Adaptations

Students with significant disabilities can participate in this lesson by listening to the discussion, and can communicate their own likes and interests by using visual aids or matching their classmates' pictures to pictures of activities they like.

Lesson 2 — Multiple Intelligence Surveys

Rationale

This lesson involves students in self-description as they respond to a survey designed as a tool for metacognition and reflection on their interests.

Individual demystification allows children to develop self-perception and a realistic self-concept by recognizing their strengths, needs, and values; they increase self-efficacy as self-awareness grows. As well, journal reflections give students a chance to reflect, identify and recognize their emotions, and evaluate their reactions regarding their learning profile.

Materials

Select the Multiple Intelligence Survey (see Appendix) appropriate for your students. Make copies and distribute a copy for each student to complete, but do not make this a reading task.

Process

- Before they begin, tell students that responding to the survey is not a competition, that what matters is that they think about each statement and decide as best they can whether it describes them, or how they think, or how they feel. Read the instructions for Part 1 of the survey to, or with, the students.

- As you begin, tell students that no one is perfect, that everyone has some strengths and challenges, and that's OK. It is vital that you emphasize this. Otherwise, children will answer according to what they think you want them to say, not what they actually believe.

  - With the students, read each statement in each section of the survey aloud, and have them put a number 1 on the line if they believe the statement is true for them most of the time, and to just leave it blank if the statement is not true, or not very often true.

- As you finish each section, have students add up their 1's and write the Total. Remind them that whether they have marked 1 or 4 or 10 statements in any section is not important, that the Totals for each section take on meaning only when placed in the bar graph in Part 4.

  - To avoid students comparing scores, tell them the scores don't matter. Whether they got a 4 or a 7 is irrelevant; what matters is their relative strengths and challenges.

- When you have finished all 9 sections (90 statements), ask the students to transfer all their Totals to the table in Part 2, then shade in the portion of each column that matches their Totals in the bar graph in Part 4.

Discussion and Journal Reflection

Were your predictions of your strengths correct? Were there any surprises for you? Why do you think this happened? *(Survey is wrong, Had not thought myself good at that.)* How do you feel about your learning profile?

Adaptations

Students with disabilities can participate in this lesson by communicating their likes and interests using visual aids, PicSyms, or PECS. Their participation depends, of course, on the student's level of functioning and degree of training with PECS, which has to be determined on a case by case basis.

Lesson 3 — Community Brain

Rationale

This lesson follows up on what the students have learned about their strong interests and abilities. It is intended to develop students' awareness of social relationships and of the skills that foster a sense of community — of their interdependence as members of their community.

All students have a chance to be the helper at times, and at other times to ask for help, which reinforces the idea that everyone has strengths and challenges. The students can use a positive framework to manage cooperative relationships, to develop communication with their peers, and to foster social engagement and inclusion.

Figure 3.2 Class Brain

Materials

Enough Plasticene for each class member to have a piece to contribute to the model of a brain. Have materials (paper 'flags" or sticky notes, toothpicks) for students to make flags. With very young children (K/1), prepare the flags in advance, or have a parent volunteer present to help.

Process

- Working together, create a model of the brain from Plasticene.
  - Give each student a piece of the Plasticene to roll into a snake. Then have them add their strip as you build up the layers into a multi-fold brain (see Figure 3.2).
- Ask students to write their name and dominant intelligence strength on a flag, and bring them together into a circle, holding their flags. There are two important points to make before the students place their flags into the brain. Explain:
  - *"Everyone in this room has something to contribute, **something to be proud of**. Whatever you wrote on your flag, shows us what you have to contribute to the community."* Give examples of actions characteristic of someone with a particular type of intelligence. (e.g., *"If you are 'interpersonal,' you can be a friend to a new student or to one who needs someone to hang out with at recess. If you are "bodily-kinesthetic," you can coach others in your skill.)*
    "We all have strengths and challenges, so all of us will be helpers sometimes, and 'helpees' at other times. When you need help in an activity we are engaged in, look for someone with strength in that area."
  - *"This is a **commitment to our community** and to yourself: When someone asks you for help with a task, leadership means that you will not make fun of them, nor will you do the task for them, but you will help them learn how to do what you are able to do, or to understand what you have learned to know."*
- After this discussion, have students place their flag in the appropriate area of the Plasticene community brain.
- As a teacher, be sure to call on your students for help at times (e.g., to draw on a chart for you, or to fix something), using the brain model.

Adaptations

For students who are significantly disabled and who may have marked only a few statements in any category of the survey, consider what emotions they evoke in other students. For instance, do they make others smile? Are they willing to interact with others? If so, their profile might be "interpersonal."

Portage & Main Press, 2012, *Teaching to Diversity*, ISBN: 978-1-55379-353-3

Lesson 4 — Multiple Intelligences and Careers

Rationale

This lesson is intended to develop self-motivation and resiliency by building hope for students, as they see that there will be opportunities for success and even fame, regardless of their learning profile.

Involve students in an exploration of career options and life paths open for those with diverse learning profiles. When students can identify role models who have learning profiles similar to theirs and who have been successful, they may begin to develop self-efficacy and emotional resiliency, as research shows.

Materials

Set up the chart you created in Lesson 1. Collect and/or have students collect photographs of public figures and people in different areas of work, of the arts, and involved in community endeavours.

Process

- With your students in a circle around the chart that you created in lesson 1, discuss the range of activities involved in different types of work done by well-known people in your community, and what strengths each might have in one or more of the intelligence categories.

- As you go around the circle, brainstorm careers for each category and some well-known people who have strengths in that field; for example, a popular radio presenter (*strong verbal-linguistic abilities*); a soccer coach (*strong bodily-kinesthetic abilities*); and so on. It is critical, during this discussion, to point out to students that, no matter the nature of their profile, they can be successful in whatever work or career they choose to pursue and train for.

- If students need an assist, hand out photographs of public figures that students might recognize, or figures in settings that help identify their field (*sports; music; technology; sciences; local, provincial, national politics;*) have students discuss the person's career and what their learning profile (*strengths and challenges*) might be.

- As an extension, you can have students research and write a brief biography of someone with a profile similar to their own. This task might help them see that someone just like them has been successful.

Adaptations

For students who are significantly disabled, there are a few possibilities. They can, of course, be a part of the discussion and brainstorming. When it comes to the biographies, they could work with a partner who has similar strengths (e.g., they both enjoy music), or they could explore other persons with disabilities similar to their own (for instance, there are biographies of people with autism, Down syndrome, and so on).

Portage & Main Press, 2012, *Teaching to Diversity*, ISBN: 978-1-55379-353-3

Lesson 5 — Multiple Intelligences and Interdependence

Rationale

In this lesson, we shift our focus from self-awareness and self-respect to focus on respect for others and respect for diversity. Students in the school years are naturally egocentric; they think everyone should know, like, and believe what they do (e.g., How could you not like hockey? What's wrong with you?)

   We cannot teach students to value diversity until we teach them to see that their life and the world are better for it. As students become aware that a community actually requires diversity in order to function, they learn to value people who are different from themselves. This focus helps create social awareness of the value of diversity and helps students develop respect for others.

Materials

Write the names of the nine intelligences under discussion on paper slips and place in a small container.

Process

Place students in nine groups; then have each group pick a slip of paper (intelligence) out of the container. Ask students to develop and write a role play, which they will perform.

- *"What if everyone were _____? For instance, what would the world be like if everyone were verbal linguistic?"* After students have performed their role-plays, discuss:
  - *"What are the pros and cons of everyone being the same?"* (e.g., Everyone would be talking, but there would be no roads, no cars, which would lead to a sense of "chaos" and disorganization.)
  - *"What are the benefits of diversity to a community?"*, *"How do diverse others support our lives?"* (*e.g., Someone builds our houses; ... performs on TV, ... programs computers*). You are trying to lead students to see how diversity benefits THEM.
- Next, ask students to write and perform a second role-play. They can either focus on the same intelligence, or you can place all the intelligences back in the hat and redraw.
  - *"What would the world be like without people who have strength in _____?"* (e.g., What would the world be like if no one were 'visual-spatial'?)
- After students have performed their role-plays, discuss:
  - *"What would be missing from the world, from your life, without other people with different likes and abilities than you?"* (e.g., no graphics for video games, everything is grey.) Here our goal is to have students recognize that they would be missed if they were not exactly who they are, and that they would miss other students with different abilities than them.
- Journal reflection: *"Why is diversity necessary? How would your life be more difficult without it?"* (e.g., "I would have to build my own house"; "...make my own music.)

Lesson 6 — Valuing Diversity

Rationale

This lesson gives students the opportunity to reflect on the advantages and disadvantages of working with others who may be similar or different. In many jobs today, the ability to work with diverse people is important — people with strengths similar to yours and some with strengths that you don't have. For instance, a technology company might have different departments — software developers, computer programmers, graphic designers, marketing and promotions staff, and sales representatives. Within each department, employees might share some strengths, but in order to create a successful product, the developers will have to collaborate with the graphic designers and the sales people, and vice versa.

Students, too, must learn to negotiate with their peers about when and how to choose and work with partners and group members, whether they have similar or differing learning profiles. The lesson is meant to build students' explicit awareness of the value of diversity, to explore the pros and cons of working with similar and different types of learners, and to see value in all. Students thus develop social awareness and relationship management skills.

Process

- Break students into groups according to MI strengths in learning profiles (i.e., all the kinesthetic learners work together, and so on).
  - Assign a topic (e.g., *Show me what you know about ___*). Here you can choose a curricular topic you wish to study, and use this as a formative assessment to see what your students know.
  - Tell students they must use at least two intelligences in their presentation *(e.g., Draw and write; Act and speak*.).
  - Discuss:*"What were the advantages and disadvantages of working with people of like mind/ learning style to you?"* (Possible responses: "Well, it was easy to decide what we wanted to do, but then everyone wanted to draw and no one wanted to write.")
- Re-arrange the students into groups of mixed intelligences.
  - Assign a second topic (e.g., *Show me what you know about ___*).
  - Tell students they must use at least two intelligences in their presentation on the topic selected (e.g., Draw and write, or act and speak).
  - Discuss: *"What were the advantages and disadvantages of working with people of different mind/learning style to you?"* (*e.g.,* Well it was hard to decide what we wanted to do, but then it was easy to divide the labour.)
- Discuss: "In the world, we have to be able to work with and relate to both people who think like us or do what we do, and people who think and work differently.

  "Sometimes it is useful to work with people who have the same interests as you, and sometimes it is useful to find partners or team members who have complementary skill sets. You cannot have a hockey team made up only of goalies."

Portage & Main Press, 2012, *Teaching to Diversity*, ISBN: 978-1-55379-353-3

Lesson 7 — Goal Setting

Rationale

This lesson is intended to develop students' self-awareness, particularly their ability to set goals, to plan and organize, and to recognize the need to develop strength in these areas and to challenge oneself in areas of weakness. Perhaps more importantly, sharing goals in community creates a sense of interdependence, as students learn to count on each other for help, to trust that they can be vulnerable, and to become the kind of friends who can be strong for each other.

It is vital that we allow, encourage, and expect students to set goals in areas of strength. Too often, we imply that goal-setting is all about getting better "at what you're not good at." But greatness is truly achieved by setting goals in areas of our strengths. If someone had said to Mozart, "You are good enough at music, but you need to work on your spelling," the world would have lost a great talent!

Give students the opportunity to reflect on what is important to them and to set goals in their strengths. Also help them learn to use their strengths to overcome challenges, and explore stress management techniques for dealing with challenge goals.

Process

- Discuss the process of setting goals.
  - It is important to set goals in both strengths (*"How are you going to develop your talents?"*), and challenges (*"What do you want to get better at?"*).
  - Emphasize setting goals in one's strengths! Tell the kids *"There would be no Mozart, no Lebron James if someone had said to them, "You're already good enough in music/basketball. You really need to work on ___"!*
  - Students tend to write goals they think their teachers or parents want to hear, like "getting better at math." Remind them that *"goals must matter to you, or you won't work toward them."*
- Goal #1
  - Have students individually set a goal in their strength.
    - How will they develop their talent? (*If a strength is athletics/hockey, what do they want to get better at? — their conditioning, stick-handling?*)
  - Make a plan for how they will do that.
- Goal #2
  - Discuss goals in areas that we find challenging — the areas we cannot improve on our own. (*Goals in challenge areas require community support. You have to plan who will help you, how they might help you, and how you can gain their support.*)
  - Have students set a goal in a challenge area.
    - What is important to you?
    - Make a plan, and decide who you need help from.
- Class discussion
  - Gather students around in a circle and ask them, one at a time, to share their goals.
  - After the individual has shared, ask the student, "How can we help you?" It is important to have students articulate how their peers can help them, as this builds trust and teaches students how to communicate their needs. Emphasize that all members of the community are responsible for supporting each other in reaching our goals.

Portage & Main Press, 2012, *Teaching to Diversity*, ISBN: 978-1-55379-353-3

Lesson 8 — Data Analysis
(Optional — for older students)

Rationale

This lesson is intended to develop students' social awareness of common misconceptions about what "intelligence" is, and about the diversity of learning profiles. It is an opportunity to explore concepts such as societal bias and its influence on individuals.

Students explore societal views of intelligence, and reflect on how society's views have influenced their own view of themselves and others. For example, one student produced a survey asking people which person they thought was smarter: Einstein or Michael Jordan. He then reflected on the value of scientific thinking versus kinesthetic and interpersonal intelligence, and the general tendency to underestimate the use of other intelligences within athletics; for instance, how "logical-mathematical" plays into strategies in sports.

Process

- Have students create their own survey on multiple intelligences (*e.g., "Which of the following activities is your favourite?" "Who do you think is the smartest?"*).
- Tally the results.
- Record the results, using a variety of graph types.
- Discuss:
  - *"What does this say about how we view intelligence and the distribution of intelligences?"* (e.g., We think Einstein is smarter than Michael Jordan, but more people are bodily-kinesthetic than logical-mathematical.)
  - *"Would the results be different in another culture?"* (Is bodily-kinesthetic intelligence viewed more positively than logical-mathematical intelligence in some societies?)
- Journal/Discussion: Reflect on how the culture and society in which you have grown up influenced how you think about yourself and others?

Portage & Main Press, 2012, *Teaching to Diversity*, ISBN: 978-1-55379-353-3

Lesson 9 — The Brain and Disabilities

Rationale

This lesson is intended to develop students' social awareness, particularly their awareness of and empathy for the challenges that people with disabilities face. We try to encourage students to reflect on their personal, moral, and ethical responsibilities within diverse communities. At the same time, we must make students aware that having a challenge in one area does not mean that you are challenged in all areas — people with mental or physical challenges can be capable in many ways. We try to challenge students' perspectives and develop their respect for others through role-plays.

It is important to help students become aware of the relationship between the intelligences and some of the disabilities their peers and classmates may face — place disability in the context of ability. Research into the outcomes of the Respecting Diversity (RD) program indicated students found this discussion to be one of the most powerful.

Process

- Discuss with students:
  - "We all have strengths and challenges, but what would it be like to have a severe challenge in each one of the intelligences?" (e.g., visual-spatial: blindness)
- Work through each intelligence, noting the associated disabilities, and the potential abilities. (e.g., *"If you are quadriplegic and in a wheelchair, does it mean you are not intelligent? No, because you can be smart in all these other ways."*) Then, have students work with partners, or in groups to role-play what it would be like to be.

 Verbal-Linguistic: learning disabled, hearing impaired, mute

 Visual-Spatial: visually impaired

 Logical-Mathematical: dyscalculia

 Bodily-Kinesthetic: physically challenged, ADHD

 Musical-Rhythmic: tone deaf

 Interpersonal: conduct disorder, non-verbal learning disability (NVLD), autism spectrum disorder

 Intrapersonal: anxiety disorder, mood disorders, autism spectrum disorder

 Naturalistic: phobias

 Existential: developmental delays, challenges with conceptual understanding, higher order thinking

- Discussion and reflection:
  - *"If you had a severe challenge in one of the nine intelligences, what other activities could you do to prepare for a career?"*
  - *"As a non-disabled person, what could you do to support community members with disabilities?"*

Portage & Main Press, 2012, *Teaching to Diversity*, ISBN: 978-1-55379-353-3

Derrick

In my grade 6/7 class, a student named Derrick struggled with impulsivity and aggression. He had been in trouble, both in the neighbourhood and in school, many times over. Now in grade 7, he was reaching an age where that trouble could become serious.

We began to work through the Respecting Diversity program, and made our way to the goal-setting activity. We came into a circle to share our goals. As each student shared, I asked them, "And how can the community support you?" I wanted it to be clear that I expected students to support each other in reaching their goals. Most students set goals in either academic or athletic areas, and we were able fairly easily to create a plan to help them reach their goals. When we reached Derrick, he hesitated and then quietly said, "My goal is to not get suspended this year." So I asked him the same question, "How can the community support you?" He shrugged. He really did not know what anyone could do to help him. He believed he was a bad kid, and it was his fault.

So I turned to his classmates, who had grown up with him, and asked them, "When does Derrick get in trouble?" The answer came quickly. "At recess, usually when we're playing, and there's an argument, and he gets mad." When I asked for an example, they said they had been playing soccer and there was an argument over whether something was a goal or not. I turned to Derrick and asked him if this sounded right. He nodded. I didn't need to know the outcome of the argument. It was written all over his face (he had smashed another kid's head into a pole). So I talked to all of the students about impulsivity.

I explained that all of us, when we are emotional, have a hard time thinking logically, and we just react. Some of us have stronger emotions, and are more easily triggered than others. Just like in learning, we all have our strengths and challenges. Derrick's face was heartbreaking — such a mixture of sadness and relief that I wasn't painting him as a bad kid. I turned to the class and Derrick, and said, "I am a very emotional person, too. There are some things I can't do, like watch horror movies or read really sad books, because I get nightmares." The kids laughed. I continued, "And people who are my friends don't ask me to do those things; they go other places with me. If we all know that Derrick gets in trouble when there are arguments over sports, how could we help him?"

The kids looked blank: "You mean not play sports?" I laughed, "No, I don't mean that. But if you are Derrick's friend, and an argument starts, what could you do?" After some discussion, the kids came to understand that being Derrick's friend might mean getting him out of a bad situation. Now some people might feel that's too much to ask of students. But I don't buy that. It is not that hard for one of his buddies to say, "Hey, D, forget it and let's get out of here." If he doesn't go, that's not their fault, but they can try. That's like taking the car keys away from a drunk friend. Looking out for a friend is part of caring about someone. I think that's a good lesson for kids.

So again, we came up with a script. His classmates would suggest to Derrick that they all leave and go do something else. It was his responsibility to take that cue — if he wanted to reach his goal. If he didn't take the cue, the kids were to send someone in to get me. Only once in the year did that happen — and I made it only part way out in the field when Derrick saw me, and came walking over. He made it through the year without suspension. As much as Derrick benefited from that community, I think his friends learned even more. They became mature, empathic leaders who were not afraid to speak out.

Portage & Main Press, 2012, *Teaching to Diversity*, ISBN: 978-1-55379-353-3

A reflection by one of Derrick's friends:

> I agree with the fact that teachers should give children the right to speak and stand up for their beliefs especially when it comes to older students. This is important because when young kids begin to get more independent, nobody will be there to hold their hand and guide them to wherever they need to go. So it's better if children start off independently so that they can have a strong foundation and be confident to voice his/her opinions when the future gets tough. The voice of the learners needs to be projected to the teacher in order for a class to function smoothly which is why class meetings are a key to a healthy social community. This way, peers can be recognized for their leadership, teamwork … etc., teacher can be notified of changes that may need to be made in the class, and obviously, it will be a happy community. A democratic classroom has made a difference in my school life because now I am willing to help others, ready to give input in social activities, and ready to listen to others' comments. I felt like, for the first time, I was as loved at school as I was at home, and everyone was behind me. It was a family, and we all helped each other, had fun, and learned a ton! —Grade 7.

Extending the Program across the Curriculum

The two methods of extending the RD program into the daily life of a classroom community are discussed in greater detail in later chapters 4 and 5, but let's consider the following two brief suggested extensions:

1. Use the language of multiple intelligences in activities across the curriculum to reinforce the notion that we all have strengths and weaknesses. This awareness gives all students a chance to develop leadership skills and self-esteem based on their strengths.

   a. *Language Arts*
   - When discussing ideas and activities related to readers' theatre (bodily-kinesthetic), add musical elements to students' performance of plays or scenes from books (musical-rhythmic).
   - Give value to students' illustrations (visual-spatial) of their understanding of material read or discussed.
   - Write sportscasts (bodily-kinesthetic).
   - Place students in groups or book clubs discussing opinions (inter-personal).
   - Explore nonfiction related to the natural world (naturalistic).
   - Discuss such themes as racism, spiritual values, and globalism (existential).
   - Discuss existential themes relating to students' lives (intrapersonal).
   - Extend some unit topics by reading or writing biographies, or exploring the learning profiles of famous people who have overcome challenges.

Portage & Main Press, 2012, *Teaching to Diversity*, ISBN: 978-1-55379-353-3

    b. *Mathematics*

- Extend logical-mathematical language to other categories when discussing ideas and activities.
- Have students develop math centres related to tangrams (visual-spatial), geoboards (bodily-kinesthetic), measurement tools (kinesthetic), musical patterning (musical-rhythmic), architecture and 3-D shapes (visual-spatial and bodily-kinesthetic), solving word problems (verbal-linguistic).
- Explore careers related to the various fields of mathematics and their origins in different cultures.

    c. *Science and Social Studies*

- When discussing ideas and activities, engage students in research explorations and investigations (verbal-linguistic and logical-mathematical); experiments (bodily-kinesthetic); murals (visual-spatial), building models (bodily-kinesthetic), cultural studies (musical-rhythmic, visual-spatial, verbal-linguistic, existential); environmental studies (naturalistic). In a science unit on brain anatomy, discuss regions related to different intelligences. Explore the hemispheres and lobes, functioning, and the concept that we all have strengths and challenges (e.g., dominant left brain or right brain).

2. Emphasize the social curriculum as extensively as the academic curriculum:
   a. Hold class meetings weekly.
   b. Set goals and reflect on strengths and challenges.
   c. Read books about diversity.
   d. Write about community issues and interdependence.
   e. Have students work in flexible groupings.
   f. Develop a class code of conduct.
   g. Weave social issues across the curriculum.
   h. Use either bibliotherapy or videotherapy.

Bibliotherapy and videotherapy are powerful techniques for resolving social and emotional issues. Teachers have always used literature to spark discussion, but bibliotherapy extends this to allow for specific issues to be addressed. For more information on how to use these strategies, visit: http://teachingwhatworks.blogspot.ca/2009/03/bibliotherapy-integrating-academics-and.html

Portage & Main Press, 2012, *Teaching to Diversity*, ISBN: 978-1-55379-353-3

RD Program Outcomes

My research into the outcomes of the RD program indicate that students' definitions of self-awareness and self-respect changed significantly following these introductory classes. A group of middle school (grades 4 to 7) students from a highly diverse and fully inclusive school district were interviewed about their experiences with the RD program. When asked whether

An article detailing the research outcomes of the RD program is available at www.internationaljournalofspecialeducation.com/articles.cfm?y=2011&v=26&n=2. (See Katz and Porath 2011.)

the program changed their thinking about themselves, almost all students said "Yes" and went on to describe the impact that exploring their strengths and challenges had on their sense of self. "It feels like I'm learning the inside of my body," one student remarked. "It was enlightening and interesting to find out what our strengths and challenges were. I was confused before, like, what am I good at?" Students noted that they had rarely thought about their "learning profile," but after the program, they felt more comfortable and accepting of themselves. "I know my strengths, and I know what I need to improve—and it's OK."

Several students commented that this newfound knowledge had encouraged them to set goals, to take risks with their learning, and to persevere through their challenges. "You set a goal with your weakness, and you challenge yourself." Some students also expressed a greater comfort level with themselves and with how others perceived them. "I felt like I could finally show people that I learn this way and not that way. Because last year was just writing, writing, writing. I'm sort of proud of it. I'm a little more happy because these people know."

A sense of belonging, of not being alone, was mentioned on several occasions. "You feel like you're not the only one, and it's OK." Students felt that they had become more confident and resilient in their sense of self "even when everyone else says you're dumb, you're—like—just because I can't do this, doesn't mean I'm dumb. I'm just as smart as them, even smarter." This confidence allowed students to become more comfortable with exposing their challenges and asking for help. "I know what I'm good at and what I need help in, and there's lots of people that could help me." Perhaps most succinctly put, "Like, about myself, I can—like, um, about the inside of my body—I can let it out."

Teachers also thought the program had a positive impact on students' self-esteem and their understanding of their unique learning profile. "It is a good way for students to understand that, just because they find certain areas of school work challenging, they are not dumb. In fact, they are all smart in some way—which builds their self-esteem."

When interviewed about whether the program had "changed how you think about others," some students spoke about the attitudes, skills, and knowledge they had gained, which affected their relationships with others. They had a growing awareness of the different strengths and challenges of their peers. Said one, "Knowing that everyone learns differently than you do makes me understand that there's different 'smarts'—everyone is smart in different ways." They mentioned their awareness of others' perspectives when facing an unusual challenge. "I really understood how they felt to be like that, how it would be harder."

Understanding, in turn, changed their attitude and behaviour toward their peers. "I can get to know them and know what their strengths are and what their weaknesses are, and like that. So I didn't bully them about that." One student described how this awareness had allowed him to initiate friendships with diverse others he might not have previously associated with. "I can, like, know their strengths, and maybe I could be friends with them—and stuff." Many students talked about how they had come to empathize with the diverse learners in their class. "Before, when I saw someone act a little different, I was, like, 'I think they are a little weird,' but now after I've seen this, I realize they're all the same as us. They just might act a little different 'cause they have challenges."

Students had begun to develop empathy for others. "You care for other people, and you think about their feelings." In particular, students talked about how the lesson on the challenges associated with each intelligence had increased their empathy for people with disabilities. "I realized how hard it is for disabled people to live. A lot of people are special in their own way—I should have known that before." However, the students differentiated their newfound empathy from pity. "I don't feel bad for them; it just taught me something so I know that everybody has strengths. It feels OK. It feels good." In fact, students learned to appreciate the value of diversity in their lives. "If you didn't have different smarts, the world would be just, like, one thing—and it would be a mess, kind of." One student summed it up: "It's good to have difference."

This attitude translated into behaviour that affected students' interactions and the class climate. Students talked about how they treated each other with respect. "They help you, and help you get better in other subjects, and they make you learn more. We 'use our manners,' 'share', and ask: *What's going on? Do you have any problems? What's on your mind?*" This awareness also translated into a reduction of negative behaviours. "Before, some people might make fun of them and then when they, like, listen to it, they stop making fun of them." In fact, not only were negative behaviours reduced, but positive support seemed to increase. "If you're being teased by other people, they might stand up for you, and tell them to stop." "You just say, 'That's OK, you'll get better next time,' and just try to make them feel better." Students also referred to a reduction in racist comments and attitudes. "You don't talk behind their back, just because they are from a different country."

Perhaps as a result of this understanding, students expressed a belief that they had developed a sense of community in the classroom. "We help, sit next to each other at lunch." "When they do something good, you respect them, kind of." One student expressed this feeling: "Since I started talking, and started getting around, being partners and in groups, I started to learn more about how you have to work as a team, and, um, to be good to each other."

Teachers felt the program had helped the students to become better acquainted with one another. "I liked the lesson with the community brain—it really helped the students appreciate each other. My students enjoyed the program." Teachers,

Portage & Main Press, 2012, *Teaching to Diversity*, ISBN: 978-1-55379-353-3

like students, noted that there was a greater level of comfort in facing challenges. "They realized how everyone can contribute, and it's OK to ask for help." "Students who had difficulties in specific areas, for example, Math, felt comfortable asking for help." Several of the teachers commented in particular on the final lesson—exploring disabilities associated with the different intelligences. They felt this lesson had really improved students' understanding and behaviour related to fellow students with exceptional needs. "Most students began to think seriously about what it would be like to be severely challenged. They became more aware of our student whose behavior falls within the autism spectrum, and how they can try to include her."

Through these MI discussions, students develop an inner core, a sense of self that allows them to cope with moments of challenge in the present and hopefully into the future. When students believe in themselves, they are better prepared to deal with challenging subjects, difficult peers, exams and other anxiety-provoking situations, even, yes, difficult teachers. As one student succinctly put it, "I learned more about my intelligence. So now for every other program around the school, I think 'If you know that you're intelligent, then nothing can get on you.'" Students came to believe in themselves and felt that their peers and teachers believed in them. They had learned to say yes.

When soul enters the classroom, fear drops away (Kessler 1998/99). Students risk exposing their pain or the shame that might be judged as weakness or stupidity "Like umm, like, if you are down you don't have to, like, say it's always my fault." They can talk to some people, talk about themselves. "Yeah, like, I suck at this." By opening a window to the perspective of others, by accepting what they thought shameful in themselves, students discover compassion and begin to learn about forgiveness. "Don't think to yourself, 'I've got such a bad mark on the test, I'm so stupid.' Don't think that." They develop a deep sense of connection to themselves, to others, and to their world—and experience a feeling of being known and understood (Kessler 1998/99).

When you ask teachers why they chose this career, the answer is almost always that they wanted to make a difference. From the research literature on resiliency, we know that the single most important factor in developing emotional resiliency in children is having one significant relationship. Just one such relationship can lower rates of substance abuse, aggressive behaviour, depression, and suicide. That one person could be parent, grandparent, teacher, counsellor—it doesn't matter. Children need someone to believe in them, someone to care, someone to say, "I see you." As teachers, we hold tremendous power to affect the lives of children. Our relationship with our students and the environment we create for them can destroy a child, or heal one. It's our choice.

Portage & Main Press, 2012, *Teaching to Diversity*, ISBN: 978-1-55379-353-3

Jay

In August, as I was preparing my classroom for the grades 6/7 students arriving the following week, a woman knocked at the door. She introduced herself as the mother of a student entering my class. She asked if she could talk to me for a few minutes, so I invited her in.

"I've lost my son," she whispered.

Her grief was palpable. I didn't know what she meant, so I asked her to tell me more. Jay, it turns out, had been diagnosed with dyslexia in grade 3. The family had provided him with private speech language therapy, tutoring, and more. He had been identified as "learning disabled" by the school, and an IEP was written. He was provided with resource support and small-group pull-out for reading instruction. Jay could read, but only for a few minutes at a time, because the movement of the letters on the page caused eyestrain and headaches. His written output was extremely disordered — missing words and letters, words out of sequence, almost no punctuation. However, he was very bright, and understood all the concepts — he just couldn't express his understanding very well in writing, or so she told me.

"He is so angry," she said. "He hates school, he hates me, and he says he hates life."

I suggested she drop all the private support, and give Jay a breather. This was his final year before heading to secondary school, and I wanted him to focus on success this year. I needed to get to know Jay before I could say much more, but I assured her I would support Jay's learning in the class, and be in touch once I had a feel for where we stood.

Jay entered the class the following week. Arms crossed and eyes squinted, he just screamed "attitude." While he did not disrupt, his body language dared you to try to get him to engage or participate. He sat behind his desk, doing nothing. However, it was clear to me that he was watching and listening to everything. So I let him be. My plan was to simply let him see that this class would be different, and I knew that telling him so would not be believed. I had to earn his trust, he wasn't going to give it away. Another casualty of the system.

With the class, I proceeded through the RD program — which Jay observed, saying nothing. He filled out the survey, but put it in his bag — it was his private reflection, and that was fine with me. We talked about being inclusive, about community, about the team sport attitude that I wanted them to have as we "burned out our brains" together that year.

Then one day, the students came in from recess and said that we needed to have a class meeting. After we pulled our chairs into a circle, they explained about the arguments that took place on the basketball court because they were playing a game called "Bump." I didn't know this game, but here's the gist: one group tries to shoot a ball into the basket, while the other tries to throw a ball that knocks the first group's ball away from the basket. Apparently, the problem was that some students wanted to play seriously and by the rules, and others were just fooling around and stuffing things in the nets.

I listened with a mixture of amusement and bewilderment. There were two nets outside; the solution seemed obvious to me. So I asked the question, "Why don't you just say one net is for those who want to play seriously, and one net is for those who want to play for fun, and people can choose?" All of a sudden, a voice came from behind. "Isn't that exclusive?" he asked sardonically. His moment had come! He had been waiting, just waiting for that moment when he caught me being a hypocrite, and could prove this was just another BS story, another class and year and teacher who was filled with hypocrisy and hurt. He looked at me with angry eyes and a knowing smirk. I laughed and replied, "I don't think so, Jay. Exclusive would mean we assigned people, maybe based on ability,

Portage & Main Press, 2012, *Teaching to Diversity*, ISBN: 978-1-55379-353-3

to different nets. I suggested the kids offer a choice. It doesn't matter how good you are, if you want to play seriously, play at this net, and if not, play at the other. You might go to one net one day, and the other a different day. Choices are not exclusive."

Now, the class had been studying a unit on Steveston, a historic fishing village in the city we lived in. The area had a history of environmental exploitation and racial discrimination, including internment of ethnic Japanese after December 1941, residential schools for First Nations, and a head tax for Chinese immigrants. I had asked the students to take on a role as an immigrant to Steveston during those times, and write their story. At the end of the day, Jay came to my desk.

"I wrote a story," he said.

"OK, hand it in, and I'll read it tonight." I shrugged, trying not to make a big deal of it.

"My spelling sucks, you might not be able to read it," he mumbled.

I told him that was fine, I was pretty good at decoding, and if I had questions I'd ask, so he handed it in and left. I, of course, read the story instantly. It was so disordered that my heart broke for him. How must it feel to be a bright kid and not be able to show it? However, as I read on, I was astounded. The power of the piece was incredible. He was so able to understand suffering and discrimination, and his vocabulary and imagery were highly advanced for his age.

When he came in the next morning, I took him aside.

"Did you know you are a gifted writer?" I asked.

"Not according to my teachers the last three years," he spat, crossing his arms and flushing. I asked him if he had given them work like this.

"No."

"Then whose fault was that?"

"Theirs."

I asked him how he figured that.

"I couldn't," he said. "They told me what to write, and how to write it, and I can't write that way" he exploded, hurt and anger and frustration all over him.

I put a hand on his shoulder, turned him to me, and said, "That isn't how we work here. There are lots of powerful people who have a secretary. I will be yours. Just get your ideas down, and I will edit them and print them out for you. There is no shame in a secretary. I won't think for you. The writing is yours."

Throughout the first term, that's how we operated. Jay would write on a computer, save to a memory stick, and hand it to me. I would edit his work, mark it based on the content, and then give it back to him. As time went on and relationship was built, I was able to goad him into making some attempts at structure with a sarcastic "Ya know, you could put one period somewhere on the page." He would allow me to do very quick mini-lessons about paragraphs, or some other structural piece, and would make attempts to use them. At the end of the first term, I asked students to write about the most important thing they had learned. Most wrote about human rights, or environmental issues. Here is what Jay wrote:

The most important thing I have learned about was people. People such as me. How someone can shine a light on you even when you are in a dark place. How all people have something to contribute. Some students believe that there is no hope in life. That they will always fail. But these children have never heard of hope for the better, of MI and that there is something for you. I used to say that hope was a bunch of lying crap but I have seen now that there is hope in the world for people like me and others.

Portage & Main Press, 2012, *Teaching to Diversity*, ISBN: 978-1-55379-353-3

His mother sent me a card that Christmas:

Dear Ms. Katz,

Thank you, thank you, thank you for transforming my son. I see the real Jay again and it is wonderful. Thank you for your kindness and patience.

At the end of the year, I announced that I was moving to a new school. Jay wrote me a card.

Dear Ms. Katz

This year has been fantastic, it has change my life and the way I look at school too. You may not know it but I respect you more then any other person in my life, Because you were the only teacher that even gave me a chance before kicking me out of class, Also you have taut me so much but the most important thing I learned from you was too believe in myself and never give up no matter what anyone says. I wish you all the best at tait and good luck.

From J

Spirit Buddies

As I read the literature on social and emotional learning, I began to think about how we could inject spirit and connection into our classrooms. The RD program starts us off, but we must find ways to maintain the feeling and the daily connection on an ongoing basis. Unfortunately, some students arrive at school in the morning having made no connections. No one has said "Good morning," or asked "How are you feeling today?" or sent them off with "Have a good day." Some students, too, are not greeted by anyone upon their arrival at school. They don't have friends waiting for them on the front steps or in the halls, and they enter our classrooms each day in relative obscurity.

Portage & Main Press, 2012, *Teaching to Diversity*, ISBN: 978-1-55379-353-3

How do we change that? How do we ensure every child starts every day on a positive note, experiencing a sense of connection and belonging?

I learned a practice called "Spirit Buddies" from Rabbi Shefa Gold, a spiritual teacher, and I began incorporating it into my classroom: For a few minutes at the beginning of each day, students connect in small groups of "spirit buddies" to greet and welcome each other, check in, and start the day in community. In my class, I put the students into groups of three, and gave them the first 15 minutes of the morning to meet (see Figure 4.8, p. 89). This gave me time to take attendance, to collect any monies and forms, and to handle any other necessary administrative pieces, but I, too, circulated to greet the students.

This practice creates community in that everyone knows someone, has a support network, and is welcomed to the shared space every day. If someone is or has been absent, their buddies can check on them, or fill each other in on happenings when they return. Because my students at that time were also working on active listening skills, a part of the English Language Arts curriculum, I asked them to take 5 minutes each to share. Their buddies were not to interject their own stories, but they could make supportive comments ("Like, Wow, that's cool" or "Are you OK?"), and they had to focus on really listening to each other.

The amount of time the class spends could be less than 15 minutes, but the sharing proves to be a vital part of building a sense of community in my classes. Now, in my university courses, I continue to implement this practice, and get a lot of positive feedback about it; students who have driven to the course from outside the city express gratitude for the chance to make a connection so they do not feel completely isolated. At every grade level, at every age level, humans seek a sense of belonging and connection. Even 5 minutes at the beginning of the day can go a long way to achieving this feeling.

Creating Democratic Classrooms

Creating a democratic classroom environment means involving students, on a regular basis and in developmentally appropriate ways, in shared decision-making that increases their responsibility for helping make the classroom a good place to be and learn. A democratic classroom is a vital ingredient in implementing universal design for learning (UDL), because it allows students to take ownership of their learning and to develop pro-social problem-solving skills. Such an environment also encourages student autonomy which, the research shows, is integral to an individual's development of intrinsic motivation and self-efficacy.

Five Characteristics of a Democratic Classroom

1. Students and teachers work together to make students' learning a contribution to their community.

   a. praise for students across intelligences, social behaviour

   b. service projects

To explore this idea further, visit the Johns Hopkins University School of Education website at education.jhu.edu/newhorizons/strategies/topics/the-democratic-classroom/

Portage & Main Press, 2012, *Teaching to Diversity*, ISBN: 978-1-55379-353-3

2. Students demonstrate their learning in public settings and receive public feedback.

   a. in-class presentations

   b. presentations to other classes, parents

3. Students have escalating degrees of choice, both as individuals and as groups, within the parameters provided by the teacher.

   a. students have input into schedule, grouping structures, methods of learning and representing understanding

4. Students actively work with problems, ideas, materials, and people as they learn skills and content.

   a. a problem-based learning approach, students work in teams to figure it out

5. Students are held to a high degree of excellence in both their academic objectives and their social contributions to their larger community.

   a. Students rise to high expectations, so expect your students to support each other, work together, and learn at deep levels.

Seven Principles of a Democratic Classroom

1. The social curriculum is as important as the academic curriculum.

2. How children learn is as important as what they learn; process and content go hand in hand.

3. The greatest cognitive growth occurs through social interaction.

4. The set of social skills that children need in order to be successful academically and socially includes: cooperation, assertion, responsibility, empathy, and self-control, among others.

5. Knowing the children we teach—individually, culturally, and developmentally—is as important as knowing the content we teach.

6. Knowing the families of the children we teach and inviting their participation is essential to children's education.

7. How the adults at school work together is as important as individual competence: lasting change begins with the adult community.

A democratic classroom contributes to character development because it provides an ongoing forum where students' thoughts are valued and the needs of anyone in the group can be addressed. In such an environment, students learn how to consider the needs of others, voice their own needs in appropriate ways, and find solutions that are mutually acceptable. Empowered students are motivated to assume a degree of social responsibility, as they recognize how their contributions, either positive or negative, affect others in their community. Democratic classroom management creates a support structure that develops moral reasoning by strengthening the sense of community and holding community members

Portage & Main Press, 2012, *Teaching to Diversity*, ISBN: 978-1-55379-353-3

accountable to practise respect and responsibility. Democracy mobilizes the peer culture on the side of virtue; that is, democracy creates a positive peer pressure that models pro-social behaviour.

Six Teaching Strategies in Democratic Classrooms

1. **Class Meetings:** Such meetings build community, create a positive climate for learning, and reinforce academic and social skills.

2. **Rules and Logical Consequences:** A clear and consistent approach to discipline fosters individual responsibility and self-control. The rules and consequences are decided at class meetings, and then consistently implemented.

3. **Guided Discovery:** An instructional pedagogy that encourages inquiry, heightens interest, and teaches care of the school environment. This philosophy of teaching requires students to take ownership of their learning, and requires teachers to step back and let students take on leadership.

4. **Academic Choice:** Devise approaches to give children choices in their learning that help them become engaged, self-motivated learners.

5. **Classroom Organization:** Implement strategies for arranging materials, furniture, and displays to encourage independence, promote caring, and maximize learning and positive social interaction for all students.

6. **Family Communication Strategies:** Devise ways for involving families as true partners in their children's education.

Portage & Main Press, 2012, *Teaching to Diversity*, ISBN: 978-1-55379-353-3

ST-V 6

Melissa

Class meetings are incredibly powerful tools for both social and academic learning. In a grade 1/2 class, one of the students said, "I would like to change that some people are throwing rocks at recess." (The playground has gravel in-fill). So I asked the kids, "How do you handle it when someone is doing something that you don't like, or that is unsafe?" Their only answer was: "I tell a teacher." So we structured a role-play.

I asked for a volunteer to pretend to be the person throwing rocks. Then I asked Melissa, a student with strong social skills and great leadership to play the student who was being hit by the rocks. At the time, I was teaching in BC, which has performance standards for social responsibility, so we used the language of the standards. I asked Melissa to show us a "Not yet meets" response, and she pretended to pick up rocks and throw them back. We talked about why this is a "Not yet" response. Then I asked her to show us a "Minimally meets" response. She pretended to go get a teacher. Again, we discussed the pros and cons of that action. When I asked her to show us a "fully meets" response, she said, "Please don't do that. It hurts me." When we asked her what she would do if it didn't stop, she said she would tell the rock thrower that if he didn't stop, she would have to go and get help, because it wasn't safe. Then I asked her to show us an "Exceeds expectations" response and — wait for it — she turned to the rock thrower and asked, "Do you want to play?"

Now, Melissa was exceptional, no question, but there is usually one. The exchange I had with her allowed all the other students to witness behaviour for how to handle such a situation. In classes where I haven't had that kind of leader, we have brainstormed possible solutions and weighed the pros and cons. At times, I've suggested some. We then discussed that the problem action didn't have to be throwing rocks. It could be anything that made you feel unsafe, emotionally or physically. We came up with a script:

> Ask them to play. If they refuse and don't stop, ask them to stop. Let them know it's unsafe, and that you will report them. If it continues, seek adult help.

In doing this, we not only teach social skills for problem solving, we also teach leadership, ethics, kinesthetic expression, and critical thinking. We teach kids to brainstorm solutions together, weigh the pros and cons, choose one, try it, and if it doesn't work, try plan B. How crucial is that for mathematics, poetry, and many, many other curricula and life situations?

Class Meetings

The class meeting is the best means of creating a democratic classroom environment. Arranging a face-to-face circle for the meeting emphasizes interactive discussion and problem solving. Class meetings should be scheduled weekly, but allow a meeting to be called at any time by a community member. In September, students tend to call a lot of meetings, in part because of the novelty or sense of power, and in part because the community is still forming. It is vital that the teacher respond, which sends the message that how we treat each other and how we feel about ourselves is more important than anything else. We will stop reading, math, science—whatever—to resolve an issue that makes students feel emotional or social stress. The novelty quickly wears off, but the students will have received the message that the classroom is a safe place where we have methods of resolving conflict peacefully. As the year wears on, the students will be able to resolve challenges themselves, will work well together, and teachers will not have to deal with constant conflict.

The intention of a class meeting is to teach the skills of problem solving in social situations, and to involve students in their learning community. The teacher sets safe and reasonable parameters for ideas and solutions.

Class meeting procedure

1. Students sit in a circle.

   Ask the students, in turn, to go around the circle giving compliments, and express their gratitude for the good that has happened in the community. "*I would like to give a compliment to _____ for helping me when _____*" or "*I am thankful for _____.*"

2. Go around the circle a second time, raising issues in the community with the sentence frame: "*I would like to change _____*".

3. Do not allow students to mention names when raising issues. Instead of saying "*Jack is yelling,*" say "*I would like to change that it's too noisy during _____.*"

4. Have students brainstorm possible solutions to problems raised, and discuss the advantages and disadvantages of each. At times, I have students role-play these solutions so students can see what the outcomes might be.

5. Allow students to try out solutions as long as doing them is safe, even if you don't think they will work. They will learn how to revisit their thinking, and to try Plan B. They become more realistic with experience. Students cannot learn if the teacher is always in control.

Portage & Main Press, 2012, *Teaching to Diversity*, ISBN: 978-1-55379-353-3

ST-V 7

Jason

Jason had come from a behavioural intervention program. He was one of those students who had great difficulty controlling his impulsivity and aggression. He got angry easily and never took responsibility for his actions. Whenever other kids complained about something he did, Jason insisted he hadn't done it, even if I had seen him myself. I'm not saying this to paint Jason in a negative light. I believe that kids express challenging behaviour for a reason, and that it's my job to figure out what is causing the distress and help them resolve it. I say this to set the stage for what happened next.

After we finished with our role-plays, Jason raised his hand. When I asked him to speak, he said, "It was me who was throwing the rocks." I was stunned, as were the students. So I asked him to tell me more. He said, "I just wasn't thinking, I was fooling around, and then they started yelling at me, so I got mad and threw more." This was a huge moment for us. Jason had come to understand how his behaviour made the others feel, something that adult intervention and discipline could never have shown him. We can tell him that it hurts the other kids, but it is very different for him to hear it from them — all of them — and hear them struggle to think of ways to resolve it.

It was also the first time that the other children began to understand Jason's perspective as well. I asked him what made him angry, and he replied "My name." I have heard this from other students with ADHD as well: they get tired of always hearing their name:"Jason, sit down"; "Jason, stop talking"; "Jason, Jason, Jason." One of the kids then asked him, "Well how can we stay 'Stop' if we don't use your name?" They brainstormed together, and came up with a hand signal they would use.

Was it a miracle cure? No, of course not. But it was a beginning. Jason did begin to take responsibility for his actions and to apologize when he made mistakes; and the other students tried to not use his name or yell at him. Together, we grew a lot that year and by the end of it, Jason had friends and was rarely angry in the school setting. Home was a different story. Here is a journal entry written shortly after by one of the grade 2 students from that class:

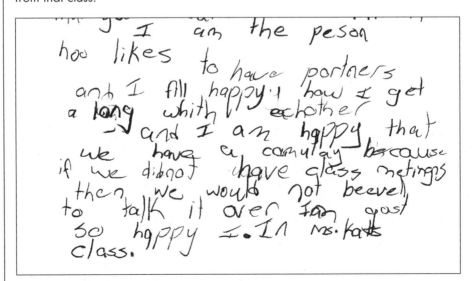

Figure 3.4 *"I am the person who likes to have partners and I feel happy how I get along with each other and I am happy that we have a community because if we didn't have class meetings then we would not be able to talk it over I am just so happy I in Ms. Katz's class."*

Portage & Main Press, 2012, *Teaching to Diversity*, ISBN: 978-1-55379-353-3

Chapter 4

Planning for Diversity—Block Two: Inclusive Instructional Practice

The logical sequence in planning for a diverse classroom, following principles of universal design for learning (UDL), begins by laying out the big picture—the whole school year for my assigned grade or combined grades. From this overview, my plans become more specific, with allocations for each term (which is a unit) and then the lesson sequence for each unit.

The School Year ➔ The Terms/Units ➔ The Lessons

The Planning Continuum

When teachers—especially beginning teachers—do not start with an overview of the school year, they may end up in a panic before June because they begin in September with great ideas for lessons, build them into a unit, and move along, only to discover in the spring that they have covered just half the curriculum. By first selecting clusters/themes/topics from the specified curriculum content for the full school year, we can organize them in sequences, combine one or two as needed, and select expectations or learning outcomes in our other disciplines. This process saves a great deal of stress about coverage, and provides logical connections for our students to relate one subject to another.

As discussed in chapter 2, nothing stays in memory that is not connected to the students' prior experience and knowledge. To help them generalize skills and knowledge across the disciplines, we must devise lesson plans and teaching strategies that help them understand how those disciplines are connected, and how their brain absorbs those connections. We can facilitate the process by integrating related curricular content. Also, in settings in which teachers teach separate subjects, the teachers of the same grade of students can find the connections between their curricula by collaboratively planning and working together. Then they can begin to team-plan for the terms or semesters in the school year and the units of study for each term or semester.

Planning the Year

For illustrative purposes, I will use grade 7 because it is half way between kindergarten and graduation from secondary. We can look first at the curriculum

Portage & Main Press, 2012, *Teaching to Diversity*, ISBN: 978-1-55379-353-3

section and the descriptions of the grade 7 disciplines on the website of Manitoba Education (www.edu.gov.mb.ca/edu).

Other provinces and territories maintain similar websites that provide information on the curriculum offered for the different disciplines, levels, and grades throughout the province—which both educators and the public can explore in detail. Let's say that, because most middle schools in Manitoba have only three terms in the school year, I want to lay out the Social Studies curriculum for those three terms.

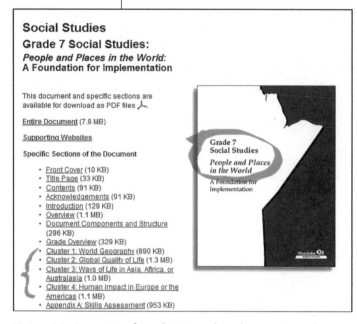

Figure 4.1 Overview of grade 7 Social Studies on Manitoba Education website

From Figure 4.1, we can see that "Grade 7: People and Places in the World" includes four *clusters*, which are thematic groupings generally corresponding to distinctions within the disciplines:

Cluster 1: World Geography

Cluster 2: Global Quality of Life

Cluster 3: Ways of Life in Asia, Africa, *or* Australasia

Cluster 4: Human Impact in Europe *or* the Americas

In order to create three themes, one per term, and have time to explore the content in depth, we will try to combine two of the four clusters into one theme. From their titles we have wide choice in combinations. One obvious option is to combine *Cluster 2: Global Quality of Life* with *Cluster 3:* Ways of Life because how people live their life impacts the quality of their life. It does not matter how you combine the clusters or when you teach them, only that you choose where connections are possible and combine in order to "cover" the key concepts by the end of the year. Then we can allocate the two remaining clusters to the other two terms.

Step 1. Aligning curricular topics with school terms

To further organize the grade 7 curriculum for my class, I complete the same process for the Science curriculum. Let's take a look at the four topical units or clusters for grade 7 Science:

Cluster 1: Interactions within Ecosystems

Cluster 2: Particle Theory of Matter

Cluster 3: Forces and Structures

Cluster 4: Earth's Crust

Looking within the clusters, we see the possibility of combining two into one. It makes sense to combine *Cluster 3:* Forces and Structures with *Cluster 4:* Earth's Crust because the movements of the tectonic plates are affected by, and create a variety of, forces and structures. Again, what matters are the connections within and among these two clusters and your ability to communicate those connections to your students. So, our first step has been to combine the curriculum clusters into more manageable units that still allow us to have the same number of curricular topics as we have terms, and report on progress in each discipline in each term.

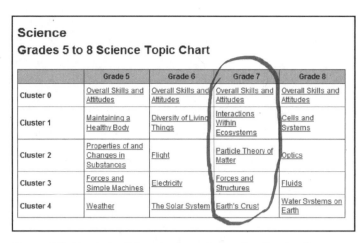

Figure 4.2 Manitoba Education's curriculum for Grades 5 to 8 Science

Step 2. Integrating curricula into thematic units

Now, our second step is to combine the topics into three integrated themes. I can choose to align Manitoba Education's Science curriculum with the Social Studies curriculum by looking for connections between the science and social studies topics. Looking at the three science clusters and the three social studies clusters, I determine which fit best together, and why. For the first theme, I see "diversity and interdependence" as a connection between Social Studies *Cluster 2:* Global Quality of Life, and *Cluster 3:* Ways of Life. My grade 7 class studied this as a unit on Canada and Afghanistan, exploring "ways of life" and "quality of life," focusing on current events and the role of human rights.

Looking at the topics within each Science cluster (Figure 4.2), we can see that the learning outcomes from *Cluster 2:* the Particle Theory of Matter (PTOM) could be related to the Social Studies clusters in the Diversity and Interdependence unit, because climate and ecology affect the ways and quality of life in the two countries. Through the first term, my class studied the water cycle in deserts (Afghanistan) and the Arctic (Canada) as a means of integrating learning outcomes for PTOM and those for the two Social Studies clusters. I chose this unit for first term because the diversity focus fit perfectly with the RD program.

For the second term (January to March), a review of the concepts in social studies *Cluster 1* World Geography and science concepts in *Cluster 3:* Forces and Structures and *Cluster 4:* Earth's Crust revealed that the theme Earth: Above and Below could allow us to make strong connections between the two disciplines. During this term, my class looked at what goes on beneath the Earth's crust, the forces involved in the movement of tectonic plates, and how that affects geography, for example, the formation of mountains. We also looked at natural and human structures, and how people try to withstand natural forces such as winds and earthquakes.

Portage & Main Press, 2012, *Teaching to Diversity*, ISBN: 978-1-55379-353-3

For the third term (April to June), I chose the theme "Canada and the Arctic" to encompass a geographic area in the Americas from the Social Studies cluster 4, relating it to "global warming" from the Science cluster "Interactions within Ecosystems." Within this theme, we could explore global warming, looking at the human impact on ecosystems and the interactions of biotic and abiotic features of the Arctic.

Again, when combining topics under one theme, what matters is that the teacher sees connections to be shared with students. This is also where regional considerations enter the choices made. Knowing my students, their experiences, their cultures, I could choose themes and combinations that make sense to them, and celebrate what they know. If my class had a large Aboriginal population, for example, we could also make connections between ecosystems and ways of life that are unique to Aboriginal peoples, which would add depth to the learning of all students.

Grade 7 School Year	September to December	January to March	April to June
THEMES CHOSEN TO INTEGRATE DISCIPLINES	**Diversity and Interdependence**	**Earth: Above and Below**	**Canada and the Arctic**
SOCIAL STUDIES "People and Places in the World"	Clusters 2 and 3 **Global Quality of Life; Ways of Life in Asia (Afghanistan)**	Cluster 1 **World Geography**	Cluster 4 **Human Impact in the Americas (Canada)**
	Skills, Knowledge, Values — Applications all year		
SCIENCES "Foundations for Scientific Literacy"	Cluster 2 **Particle Theory of Matter**	Clusters 3, 4 **Forces and Structures; Earth's Crust**	Cluster 1 **Interactions within Ecosystems**
	Skills, Knowledge, Values — Applications all year		

Figure 4.3 Grade 7 Class: Second stage of planning curriculum integration for school year

Now, having organized the four clusters for each discipline's curriculum for grade 7 into three main thematic units, one for each term, we can begin to make connections with our other disciplines, particularly Language Arts and Mathematics. We can have students read and write about our themes and use relevant mathematics topics and methodologies when investigating subtopics (Van De Walle 2006). In the related activities for the students, we can also encourage them to create related music and art (fine arts).

When curricula do not integrate well, it is difficult for students on their own to make connections to the real world, as happens when specific skills in the mathematics subtopics are taught in isolation. Although at times we need to explicitly teach students a skill for the skill's sake, it is preferable to use problem-based learning and connect mathematics to the overall theme and subtopics of a unit. Problems related to measuring, data analysis, and spatial transformations

Portage & Main Press, 2012, *Teaching to Diversity*, ISBN: 978-1-55379-353-3

require specific mathematical skills when exploring inquiry projects in combined social studies/sciences thematic units.

In the units just described, from the broad topic of World Geography, we could choose to study the Cartesian plane, use statistics about global warming as part of the study of the North, and blend in measurement through experiments related to the particle theory of matter. I had to teach measures of central tendency (mean, median, and mode), so why not use a table of statistics about income and employment in Canada and Afghanistan? My lessons were specific to the numeracy, but the learning reinforced our understanding and provided information to the students for their inquiry projects in social studies and science. This is true curricular integration.

Step 3. Sequencing themes and topics

The final step in the process for planning the year was to decide which theme to teach in each term. Sometimes there is a logical sequence conceptually (e.g., formation of the earth might precede geology); other times, there is a logical sequence seasonally (e.g., you might want to study plants in spring). Again, as long as you "cover" the key concepts by the end of the school year, you can choose any combination in any order that you believe will work for you and your students, and that assures integration.

Grade 7 School Year	September to December	January to March	April to June
THEMES CHOSEN TO INTEGRATE DISCIPLINES	**Diversity and Interdependence**	**Earth: Above and Below**	**Canada and the Arctic**
SOCIAL STUDIES "People and Places in the World"	Clusters 2 and 3 **Global Quality of Life; Ways of Life in Asia (Afghanistan)**	Cluster 1 **World Geography**	Cluster 4 **Human Impact in the Americas (Canada)**
	Skills, Knowledge, Values — Applications all year		
SCIENCES "Foundations for Scientific Literacy"	Cluster 2 **Particle Theory of Matter**	Clusters 3, 4 **Forces and Structures; Earth's Crust**	Cluster 1 **Interactions within Ecosystems**
	Skills, Knowledge, Values — Applications all year		
MATHEMATICS	**Statistics and Probability** (Data Analysis)	**Shape and Space** (Measurement)	**Shape and Space** (Transformations)
	Number concepts and numerical operations all year		
LANGUAGE ARTS	Integrated all year long		
FINE ARTS	Integrated all year long		

Figure 4.4 Grade 7 Class: Final plan of school year, combining themes and topics in all disciplines

Portage & Main Press, 2012, *Teaching to Diversity*, ISBN: 978-1-55379-353-3

Strategies for Variations on the Year

Challenge 1: Multi-grade classrooms

1. Create a two-year plan: In a class combining two grades, for instance grades 6 and 7, you will have the students for two years. So you can take the three themes from grade 6 and the three from grade 7, and spread them over two years. You might do two grade 6 and one grade 7 theme in Year A, and then do two grade 7 and one grade 6 theme in Year B. Thus over the two years, students cover all the topics. It does not matter that grade 6 students will do a grade 7 topic and vice-versa.

Our curriculum is a spiral curriculum. It follows strands such as life science or history and builds on itself. In different provinces, topics appear at different grades, because any topic can be taught at any level—we can talk about habitats in grade 1, or grade 4, or grade 10, or do a PhD on them. The topics are flexible—the depth to which you take them depends on when they are introduced—and in any class, you have a range of ability and knowledge whether you have a single grade or a combined one, which means that you have to differentiate your instruction.

> The concern that a student's family might move and the student would miss a particular topic is matched by the concern that the teacher in the new school might cover the topic in third term and the student ends up doing it twice, missing whatever was taught in first and second term. In the end, *students who are learning how to learn* can find any missed information. No one's life has been ruined because they missed their grade 6 class on plants.

2. Recombine units: You can do a second level of thematic combination. In our spiral curricula, topics recur every year, with new perspectives— one year in Science, students study animal life cycles and the next year, plant life cycles. You can combine them into a unit on life cycles. Social Studies units on communities move out from local, to provincial, to national, and to global. History moves out through various periods, and Geography expands from local through particular areas to cover the globe and move out into space. Looking for combinations, you might combine the grade 6 "national" government unit with the grade 7 "global" communities unit into a "Canada and the world" unit. Such combinations allow you to take the three grade 6 units and the three grade 7 units, and combine them into three large units.

Challenge 2: In discipline-specific settings

1. Collaborate with teachers of other disciplines: Discipline-specific teachers in middle grades and secondary school teachers who teach only one discipline would need to collaborate when planning a whole school year. Colleagues who have taught together, sometimes for decades, may have worked in such isolation that they truly do not know the content of each other's courses. So when the school is implementing collaborative planning, these teachers are surprised to realize the connections that exist within their courses—themes like sustainability, Canadian social history, and safe handling of equipment. Collaborative planning means that, working together, you find the connections between your curricula in order to team-plan units of study for the term or the year. But you each teach your part of the unit's content.

As an example, with a grade 11 history course focused on the period between World War I and World War II, all teachers on the team decided that each would approach their discipline through the lens of this time period—innovations in technology and the sciences (chemistry, physics, and power mechanics), literature, economics, and so on. As far as the students knew, they spent the semester studying "Between the Wars." As they went from class to class, the teacher of each discipline directly linked their lessons with topics the students were dealing with in other disciplines. Some teachers chose to plan co-operative lessons and assignments; for example, the Power Mechanics teacher and the Physics teacher did a project about the evolution of the engine for flight. All over the school, these students were talking about the wars and what they were learning. Other themes ideal for collaboration are sustainability, global warming, interdependence, and health sciences, which run through many curricula. If your colleagues are not able or willing to collaborate, ask a few of them what they are teaching during a term or semester. Then find connections in your own course content and help the students make connections by planning a unit in a universally designed way, even if discipline-specific.

Numeracy in all themes

Glenys MacLeod, a numeracy consultant in a large urban school division, was a participant in my 2011 summer institute. When I talked about choosing a strand of mathematics that fit with the theme, Glenys mentioned the current concern in mathematics education is that teachers tend to deal only once a year with particular subunits in the mathematics curriculum (like fractions or measurement), then students don't encounter the topic again until the following year. This means that students have long gaps between exploring math concepts, and do not see how they apply across multiple units and content. When I asked Glenys to suggest an alternative, she said that aspects of each strand should be addressed in each thematic unit, much as reading and writing are.

Planning the Units

For our plan of the school year, we had a curriculum to deliver, and we were simply organizing the sequence of the units. For planning the units, we begin to take into consideration the diverse nature of our learners, aware that they differ in background knowledge, skills, and pace of learning. We also recognize that they learn best in varied ways, so we cannot assume that we can deliver the same curriculum content at the same pace and in the same way to all grade 7 students. How do we meet such diverse needs? We start at the end.

Planning with assessment in mind

Traditionally, teachers planned a unit, taught it, and then assessed students' understanding at the end of the unit. This sequence left no opportunity to re-teach material if the students had not understood it, and it was inefficient. Without first assessing students' knowledge, teachers might have been teaching material that students had already mastered, or their planning might have assumed the students had knowledge or skills that they actually lacked. With backward design (Wiggins and McTighe 1998), teachers do their planning with the desired result in mind. After deciding on the essential understandings for the unit, they determine how to assess whether students have mastered them. Then they *assess where the students are now* before they develop a plan of instruction to take students *from where they are to where they need to be.*

Determining essential understandings

Although we teach with the learning outcomes in mind, no one can cover them all. More recently, teachers have been encouraged to let go of specific learning outcomes and focus on the depth and meaning in the curriculum. Some provinces and school divisions have even gone so far as to identify *essential outcomes* for teachers. However, there is a difference between an essential outcome and an essential understanding.

Understanding is a conceptual approach, which emphasizes thinking. *Outcome* is a skills-based approach, which emphasizes performance.

One teacher I worked with insisted she covered all the outcomes, and her students did well on her tests. When I asked her whether her students would still do well if she gave the same test a few weeks from now, she laughed and replied, "Of course not." Well, if students cannot remember what they learned, then they have not truly learned anything, and you have not really taught anything — nor have you covered the curriculum.

The emphasis on performance has created passive learners, leaving one of the biggest problems we face in our schools. Such learners have no motivation to think deeply, to seek insight, to make connections, or to go above and beyond. As a university professor, I see this even in adult professionals. They just want to be told what I am looking for, so they can regurgitate it and get their mark. I want my students to think. I tell them their brains should be burnt out by 3:30 in the afternoon. So I look for the essential understandings of the unit:

> *What is it I want my students to understand, in a deep and profound way?*
>
> *What are the big ideas from this unit that they will carry with them across disciplines and will retain years from now?*
>
> *Why do we bother to teach this?*

It may be helpful to examine the general learning outcomes (GLOs) or summaries in your curricula and highlight key words. The conceptual structure of Manitoba Education's Social Studies curriculum sets out six general learning outcomes that apply from Kindergarten through Grade 12 and are the basis for the specific learning outcomes at each grade:

1. **Identity, Culture, and Community:** Students will explore concepts of identity, culture, and community in relation to individuals, societies, and nations.

2. **The Land:** Places and People: Students will explore the dynamic relationships of people with the land, places, and environments

3. **Historical Connections:** Students will explore how people, events, and ideas of the past shape the present and influence the future.

4. **Global Interdependence:** Students will explore the global interdependence of people, communities, societies, nations, and environments.

5. **Power and Authority:** Students will explore the processes and structures of power and authority, and their implications for individuals, relationships, communities, and nations.

6. **Economics and Resources:** Students will explore the distribution of resources and wealth in relation to individuals, communities, and nations.

To move from these big ideas in planning our first unit/theme "Diversity and Interdependence" for our grade 7 class, we look at the learning outcomes set out in the curriculum and synthesize them into essential understandings. At the same time, we have to consider the developmental stage of our students—primarily 12- to 14-year-olds. What is appropriate for them to know about the quality of life around the world?

Secondary school teachers often raise the issue of provincial exams at this point. It is a legitimate concern. Yes, I wish government ministries would give their head a shake, but they have political agendas to balance with the educational ones. So for now, we are stuck with the exams. To their credit, they have tried to move away from the rote details, and ask deeper questions, at least in some exams. The bottom line is this: if secondary school students have a deep understanding of the important concepts in the course, they will be able to tackle the provincial exam much better than if they try to memorize a million details, only to discover they "studied the wrong stuff" for the exam.

Portage & Main Press, 2012, *Teaching to Diversity*, ISBN: 978-1-55379-353-3

Learning Outcomes for Quality of Life (QOL)	
• Describe the impact of various factors on citizenship rights in Canada/the world.	• Compare and contrast various types of power and authority.
• Describe the impact of various factors on quality of life in Canada/world.	• Explain the relationship between power and access to wealth and resources.
• Give examples of ways in which QOL may be enhanced within a democracy.	• Identify various individuals who influence world affairs.
• Describe ways in which their personal actions may affect QOL for people elsewhere in the world.	• Give examples of the uneven distribution of wealth and resources in the world and describe the impact on individuals, communities, and nations.
• Recognize Remembrance Day as a commemoration of Canadian participation in world conflicts.	• Respect the inherent dignity of all people.
• Identify diverse cultural and social perspectives regarding quality of life.	• Acknowledge that the rights of citizenship involve limitations on personal freedom for the sake of collective quality of life.
• Describe the impact of discriminatory attitudes and practices on quality of life.	• Be willing to contribute to their groups and communities.
• Describe the influence of various factors on personal identity.	• Be willing to take action to support quality of life for people around the world.
• Give examples of events and achievements that enhance understanding among peoples and nations.	• Respect others' rights to express their points of view.
• Identify reasons why people emigrate.	• Value the contributions of international agencies and humanitarians to QOL.
• Give examples of global cooperation to solve conflicts or disasters.	• Demonstrate concern for people who are affected by discrimination, injustice, or abuse of power.
• Identify various international organizations and describe their role in protecting or enhancing global quality of life.	• Appreciate the positive contributions of various individuals to world affairs.
• Identify universal human rights and explain their importance.	• Appreciate that QOL is not solely determined by access to wealth, resources, and technologies.
• Give examples of government decisions that affect quality of life.	

What do you think are the essential understandings in this list? What is really important here? What should a 13-year-old understand about this topic? There are a few ways to complete this process. If you have a big picture mind, you can probably scan these and say "This is really about _____." For others, try to see what ideas repeat by cutting them up and sorting them into piles. Here are my "essential understandings" for this Social Studies cluster.

Students will understand that…

1. people around the world are diverse in their quality of life (QOL), and how they define it.

2. many factors contribute to QOL and our understandings of it.

3. human rights and discrimination have significant impact on QOL.

Portage & Main Press, 2012, *Teaching to Diversity*, ISBN: 978-1-55379-353-3

Because we have combined two clusters, we have another set of learning outcomes to consider for Ways of Life in Asia, Africa, *or* Australasia:

Learning Outcomes for Ways of Life	
• Identify elements that all societies have in common. • Give examples of cultural factors that shape ways of life in a society of Asia, Africa, *or* Australasia (A, A, AA). • Give examples of the artistic expression of culture in a society of A, A, AA. • Describe the influence of westernization in a society of A, A, AA. • Describe factors that affect health in a society of A, A, AA. • Describe characteristics of indigenous ways of life in a society of A, A, AA. • Identify on a map the major cities, landforms, and bodies of water of a society of A, A, AA. • Give examples of the influence of the natural environment on ways of life in a society of A, A, AA. • Identify historical events that continue to affect a society of A, A, AA.	• Give examples of the impact of government and the justice system on ways of life in a society of A, A, AA. • Identify major economic activities in a society of A, A, AA. • Describe the impact of urbanization and industrialization on indigenous peoples in a society of A, A, AA. • Give examples of the impact of changing technologies on ways of life in a society of A, A, AA. • Identify issues related to work and trade in a society of A, A, AA. • Be willing to broaden personal perspectives and experiences beyond the familiar. • Appreciate the importance of cultural and linguistic diversity in the world. • Demonstrate interest in ways of life of other societies in the world. • Demonstrate concern for the loss of indigenous ways of life.

We repeat the process of synthesizing, and look for the essential understandings:
   Students will understand that...

1. many factors affect life in Asia, Africa, *or* Australasia.

2. humans impact their environment.

3. environments impact human societies.

4. sustainability requires a balancing of economic, environmental, and cultural factors.

5. our personal choices affect our environment.

Portage & Main Press, 2012, *Teaching to Diversity*, ISBN: 978-1-55379-353-3

Finally, we look at the learning outcomes for the Science cluster selected:

Learning Outcomes for Particle Theory of Matter	
• Evaluate different types of thermometers using the design process. • Demonstrate the effects of heating and cooling on the volume of solids, liquids, and gases, and give examples from daily life. • Compare the boiling and melting points of a variety of substances and recognize that boiling and melting points are properties of pure substances. • Explain what scientific theories are, and provide some examples. • Describe the particle theory of matter and use it to explain changes of state. • Differentiate between the concept of temperature and the concept of heat. • Demonstrate how heat can be transmitted through solids, liquids, and gases. • Plan an experiment to identify materials that are good heat insulators and good heat conductors, and describe some uses of these materials. • Use the design process to construct a prototype to control transfer of heat energy. • Recognize that heat energy is the most common by-product of energy transformations, and describe some examples. • Identify different forms of energy that can be transformed into heat energy.	• Differentiate between pure substances and mixtures by using the particle theory. • Differentiate between two types of mixtures-solutions and mechanical mixtures. • Classify a variety of substances used in daily life as pure substances, solutions, or mechanical mixtures. • Identify solutes and solvents in common solid, liquid, and gaseous solutions. • Describe solutions by using the particle theory of matter. • Demonstrate different methods of separating the components of both solutions and mechanical mixtures. • Identify a separation technique used in industry, explain why it's appropriate. • Experiment to determine factors that affect solubility. • Describe the concentration of a solution in qualitative and quantitative terms, and give examples from daily life when the concentration of a solution influences its usefulness. • Demonstrate the difference between saturated and unsaturated solutions. • Discuss the potential harmful effects of some substances on the environment, and identify methods to ensure their safe use and disposal.

I want to narrow this list down, because I want the students to understand that Science is actually born of a creative and curious mind: Someone wondered about what they observed in our world—"How did that occur? And why?"—they investigated, and perhaps experimented and figured it out. So to paraphrase the list, I chose the following essential understandings for the Science:

Students will understand that

1. scientific theories help us understand our world.
2. the particle theory of matter (PTOM) explains how things (matter) exist in and change states.
3. heat is a form of energy transfer that affects matter.
4. matter can be classified in a variety of ways.

These choices mean that my teaching and my assessment will be focused on these four big ideas, and everything we do in the science strand will help the students reach a deep level of understanding of them.

Portage & Main Press, 2012, *Teaching to Diversity*, ISBN: 978-1-55379-353-3

When we put together the essential understandings in our combined Social Studies and Science curriculum units, we have:

Students will understand that…

1. people around the world are diverse in their quality of life (QOL), and how they define it.
2. many factors contribute to QOL and our understandings of it.
3. human rights and discrimination have significant impact on QOL.
4. individuals and groups can impact human rights and the QOL for themselves and others.
5. our personal choices impact global QOL.
6. many factors affect life in A, A, *or* AA (Canada and Afghanistan).
7. humans impact their environment.
8. environments impact human societies.
9. sustainability requires a balancing of economic, environmental, and cultural factors.
10. our personal choices affect our environment.
11. scientific theories help us understand our world.
12. the particle theory of matter explains how things (matter) exist in and change states.
13. heat is a form of energy transfer that affects matter.
14. matter can be classified in a variety of ways.

I have one term of three months within which to teach my students these fourteen topics, some of which I can combine—for instance, statements 5 and 10 both refer to how personal choices affect the world around us. At age 13, students have begun to understand that what they do affects not only their immediate environment but also the people and environment around the world. So by synthesizing these understandings, I end up with nine essential understandings:

1. People around the world are diverse in their ways and quality of life.
2. Many factors contribute to quality and ways of life, and our understanding of them.
3. Our personal choices impact our world.
4. Sustainability requires a balancing of economic, environmental, and cultural factors.
5. Compassion and respect are necessary attitudes for sustainability.
6. Scientific theories help us understand our world.
7. Matter can be classified in a variety of ways.
8. Heat is a form of energy transfer that affects matter.
9. The particle theory of matter explains how things (matter) exist in and change states.

Having consolidated the big ideas into nine essential understandings, and with three months to teach them, I can, as a teacher, take a deep breath, and be creative and focused in my teaching. At this point also, we can consider regional and cultural factors within our group of students. We can also bring in the perspectives of often marginalized populations and enrich the learning, not simplify it.

What would Aboriginal culture deem essential in learning about ways of life?

How is this the same or different from other cultures?

How does urban versus rural life affect our thinking?

Creating inquiry questions

We need to consider how to lead our students to inquire into these topics, which means we have to turn our essential understandings into essential questions. We want questions that lead our students to discover the concepts themselves, wrestle with them, and synthesize their own understanding of them. Creating questions can be as simple as putting "who, what, when, where, why, or how" in front of the essential understanding. For example, we could ask "How are people around the world diverse in their ways and quality of life?" To get at the factors involved (e.g., politics, economics), we simply change the "How..." to "*Why* are people around the world diverse in their ways and quality of life?"

Such an approach can be effective, at times. However, it tends to encourage the "correct answer" type of activity, like the poster with twenty downloaded facts and two pictures on it that students read orally in a presentation. But, have they really done any deep critical thinking about the topic? They have not had to wrestle with the issues, to see the conflicts and inconsistencies, or to develop a personal connection and viewpoint—all of which require true intellectual inquiry and critical analysis. They have simply "met the criteria." I want more, much more, from education and from my students. So how do I get them to think? How do I make this personal and challenging, and yet multi-levelled for diverse learners? The key is in the question and in the approach.

One approach to inquiry is to devise open-ended questions using the higher levels of the progression shown in Bloom's taxonomy (Figure 4.5). By asking open-ended questions, we allow students to take their learning to their best level. For example, in the first unit, the question "How would your life be different if you moved to Afghanistan?" allowed students to personalize the differences in ways of life and in human rights. When the girls in the class realized their lives would change a lot more than the boys' lives, some fascinating discussions took place. For this unit, then, we might pose some of the following questions:

- *Would your life be different if you lived in another country?*
- *What would make it different?*
- *In what ways do the choices you make affect the world around you?*
- *How can we sustain our environment and way of life?*
- *Why do scientists propose theories?*

Portage & Main Press, 2012, *Teaching to Diversity*, ISBN: 978-1-55379-353-3

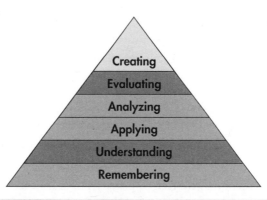

Cognitive Domains	Examples of Key Words Describing Capability
6. Creating Can the student create a new product or point of view?	assemble, construct, create, design, develop, formulate, write
5. Evaluating Can the student justify a stand or decision?	appraise, argue, defend, judge, select, support, value, evaluate
4. Analyzing Can the student distinguish between the different parts?	appraise, compare, contrast, criticize, differentiate, discriminate, distinguish, examine, experiment, question, test
3. Applying Can the student use the information in a new way?	choose, demonstrate, dramatize, employ, illustrate, interpret, operate, schedule, sketch, solve, use, write
2. Understanding Can the student explain ideas or concepts?	classify, describe, discuss, explain, identify, locate, recognize, report, select, translate, paraphrase
1. Remembering Can the student recall or remember the information?	define, duplicate, list, memorize, recall, repeat, reproduce, state

Figure 4.5 Adapted from Bloom's *Taxonomy of Educational Objectives, Cognitive Domain,* revised by Anderson and Krathwohl 2001

- *What is the purpose of the particle theory of matter?*
- *What is matter? Does it matter?*

Another approach has been suggested in the work of Jeffrey Wilhelm (2007) in which he suggested taking an approach based on professions. As an example, we might develop an activity in which the students are told that the United Nations wants to send them to investigate human rights and environmental issues in Afghanistan, and they have to report back. The U.N. also requires that their team include an anthropologist, an environmental scientist, a medical doctor, and a theologian. From this added detail about their team's role-play, the students would learn the "kind of mind" that different disciplines employ in their line of work, and how they can work together.

We know where we are leading our students, but we still need to plan with the end result in mind. What kind of summative assessment or evaluation would allow the students to show what they have learned or to demonstrate mastery of the important concepts and skills? For a grade 7 student, what would constitute a good answer? If one of the girls said, "I would have to wear a veil and stay inside," does this answer "fully meet the expectations"? Some might say yes, but I don't think so. "Girls wear veils" is just factual recall. But I want my students to have debated the why.

- *"Why are women thought of so differently?"*
- *"Why would a young girl be seen as improper in dress?"*
- *"What does this say about sexuality, gender, social roles, human rights?"*
- *"How do secular versus theistic models of governments affect their citizens?"*

In the Science part of the unit, I want my students to explore not only what the particle theory of matter is, but why it is important. Why do we care that heat increases the vibration of the molecules, which spread apart, start moving faster, and become a gas? Well, if you live in Afghanistan, where desertification and droughts are significant issues, then it matters. If you live in Canada's North where the permafrost is softening, then it matters. This application to one's personal space is where students become engaged, see the real-life application to what they are learning, and come to understand the scientific process and science's contribution to our world. This is evidence of the depth of their learning.

Creating Rubrics for Assessment for, as, and of Learning

In order to assess diverse learners, we have to use diverse methods, but not different standards. We should hold high expectations for all learners, but recognize that *learning is a developmental process*, one which students enter on any given topic (or for any given skill) at different points along the continuum, and which they will likely leave at different points.

- We need a way of outlining the continuum, the conceptual scope and sequence of what we are teaching.
- We need to differentiate our assessment. Whether students do a role-play, a written report, or a piece of art, we should be able to assess their understanding.
- We need to ensure that we assess what we want to know about our students' learning.

If I am assessing the students' understanding of the particle theory of matter, it is inappropriate to give a timed written test. The learning objective states "can describe ___", "can analyze___," but does not add "in writing." It means "assess their thinking" and assign a mark according to the depth of thought revealed in the response, whether that response is a model of the molecular structure, a painting of it, a diagram, or a written description. All such formats for the response can be assessed for the scientific content.

In one class, my students had been learning about biotic and abiotic features of an ecosystem and, later, we went on to explore interaction or interdependence. One group that included some kinesthetic learners was studying the desert, so I gave them the option of creating six yoga poses that reflected three biotic and three abiotic features of the desert. A biology teacher who saw the students' video said, "Well, I can't mark yoga for science." Really? Why not? Would you give the students an item on a test with the direction to "List three abiotic and three biotic features of the desert"? If so, what's the difference? If my students got up to perform and said: "Here are three yoga poses demonstrating abiotic features of the desert," and then showed "snake," I would know that they didn't understand *abiotic*. But when they did *sandstorm*, *dune*, and *heat*, I gave them full credit.

Let's focus on how we determine the conceptual development that we expect the students to demonstrate. For starters, don't reinvent the wheel. Many curricular programs come with rubrics for assessment. The BC Ministry of Education, for example, has performance standards for literacy and numeracy on their website—use them. However, in science and social studies, rubrics are rare, or are specific to an activity, not a concept. So we have to make our own rubrics for our combined essential understandings—a challenging task at first that gets much easier with practice. To begin, use the concept of a pyramid:

- *What will all your students understand at the end of the unit?*
- *What will most of your students understand at the end of the unit?*
- *What will some of the students understand?*

Use the essential understanding in your "fully meets" column because, if it is *essential*, then it is what most of your students should understand. Then, to stretch it developmentally, add others verbs in front of the stated essential understanding. I use Bloom's taxonomy (Figure 4.5, p. 73.) to do this. For the essential understanding "People around the world are diverse in their ways of life," I think about what is realistic to expect of most grade 7 students. Is it "can describe" how people around the world are diverse in their ways of life? Is it "analyze how people…"? Then, I think about what students would need to know or be able to do to gain that understanding, that is, "What should all grade 7 students be able to understand?"

A note on language: Some provinces have provincial language for rubrics. BC, for example, uses "C-: Not yet meeting expectations," "C: Minimally meeting expectations," "B: Fully meeting expectations," and "A: Exceeding expectations." If your province requires consistent language, then use it. However, if you have a choice, get rid of the "Not yet…" wording in the first columns of your rubrics. It's negative and not reflective of what we understand about learning, which is that "It's a process." I prefer using language like "Beginning…" in these statements because the left column of the rubric is supposed to be the point at which your students begin. In other words, on a grade 7 rubric, the "Beginning…" column should state what you would expect a grade 5/6 student to know about the topic.

The details of provincial curricula spiral through the grades: in Early Years, for example, children learn about "living and not living" ; in the next grades, the topic becomes "life cycles"; then "classification systems"; then "biodiversity"; and so on. When I teach "life cycles," the "Beginning…" column of my assessment rubric says something about understanding "… the characteristics of living things." If I look at prior grades in the curriculum cycle, I can see the stated expectations of what students would have learned by the end of that year. Most students would then start the first unit in the subsequent grade with that level of understanding. So the beginning column of your assessment rubric should describe what you expect students will come in with, and the other columns in the rubric outline your expectations of where they will go.

Using Bloom's taxonomy (Figure 4.5), focus on making the rubric statements show the *developmental* levels of thinking, rather than the *quantitative*. Quantitative language "knows *some* of the ways, knows *most* of the ways" is deadly in a rubric because, first, it implies a race to memorize the most facts and, second, students will instantly ask "How many is most?"—but the assessments of conceptual understanding are not numerical. Instead, the words that show developmental progress move through Bloom's stages of thinking, for instance, from *recognize*, to *describe*, to *analyze*, to *synthesize* or *apply*. So a rubric for this unit might look like Figure 4.6.

Student input

It is always important to have student input into the criteria for their assessment. However, this requires a delicate balance when asking students to describe progressive stages of conceptual thinking rather than of skill levels. On the one hand, we have not yet introduced the concepts to our students, so we cannot expect them to grasp the development of the concept; on the other hand, if we wait to develop the rubric with them, we would not have the goal in mind as we do our planning. So, how do we resolve the conflict? We create a rubric, but as we progress through the unit, we flexibly alter it, if needed. Thus, as my students engage in their learning activities, we share our thinking, relate it to the original rubric I shared with them, and say, for example, "How is this a powerful example of analysis or creativity?" As the group or the class discusses what we believe makes some perception "powerful" or "profound," we may alter the wording of the rubric to reflect that perception. In my experience, the students actually exceed the statements in my original rubric—they are amazing when given the opportunity.

Formative assessment

Now that we know what we want the students to know by the end of the unit, we need a snapshot of their knowledge and understanding as the term begins. Where are we at this moment? What do they already know about ways of life around the world? about the particle theory of matter? about global warming? about human rights? We can use a variety of quick, formative assessments to determine this: group discussions; know-wonder-learn charts, and brainstorming provide a quick sense of our starting points. Once we know where our students are in their thinking, we know where we can begin. One group of teachers decided that they should start with basic lessons:

- *What are human rights?*
- *What is the difference between "way of life" and "quality of life"?*

Portage & Main Press, 2012, *Teaching to Diversity*, ISBN: 978-1-55379-353-3

DISCIPLINES	Beginning to develop (C-)	Approaching expectations (C)	Fully meeting expectations (B)	Exceeding expectations (A)
SOCIAL STUDIES Essential Understanding 1	Recognizes that daily life differs around the world	Able to describe differing ways of life around the world	Able to describe differing ways of life, and assess diverse concepts of quality of life	Argues reasons for diverse ways of living and concepts of quality of life, with justification
Essential Understanding 2	Understands that where you live affects your way of life in simple, linear ways	Can explain factors that contribute to a person's way of life (e.g., where you live, economics)	Can explain factors that contribute to the quality of life and to different ways of life, and our understandings of both	Infers, and gives opinions about definitions of quality of life and the reasons for them
Essential Understanding 3	Understands that we affect our environment	Explains how personal choices affect the environment	Explains how our personal choices impact our world, including both the environment and other people and cultures	Analyzes the interdependent relationship between Canada and other nations and cultures in the world
Essential Understanding 4	Describes environmental issues	Describes environmental issues and their causes	Analyzes how and why sustainability requires a balancing of economic, environmental, and cultural factors	Proposes a plan for sustaining an ecosystem Plan is logical
SCIENCES Essential Understanding 1	Understands that all things are made of matter	Defines states of matter, solutions	Explains how matter can be classified in a variety of ways, with supporting examples	Compares and contrasts classification systems
Essential Understanding 2	Understands that scientists study how the world works	Explains why scientists postulate theories (trying to figure out how the world works)	Explains the connection between wondering, theory, and experimentation	Argues the role of science in "progress" (i.e., the pros and cons)
Essential Understanding 3	Recognizes states of matter (solid, liquid, gas)	Gives examples of changes of state	Explains the particle theory of matter (PTOM) as a theory of how things (matter) exist in and change states	Connects the PTOM with environmental issues, such as global warming and desertification

Figure 4.6 Sample rubric for two disciplines in an integrated unit of study

- *Where is Afghanistan and what is the environment like there?*
- *What are the characteristics of a solid, a liquid, and a gas, molecularly?*

Each group of students is different, but once we know where our starting and ending points are, we can plan our instruction.

Portage & Main Press, 2012, *Teaching to Diversity*, ISBN: 978-1-55379-353-3

Some students already know the answers to these questions because they have the background knowledge that we are trying to build in the rest of the students. But as teachers, we now have goals in mind for our students, and we use an open-ended lesson to engage all our learners. Learning involves discovery, problem solving, critical thinking, and cooperation. We don't want to just deliver curriculum, we want our students to discover it through their own investigative thinking.

Inquiry and discipline-based instruction

Success in postsecondary requires that students have a good understanding of the disciplines they have chosen. In Biology, for example, how does a biologist think? What kinds of problems do they face in their research or their work? What skills and vocabulary are integral to the discipline? How do the answers to these questions differ for a chemist, an anthropologist, or a historian? Members from each of these professions might be required in an investigation of an archaeological dig, and have to work together, but they all work from different perspectives. Introducing young children and youth to "Thinking like a ... (profession)" helps to form schemas for them. As we approach our unit, we can "think like a biologist or an anthropologist."

Now, if we pose these questions to the students, and plan activities and resources that will allow them to discover *their* answers, we will be on our way. We can provide resources with varying reading levels, formats (videos, websites, guest speakers), and depth of content. Students will answer the questions with varying levels of complexity, but we will all be investigating the same questions. A student with severe disabilities can come to understand that people in other countries live lives quite different from ours. A gifted student can be introduced to ideas such as secularism versus theocracy, sexual discrimination, and the impact of war. Students vary as well in the formats they choose for their response: one student might make a picture book to show their learning, another might choose a musical format. Such differentiation of content, process, and product allows diverse learners to belong to the same learning community and work alongside each other.

Jeffrey Wilhelm (2007) goes a step further in his work with inquiry. He suggests guiding a theme with an overarching inquiry that really gets to the heart of what we are learning—"big questions" like "big ideas" really teach to the heart, mind, and spirit, and help guide all aspects of the learning community. In our first unit "Diversity and Interdependence," we might use questions like "What makes a good life?" or "What is interdependence?" or "What is harmony?" to explore the relationships within our classroom community, as well as in the larger communities we have chosen to study. And doing so with diverse learners means we have to consider how best to do so in ways that everyone, regardless of language proficiency or cognitive level, can participate.

Differentiating instruction for multiple intelligences

Students learn in a variety of ways and at varying paces, so for all students in our class to succeed in mastering the concepts and skills that we deem essential for our unit, we have to present the material in a variety of ways—and allow students to show their mastery in a variety of ways. I use Multiple Intelligences Theory as a framework to ensure that I am doing just that—using multiple modes of teaching and responding. It ensures balance in my teaching.

As teachers, we tend to teach to ourselves. When I do workshops, I sometimes have my adult participants play a game called "Stand up if you are... ," for example, Musical-Rhythmic or Bodily-Kinesthetic, and so on. Then I say "Stand up if you use a lot of music in your class" or "Stand up if you have your students move around a lot." Of course, we see that the standees are themselves musical, so they use a lot of music in their class; those who are physically active involve their students in kinesthetic activities. But what can we do for the student whose learning profile doesn't match our own? Many students can remember the words to a song better than they can retain the words to a poem. How do I offer these students a chance to learn through their strength?

I don't have to sing in order to suggest that my students "Write a song about ____" or "Create sound effects to back up ..." a written piece, and so on. By differentiating my instruction through the lens of the multiple intelligences that I presented to and discussed with my students during the RD program, I know that over the course of the unit I will have taught through visual, auditory, kinesthetic, and other modalities, and I will have varied my groupings (because of interpersonal and intrapersonal intelligences), and I will have added in fine arts like drama (bodily-kinesthetic), art (visual-spatial), and music (musical-rhythmic). It also connects our academic life to the RD program and to the social and emotional work we did at the beginning of the year.

Working with multiple intelligences

When I discuss working with multiple intelligences, many teachers ask me, "But aren't you labelling students?" and "Aren't they going to want to work only in their strengths?" My response: "No, I am not," and "No, I won't let them."

We have to be explicit with our students. Learning profiles showing strengths and challenges in the range of intelligences change over time; we can intentionally develop a given intelligence; and life circumstances may also change us. Although a person's particular learning strength might be true now, it is not a permanent condition. A "strength" is only a potential that needs development. Mozart had great potential in "musical-rhythmic" intelligence, but had there been no piano in his home, it might never have been developed.

In my classroom, students rotate in cooperative teams through work centres focused on one of the intelligences, so that the students have a chance to develop an understanding of them all. This is how we ensure that our students do not get stuck learning in only one way. The activities stimulate all the different areas of the brain so that students develop neurologically, as well as academically. The rotation also gives different students an opportunity to shine and to be a leader at different stations. The student with autism might be the best at the visual-spatial centre, but might require the support of their team at the verbal-linguistic centre.

Portage & Main Press, 2012, *Teaching to Diversity*, ISBN: 978-1-55379-353-3

ST-V 8

Sara

Sara was in grade 6. Her previous teachers considered her to be bright, but immature and distractible, with socially inappropriate behaviour. When Sara entered the class, she immediately stood out. She had great difficulty sitting still, and was almost always either talking to someone or playing with the dozens of small toys and gadgets she brought to school. Sara came from a split family; her father was in Hong Kong managing the business, while her mother was in Canada with Sara and her younger brother.

In class, Sara was completely unfocused, and unmotivated. She laughed off any attempts to re-engage her. Sara was not rude or disrespectful; she was just very honest about herself. When asked whether she understood something, she would answer, "I might if I could stop thinking about eating my lunch," and other such truths. I tried many strategies: squeeze balls to hold, yoga balls to sit on; partners of various types; choice in activities. In the middle of an activity, Sara would approach me, like a much younger child, and say things like "Ms. Katz, did you know I love pork?" Other students found it hard to relate to Sara. She presented as so much younger, with a fascination for silly games and toys. She often annoyed others with constant fidgeting, poking, and talking.

I worked hard to find a few peers willing to work with Sara and befriend her. She had a dry sense of humour, which I noted appreciatively, trying to model my recognition of her strengths for other students. Sara became aware of this, and thanked me for being "the only teacher who liked her." The one activity that Sara seemed to engage in was music. It was clear she loved it, so I tried to offer opportunities for her to express herself through music. One day, in the midst of a unit about immigration, Sara approached me, carrying a paper in her hand. "Would you like to see something I wrote?" she asked. When I said "Sure," Sara handed me this page:

You.
Buried.
In that dark, silent coffin.
The you that cannot be seen.
Will we lose it someday? The light we held onto.
The memory of you. The memory of me.
As I watch people bury you
A single tear.
Two tears.
Three tears. Many tears that cannot be counted
Trickles down my cheek.
My tears, cry for me.
Family friends around me
Rubs my shoulder.
"Don't cry"
They tell me.
I ignore them.
They don't understand.
How much I need them.
My family.
I think.
It is unfair.

People I love die first.
Buried.
Alone in the silent darkness
The you that cannot be seen.
I shoulder the burden.
And leave it behind me.
I force on a smile.
And wave farewell.

Portage & Main Press, 2012, *Teaching to Diversity*, ISBN: 978-1-55379-353-3

I was speechless upon reading it, and asked Sara to tell me more about it. She said, "It's the lyrics to a song. I write them all the time." I asked her if she composed music for them. "No, I just listen to my IPod, and then I change the song lyrics to get my thoughts out," she answered. She agreed to bring in more for me to see. The next day, Sara arrived with a 4-inch binder filled with lyrics.

When I asked Sara how long she had been writing, she answered flatly, "Years." I asked her what her mom thought of her songs, and she blithely answered, "She doesn't know." You see, Sara's mother didn't speak English well, and Sara didn't speak Cantonese well, so although they could get by for everyday conversation, she could not translate the power and depth of her poetry into Cantonese. When Sara's mom had been to parent-teacher conferences, translators informed her that Sara was immature, unfocused, inappropriate, and falling behind, but they had no idea of her daughter's depth.

I asked Sara to walk with me after school, and we talked for a long time. She chose very deliberately the mask that she wore. She had not shown her songs to anyone before because "they wouldn't get it." Her peers were silly, she thought, so she just found relief in her own imagination. I asked her if she would share her songs, but she refused. However, she did agree to have a conference with her mother and a translator. Her mother left in tears, saying only a whispered "Thank you."

Later in the year, Sara came to me and said, "I have one you can share."

Me

I walk down the school hallway
As I pass, people stare
*How **hideous***
One says
No, I'm not hurt at all
*I'm **proud***
*Because I am being **me***
And I don't care what people think
Not
At
All
I sit at my desk
And I wonder
***Why** do people **bother**?*
*Trying to **act** and be the **same** as everyone else*
*It's just plain **stupid***
Stupid
Stupid
Stupid
A person comes to me and says
*How about you go home after school and get some **new** clothes*
*You could even **throw** those **away** after*
*They **disgust** me. **No. Us**.*
*And they walk **away***

Portage & Main Press, 2012, *Teaching to Diversity*, ISBN: 978-1-55379-353-3

No
*I'm not **hurt** at all*
I get home
I go to the mall
*d buy more of the clothes that are **me**, not the **same** as everyone elses'*
*The people at the mall **stared** at me like I was an **alien***
This morning at school
The person walks over again
*You are **disgusting**. Go get new clothes*
They say
*You **can't** tell me **what** to **wear***
I say
*The person **smirks***
We'll see
They say
The next day
*I chop my hair **short**, right to my neck*
Before, it went all the way down to my back
*You're **crazy**, **insane**, out of your **mind**. Are you even **human** at all?*
They tell me
*Now, that **hurt**. I was almost **angry***
*You're a **freak***
They say
*Well that's **who** I am. You'll just have to **deal** with it*
I tell them
*And **I** stand up*
And I am the one to walk away this time
*Leaving **them in shock***
*I **smile***
*I am **happy***
*I am **proud***
*Of **Myself***
For being
*An **absolutely***
Perfect
Me

Her fellow students were shocked. We had a long discussion about judgment and perception. They asked her who had treated her that way, and her response was a deeply felt "The world." The students had not themselves said those specific things, but Sara's perception was that people had judged her "by her outside," and so she played it up as an act of resistance and internal resiliency.

After that, Sara wrote many songs related to our themes, almost always "exceeding expectations" conceptually. Music gave her voice, and strength, and hope, which is why it is so vital that we offer our students the opportunity to learn in different ways — and give voice to the voiceless.

Portage & Main Press, 2012, *Teaching to Diversity*, ISBN: 978-1-55379-353-3

If T. or Cole had been in such a classroom, they would have excelled at building the model or creating the visual image. Their talents would have been honoured and developed, and they would have been seen as "smart" by their peers and themselves. We would have seen far less avoidant and negative behaviour. All students' strengths are valued in such a classroom, and when they are being evaluated for their final projects, they can choose to show their learning through their strength.

Practically speaking, many resources available for teachers have activities focused on the different intelligences. Books, websites, lesson plan models are, indeed, out there. The key is to look for lesson ideas that hit on the essential understandings. If, for example, I take an essential understanding for "the particle theory of matter explains how things (matter) exist in and change states," I can begin to look for lesson ideas that would approach this content visually, kinesthetically, musically, and so on. I could have the students compare images of the molecular structures and hypothesize about why they are different, which would be a visual-spatial activity. I could have the students act out the movement of molecules in different states—a kinesthetic activity. Musically, I could have the students compose a "Proton Symphony" using GarageBand or musical instruments. They could create a musical piece that reflects the sounds of solids, liquids, and gases—the sounds they hear from them (e.g., running water, air coming out of a balloon) or the sounds they would hear if they were a proton living inside a solid, liquid, or gas.

As you become more familiar with the intelligences (and some of the best lesson structures for them), it gets easier to do. I map out the ideas on an MI web or instructional planner (Figure 4.7) to be sure they are balanced. I google lesson plan ideas, then plug them into my web. I might google "lesson plans + PTOM," then look for good ideas that would fit under visual, musical, or kinesthetic. You don't have to reinvent the wheel, just balance them. Brainstorm as many activities as you can for each essential understanding. Focus on differentiating modalities and the complexity of concepts—we have 3-month units and we want to go deep. You will have more to choose from when devising the sequence in the next step—you don't have to include every intelligence for every essential understanding.

After I have my web with a full unit's worth of ideas for lessons/activities, I begin planning the sequence and delivery model for all lessons to facilitate my students' mastery of the essential understandings. At this point, "gradual release" enters the plan at the unit level. What are the whole-class, teacher-led activities that I can begin with to build my students' basic vocabulary, skills, and conceptual knowledge? I choose the ones that suit the first week or two of the unit.

Which activities can I then use at the work centres for group activities? My students will work on these cooperatively to scaffold their learning as they investigate the inquiry questions posed for them. The students' rotation around all the centres generally takes about 15 days, or 3 weeks. There are 9 stations but for some stations, the students need more than one day. I decide which centres will be activities at which the group will create one product, and which centres will be for individual activities in which students can share ideas, but each creates their own

Intrapersonal	**Whole Class** 1. Science in my life: solutions, solvents, heat, and so on **Individual** 1. Journals: What makes my life a "good life"? 2. Using a Venn diagram, compare your life in Canada with your imagined life in Afghanistan
Existential	**Group** Why should we care about the lives of people around the world?
Bodily-Kinesthetic	**Whole Class** 1. Experiencing discrimination: Separating classmates by hair colour 2. Science experiments re PTOM 3. Construction of prototype re heat conduction, PTOM **Group** 1. Role-play: Gender roles in Canada and in Afghanistan 2. Role-play: States of matter
Visual-spatial	**Whole Class** 1. Video: Life under the Taliban **Individual** 1. Art: 3-D & 2-D landscape of desert, showing water cycle 2. Art: Human rights
Musical-Rhythmic	**Group** 1. Compose a song written by a child living in Afghanistan 2. Proton Symphony: Sounds of matter in various states
Interpersonal	**Whole Class** 1. Study of *UN Charter* 2. Field trip: Womyn's Centre **Group** 1. Choices we make that impact people around the world: choice of song, art, play, written response
Verbal-Linguistic	**Whole Class** 1. Literature circles 2. Newspaper search **Group** 1. Poetry, chants 2. Debate: Should Canada be active in Afghanistan?
Naturalist	**Whole Class** 1. Experiment: Particle theory of matter **Group** 1. Landscapes of Canada and Afghanistan 2. Particle theory of matter: Deserts and the Arctic
Logical-Mathematical	**Group** 1. Compare measure of precipitation, temperature, and so on in Canada and Afghanistan 2. Economics and quality of life: Prepare budgets for food, housing, and material needs

Figure 4.7 MI web of ideas for Unit 1 activities

Portage & Main Press, 2012, *Teaching to Diversity*, ISBN: 978-1-55379-353-3

product. Note that the verbal-linguistic centre is always a group activity so that struggling readers and writers can be supported. Each centre offers a few choices for each student group. If we have time, I give my students a few free-choice days at the end of the centre rotations. They can go back to any centre and do one of the activities that their group did not select.

Finally, I wonder which activities could be offered as options to students for an independent activity that they could work on closer to the end of the unit, and that would allow them to work through their strengths to demonstrate their learning. I can be flexible in how much in-class time is given to this. For example, my plan for this unit would include some opening activities introducing the concepts of human rights, way of life and quality of life, and PTOM. Then we would move into the centres and the inquiry. As a final project, I might give students some choice in how they meet the criteria, which I usually lay out with them as in the example below.

Instructions for project

Your project must show your understanding of (i.e., answer) the following questions:

1. Would your life be different if you lived in another country?
2. What would make it different?
3. In what ways do the choices you make affect the world around you?
4. How can we sustain our environment and way of life?
5. Why do scientists propose theories?
6. What is the purpose of the particle theory of matter?
7. What is matter?

You must use at least two intelligences to demonstrate your learning. For example, you could create a poetry collection and illustrate it, write a role-play or song and perform it, record a podcast, or paint a mural and present it orally. Review the rubric to remind you of what I am looking for. In other words, your project must show me that you can analyze _____, describe _____, and so on.

Another option is to create an inquiry project as a final piece, which involves group co-operation but some individual accountability. For example, for this unit, I could create an inquiry something like the following:

Your team has been hired by the Canadian government to research and then create a proposal for how to assist the people of Afghanistan to create a sustainable, and democratic, society. You must give suggestions re:

1. What needs to be done to care for the ecosystems in the country?
2. How could we reverse the desertification process?
3. What laws need to be changed or passed to create a new government that will both respect human rights and freedoms, and Islamic traditions?
4. How could the economy be sustained to create a "good life" for the people of Afghanistan?
5. What role, if any, should Canada play in this?

On your team are an environmental scientist, a biologist, a lawyer, and a specialist in politics in the Islamic world. You may present your proposal in any format you like.

This would then fit with my rubric, and no matter what format my students used, all of them would be marked against these criteria (Figure 4.6).

Planning the Lessons

With my first unit planned out, the lesson plans follow easily. Each lesson focuses on one or two of the essential understandings, and approaches them through one or two intelligences. The lessons already have objectives, flexible groupings, and differentiations. At various points in the unit, the lesson may be teacher-led or collaborative, or it may involve independent learning and student choice. Generally, each lesson also follows a "gradual release" process, beginning with my short reminder about what it is we are trying to learn: I may remind them of the inquiry question, read a short piece, or otherwise hook them into the learning. At this time, I may also discuss behavioural expectations, criteria for products and process, and any other essential bits of information. Then the students will get together to work on a designated activity (early in the unit) at their centre or on their final project, share ideas, peer edit, and so on. Near the end of the lesson, the students may do some form of metacognitive reflection, quick-write, or partner-sharing to synthesize their learning: for example, a 5-minute quick-write, a "whip-around" oral sharing of one important thing learned, a presentation of a multi-modal product like a role-play, or a favourite line from their own writing. These summative moments are important both to understanding and to memory, so I pace my lessons in such a way that there is time at the end for such summaries—even when we have been involved in group work or a messy hands-on activity.

At this point, I have planned out my year in a way that helps students see connections in their learning, and have developed units that differentiate content, process, and product in ways that will serve diverse learners, that focus on the essential understandings, and that promote higher order thinking. I also have a rubric with which to assess my students' progress and mastery. The unit includes content from science, social studies, mathematics, language arts, and fine arts.

Yes, this takes some time. Does it sound like too much work? It really isn't. The schedule of the work is different because it is front-end loaded. It has to be ready to go at the beginning of each term, but then I have no preparation for the rest of the term. Remember that we only have to do this once per term, not every few weeks, as happens with smaller units. The first few times you do it, you will spend a long time, learning the process of determining EU's, building rubrics, planning MI lessons, but it will get much easier and faster. I can now put together a unit, from scratch, in a couple of hours.

Accommodations for exceptional needs

The unit I have prepared is one that all students can be a part of. As they progress through the centres, they work together as a team, supporting each other's learning.

Portage & Main Press, 2012, *Teaching to Diversity*, ISBN: 978-1-55379-353-3

As well, because we have done the RD program, and they know each other's strengths and challenges, they are empowered to problem-solve together.

UDL is designed so that we do not have to retrofit—we do not have to make changes to our unit to accommodate or provide access to diverse learners. There will always be a small percentage of students who need very specific supports, such as Braille books or augmented communication devices. These "ramps" are meant to allow them to enter into the unit. They can then participate with their peers, and we do not need to give them a separate program.

We can also anticipate some common challenges, and provide supports that will be available to all our learners. Although some students struggle with focusing their attention on task, actually, all students can benefit if we "chunk" our activities (i.e., introduce them a few steps at a time), take breaks for physical movement, and provide visual supports for activity instructions. When you know that many students have difficulties remembering or sequencing multi-step instructions, put instructions with visuals on the board. This allows students to recheck for themselves the procedures and process for the tasks, and you support student learning without singling out some students. Tape or mount class schedules and programs on the board for everyone to see. Lots of students benefit from a system of cues for schedules, behavioural expectations, and task break-down.

Students with significant or even severe disabilities may appear to be unable to join in, or activities may seem inappropriate for them. This is simply not true. Even 2-year-old toddlers imitate everything around them, so a student with the "mental age" of a 2-year-old will do the same. To counter the arguments of people who say that such a student does not belong in a secondary school classroom, I say that if we put all students living with an autism spectrum disorder in one room, their only peer models will be children with a range of autistic behaviour, so they learn only how to be more autistic. When in a regular classroom, these students can observe and then model more age-appropriate behaviour, language, and thinking—from which they will learn. There is nothing wrong with letting a student sometimes just listen or observe. That is usually what we all want to do when first learning a skill.

Students with special needs should not be left on the periphery of classroom life. When teachers provide differentiated activities, students with disabilities can participate—perhaps drawing the art for an activity, playing a role in a dramatization, singing along with a song, or contributing ideas to a story. They can use technology to contribute images and ideas, and will learn at their own pace and conceptual level without holding others back. They can actually bring new perspectives that enrich the learning of others. These students can learn to use a microscope, watch films or texts of historical events, or build a model. In other words, they can learn significant parts of the content and discipline-specific skills that the others learn. They also benefit from seeing their peers focus attention on a project and apply team discipline in collaborative activities.

Sometimes, although a task is common to the group, the goals for accomplishing the task may be different for each student. For example, in a

Portage & Main Press, 2012, *Teaching to Diversity*, ISBN: 978-1-55379-353-3

Karl and Mitchell

Three of my boys were at the musical-rhythmic centre. Their task was to write a song that explorers would have sung about the challenges they faced. Karl, one of the boys, had significant disabilities, being in grade 6 but reading at about a grade 1 level. However, his strength was in musical-rhythmic intelligence. He loved music, and he listened to his iPod often to calm himself and deal with sensory challenges. The boys were writing a rap, and I approached the group to see how Karl was going to be included in the activity. As I approached, Mitchell, who had taken the lead in the group, put up his hand in a stop gesture and said, "It's under control!" So I backed away and left them to work.

A little later, Mitchell approached me quietly. "Miss Katz," he said. "Karl is musical-rhythmic, right?" I said, "Yes, but he may struggle with reading the lyrics, Mitchell." "I know," he said, "so I downloaded the song onto his iPod. Can we present on Monday, so he has the weekend to listen to it and memorize it?" On Monday, the three boys stood at the front of the room. Mitchell stood in the middle, and all the boys "read" the lyrics as they rapped out their song. If you didn't know Karl, you would never have picked him out in the group, or known he wasn't reading along with the other two boys.

chemistry lab where students in high school are conducting experiments on boiling points, a student with a developmental disability might participate while learning how to measure the liquids (math), how to handle hot objects (safety), how to observe carefully and record simple information (literacy), how to use a thermometer, and also learn vocabulary such as *mix, stir, boil,* and *melt* (life skills). Such students are still interacting with their peers, developing basic scientific skills and understandings, and experiencing school life, as all other adolescents do. There is no class where students with disabilities cannot learn and contribute.

One final point: It is not just students with disabilities that we need to consider. UDL is designed, by definition, to be inclusive of all, and students who are gifted also need special consideration. No child has ever committed suicide because they were bored—the fear that we will bore our gifted learners is the least of our concerns. First, having open-ended questions and integrated curriculum will appeal to the divergent thinker. Second, using multiple intelligences in lesson planning will give these students an opportunity to be challenged in a variety of ways. Third, we can work one-on-one or with a small group of these students at any time, should we deem it necessary to provide some enrichment. Our biggest concern is how to help a group of divergent, creative, and sensitive children feel valued and connected to their peers. Small-group work can be challenging for them because their thinking is often not appreciated or understood by others, as in the story of Nate and Michael. They appear to be off-task and are dismissed. Frequently, they are silenced by bright students who are more capable of staying within the box of teacher expectations, following linear criteria for assignments, and developing "school smarts."

Nate and Michael

During my teaching practicum in a grade 2 class in Vancouver, I had a student named Nate. Like Michael (#3), Nate was a globally gifted student. While other students were reading one of the Berenstain Bears books and Mercer Mayer, Nate was reading *The Hobbit* long before the revival and the movies of Tolkein's work. Conferences with Nate contained comments like "You know, Ms. Katz, I could write a book like *The Hobbit*. I could make up a fantasy world and weird and wonderful characters. But I would never think of a name like Bilbo Baggins, and it just wouldn't be the same if his name was Harry."

One day, the students were working on a class book about the seashore. Each student had a page with a letter on it. They were to record a seashore-related fact using that letter, as in "W is for whale. Whales are the largest mammals in the sea." Most students were writing about an animal. A few students came to me to say "Nate is ruining the book." I sent them back to work, and subtly cruised by Nate's desk. On his page, he had the letter "I" and had written "I is for Industry." He was up and walking around and looking at the other students' pages. Knowing that he would find a connection somewhere, I let him be. When the students' pages were turned in, I flipped to Nate's page. On it was written "I is for industry. Industry is polluting the oceans." It had a picture of all the animals that the other children had written about — floating dead on the top of the water!

It took me some work to help the other children understand that Nate wasn't "being mean" and "killing their animals." Children such as Nate often do not see why the other children are upset because, after all, he was trying to call attention to an environmental issue that would protect those animals. Nate, too, was 7 years old and just didn't understand why others didn't see what he saw. He felt rejected and frustrated and, at the time, I didn't know how to help him, though I tried.

It wasn't until many years later, when I took that gifted education course and met Michael, that I pursued the void in my knowledge related to these children, and came to understand. Explaining to Michael and his peers the difference between divergent thinking and convergent thinking made a world of difference. The students understood that neither was better than or smarter than — it depended on the task. They knew that Michael's brain was good at "having ideas" and "making connections," and their own were better at "organizing and sorting information" in logical ways. They knew that Michael got worried easily, and they would come down to my room and say, "Ms. Katz, you better come" when they saw his facial expression change.

Michael learned to understand that who he was had value and, yes, challenges. It is hard to live as such a deeply sensitive person in an often insensitive world. We did the best we could to create a supportive network around him so that, at the very least, he never felt he was alone in it. We clustered our gifted students, placing four of them in a classroom together, along with twenty-six other students, so that they had a chance, at times, to work with others who shared their experience and thinking style and, at other times, could learn to work with diverse others. This setting reduced Michael's sense of isolation as he learned that, although he was in a minority, there were others like him. Michael and I also co-wrote poetry, in an effort to give him a vehicle for expressing his thoughts and feelings. An example, written when he was in grade 4, shows the atypical sensitivity and divergence for a then 10-year-old.

Portage & Main Press, 2012, *Teaching to Diversity*, ISBN: 978-1-55379-353-3

Why?

Why does the sun rise over the hill?
Why is everything good in life a wonderful thrill?
Why does the moss creep over a stone?
Why is it that when you're sad you're all alone?
Why does the moon rise every night?
Why do you always lose something in a fight?
Why can a bird be so agile and fly?
"Why?" I ask "Why?"

I don't know what happened to Nate, but a few months ago, after eight years apart, I received an email from Michael:

Dear Professor Katz,

Hi, I'm not certain you remember me, my name is Michael XXX. I was one of your students at XXX Elementary and am now currently studying at UBC, starting my fourth year of a double major in English and History. I really hope you're doing well. My parents mentioned the other day that they had run into you a while ago, and I was suddenly struck with the immense amount of time that has passed between our last contact and guilt at not doing more to stay in touch. You certainly left an indelible mark on my personality and I am so grateful for everything. I just wanted to say hi and ask how you are. I remember that you used to write a fair amount of poetry, I'm not certain if you still do, I'm sure the responsibilities of tenure and teaching are time consuming, I still write and thought I'd share some with you (attached).

Sincerely,
Michael

Attached were a few poems, including this one:

Postscript

And yes I believe in God
amongst all the binary code:
a shameful confession in a secular age.
(I do not believe in the deer by the roadside
or the bees circling summer flowers
but I will defer to the elegiac silence
between that couple at the picnic table)
I want to deliver the message
unaltered like a newborn,
kicking and screaming at the cold,
more real than the faith I had imagined
as a postscript for my dying cells —
that constant struggle to write what I mean.

Scheduling

To be clear, students in my classroom do not spend all day in centres. In general, a teacher who has the same students all day usually has three blocks to the day: morning to recess, recess to lunch, and the afternoon. For me, the Science/Social Studies/Fine Arts units in my plan took place in the afternoons because they involved the MI centres where hands-on activities allow movement—something students needed to stay engaged in the afternoons. During the two morning blocks, I spent the first block teaching numeracy (Mathematics), and the second block teaching literacy (Language Arts).

8:45–9:00 a.m.	**Spirit Buddies** (see p. 52, Chapter 3)
9:00–10:20 a.m.	**Math Block** Calendar (Primary) Whole-class Math lessons and activities Math centres and mini-lessons Math Journal
10:40–12:00 noon	**Literacy Block** Guided reading or literature circles Literacy centres Writer's workshop Working with words
1:00–3:00 p.m.	**Theme Block** Whole-class activities: Science, Social Studies, Art, Music Multiple intelligence stations and centres Demonstration activities

Figure 4.8 Scheduling the curricula and lessons/activities to provide consistency in the school day

This organization of their school day provided my students with some consistency. They knew when they came in the morning that they should prepare their math materials. After recess, they prepared their literacy materials, and after lunch, their inquiry projects. There were fewer transitions, less down time in which we had to put away one set of materials and take out others. Of course, phys. ed., computer classes, class meetings, and other essentials were fitted in here and there, by having one subject revised to a single 40-minute period instead of a double.

Literacy across the Curriculum

Universal Design for Learning has two primary goals:

1. To develop higher order thinking and passionate learners.
2. To make the concepts and interactions in the learning accessible to diverse learners.

When we focus on literacy, we strive for the same goals.

How do we help diverse learners to think deeply and profoundly about literature and multi-media texts; to communicate their feelings, thoughts, beliefs and values in powerful and impactful ways; and to develop a love for language?

The originators of UDL strongly advocated for the use of assistive technology to help all children with disabilities (Rose and Meyer 2002). Many of the available software programs assist the students who struggle with reading and writing to take part in literary studies. Such tools offer students who would otherwise be unable to communicate a chance to focus on thinking—and should absolutely be treasured. However, these tools might not always be available in the classroom or in the school and, fortunately, they cannot actually think for the students.

Speaking, reading, and writing are symbiotic aspects of literacy. Our knowledge of vocabulary, appropriate voice and register, communication styles, and the rules of grammar and syntax within a variety of social contexts influences our ability both to comprehend others and to express our own ideas. Speaking, like writing, involves the communicator or author in an attempt to share their thoughts, feelings, and values with others. Making meaning out of their communication requires some understanding not only of the vocabulary but also of the context in which the communication takes place, some knowledge of the person communicating, and our own inferential processes.

In conversation, the way two 12-year-old boys speak to each other is likely different from how they talk to their grandmother, or their spiritual leader. Likewise, textual materials, fiction and nonfiction, may be written in formal language, in conversational language, in slang, or even in dialect to reflect the speech of characters in the text. The strategies that readers use for decoding text and comprehending language are also similar. Whether we are listening to a speech or reading a text, we use grammatical, contextual, and syntactic cues to figure out unknown words and process the language. Sometimes in order to comprehend, we have to visualize, make connections, determine importance, question, and synthesize the information. When we speak or write, we choose a voice in which to communicate, we determine the most powerful vocabulary, we structure our sentences and ideas, and we use punctuation (whether for pauses, tone of voice, or written forms) to aid the reader or listener in understanding.

When structuring literacy activities in the UDL classroom, we have to search for ways to integrate instruction into the rhythm of the learning. By connecting our reading, writing, listening, and speaking activities to the themes we are studying, we scaffold the learning for our students. Think about it—if I have to pick up a text about volcanoes and I have never heard the words *magma* or *tectonic plates*, decoding the text is likely to be difficult. On the other hand, if we have been studying "Earth's Crust" and discussing magma and tectonic plates, then when I see that word on the page—t-e-c-t-o-n-i-c, I have a model with which to decode it. Similarly, it is much easier to write about something we know, especially if we have been building it, acting it out, drawing it, and talking about it. As well, from those learning experiences, I will find it much easier to write a poem, a story, or a report about it with powerful language and detailed description. This process also works in reverse; that is, our reading and writing supports our understandings in science and social studies—it's a win-win!

Portage & Main Press, 2012, *Teaching to Diversity*, ISBN: 978-1-55379-353-3

Sensible, but you are probably wondering, "Don't we have to directly teach reading and writing?" Of course, we have to teach, but we might as well use texts connected to our themes while doing so. What does literacy instruction look like in the UDL classroom? First, I'm going to break down the process, then come back to the integration and connection. Teaching literacy in the UDL classroom is a whole other book, one I may write one day, so consider the following just an overview, not a comprehensive literacy resource.

Reading

For my overview, I want to clarify some basic vocabulary and concepts about reading instruction in two large categories—*fluency* and *comprehension*—which are, of course, interrelated. We can say, "The more fluently one can decode a text, the easier it is to comprehend," but that is not completely true for students with learning disabilities. Some students can decode a text fluently but have no idea what they just read. Other students who lack fluency and seem to miss half the words in the text are, nevertheless, capable of telling you what the passage was about. Although fluency and comprehension are related, they can be isolated in terms of strategies (Figure 4.9). In many ways, the brain is still a mystery to us.

Fluency

To read fluently, a reader should be able to instantly recognize about 95 per cent of the words as they read the text, no matter the medium. The ability to recognize the words in a text accurately and to read at a steady pace involves having a good sight-word vocabulary and fully developed word attack strategies for unknown or new words. Good sight-word vocabulary means not having to pause to figure out every single word on a page—which is when reading becomes incredibly laborious. Research shows that good readers also use context clues (*What makes sense here?*), picture clues (*Is the text illustrated?*), syntactic clues (*What kind of word belongs here?*), and grapho-phonic clues (*seeing parts of words and sounding them out*) to decode unknown words. In order to teach fluency, then, we have to help students develop sight-word vocabulary and strategies for figuring out unknown words.

All teachers teach literacy

Secondary teachers who assume that their students can read and that the English Language Arts teachers will do the rest are in error. The English teacher does not teach discipline-specific subject matter and vocabulary — for instance, how to read a chemistry text, mathematical instructions, or a power mechanics manual. Therefore, all teachers must instruct students in the vocabulary and usage specific to the topics and themes in the different levels of their discipline's curriculum — what the students interested in pursuing a career in the field would need to know. No one can do it but you!

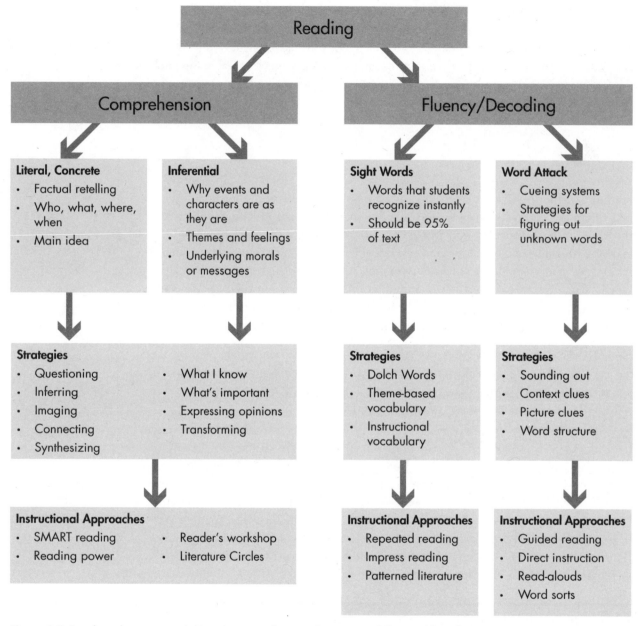

Figure 4.9 Reading deconstructed: Key elements of comprehension and fluency/decoding

Comprehension

What is it that goes on in the minds of good readers that helps them to make meaning of textual material? Regardless of the research done in this field, most agree that good readers do the following:

- They activate prior knowledge.
- They create images in their mind.

Portage & Main Press, 2012, *Teaching to Diversity*, ISBN: 978-1-55379-353-3

- They make connections to self, to other texts, and to world events.
- They question.
- They determine importance for memory.
- They draw inferences and read between the lines.
- They synthesize.
- They read for meaning and they self-correct.

On these points, we have consensus in the field. However, when it comes to teaching students to use these strategies, there are many different ideas, programs, and structures. Such gurus as Faye Brownlie, Susan Close, Stephanie Harvey, and Debbie Miller, among others, have suggested using versions of Readers Workshop, Guided Reading, Literature Circles, and other frameworks. All such programs have merit, but let me share how my literacy program worked in my UDL classroom, and the criteria you might use when choosing a framework for your reading instruction.

Reading in the UDL classroom

I believe in gradual release—a balance of teacher-led instruction, guided practice, and independent application. I scheduled my teaching of reading on Monday, Wednesday, and Friday, and my teaching of writing on Tuesday and Thursday—of course, the students both read and wrote every day. On Mondays, I did whole-class reading instruction around comprehension and fluency strategies using mini-lessons. One lesson might consist of a read-aloud piece or direct teaching, followed by having students work with a partner to practise.

During the mini-lessons, I model strategies for decoding using techniques like read-alouds, that is, while reading, I pause to talk about the connections I am making or how I figured out a word. Students with exceptional needs and those who are just learning English might have a hard time processing the amount of language in the reading piece or the pace of reading, so a teacher may need to read chunks of text, stop to process or change tone of voice for emphasis, or add props, puppets, pictures, or PicSyms to manipulate. Make it fun! Have students quickly act out a scene or do a tableau.

Let's take an example. To teach students about imagery, I chose the book *Feathers and Fools* by Mem Fox (2000) because it has rich, descriptive language and introduces the "fear of difference," a topic for my social-emotional learning goals. I asked the students to "listen for words that made pictures in their minds," and I chunked the book into three parts, reading one part at a time. Students folded their papers into three sections. After each section, they talked to their partner about the words they had heard that created images in their minds; then they drew or recorded these words and images. Here is an example:

> Technology can be invaluable in supporting students who are struggling readers. There are many supportive software programs, including read-aloud programs like Kurzweil, audio books, and fluency programs.

Portage & Main Press, 2012, *Teaching to Diversity*, ISBN: 978-1-55379-353-3

Figure 4.10 Imaging 3 text chunks of a story: Student response

Portage & Main Press, 2012, *Teaching to Diversity*, ISBN: 978-1-55379-353-3

On Wednesdays and Fridays, my students engaged in literature circles. I am a fan of Faye Brownlie's structure for these, discussed in her book *Grand Conversations, Thoughtful Responses* (2005), which I highly recommend. The whole process allows diverse learners to read and share literature together, to self-pace, and to work in heterogeneous groupings. By removing the old roles that were part of literature circles, the process requires much deeper thought. With children in the younger years, we used picture books; in later years, chapter books, and the books were all related to our theme. If I taught "imagery" as expressive language on Monday, then the students talked about the images they formed as they read during their book club meetings. Afterwards, students responded in double-entry journals, writing about the section of the book they had read, and their images as they read it. So we went from teacher modelling (during the read-aloud) to guided practice (with a partner, then with their book clubs), to independent application (in their personal journals).

Literature response centres

As you teach different strategies for fluency and comprehension, your students' responses in their journals will change over time. The journals in Figures 4.10 and 4.11 focus on inferencing and author's message.

Primary/Early Years responses: Note how at this age, students tend to retell the story at length.

In Middle/Senior Years, students will summarize or focus on a critical event for their response (Figure 4.12).

Journal entries create a good connection between reading and writing, as students use language from the text in their responses. During literature circles, I conferenced one-on-one with students to talk about their reading. I also responded in their journals, giving them feedback about what they were doing well, and what I would like to see (Figure 4.13).

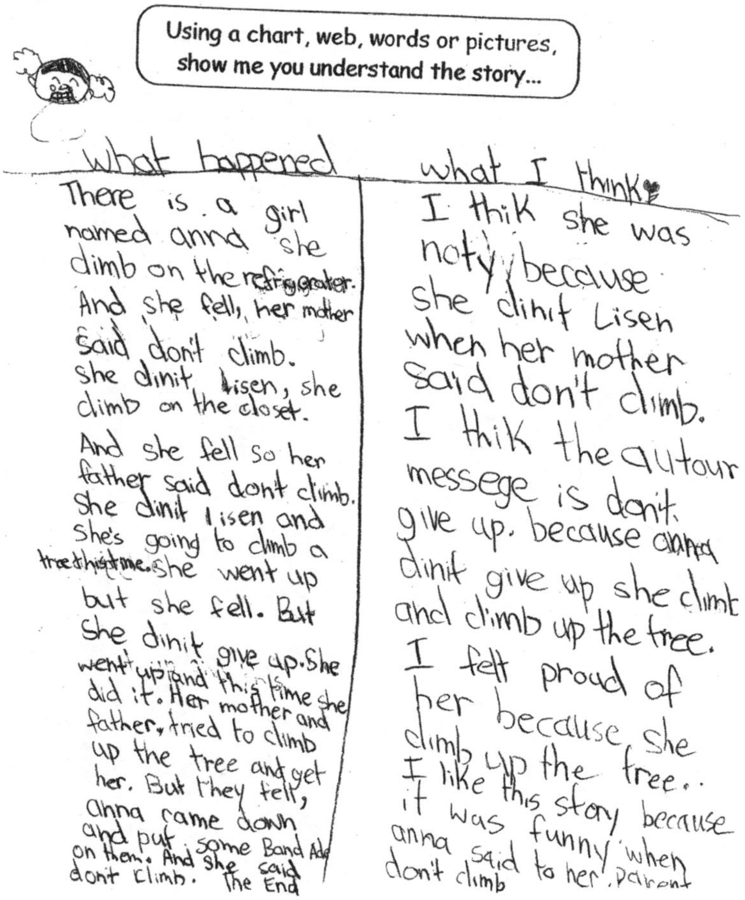

Figure 4.11 Primary: Double-Entry journal

WHAT I THINK

The book "Gathering has a very strange ending. Kira has changed a lot from the book's beginning. She is growing much more independant and responsible. She feels responsible for Matt and Jo. After her mother died, she became almost like a mother to other little Kids as she grew up. She had been looking for her father from the begginning and now that she finds him, she refuses to go with him. She is becoming a leader. She reminds me of Harry Potter, who like Kira "have leadership thrust upon them, and take up the mantle because they must, and find to their own sqrise they wear it well." Gathering Blue is an astanding story that remind me of many others that give me the same message. Lois Lowry has a weird way of saying it, but she is teaching me how to overcome any challenges I face in my future life,

Figure 4.12 Middle Years: Double-Entry journal

Portage & Main Press, 2012, *Teaching to Diversity*, ISBN: 978-1-55379-353-3

What I Think

What You've Done Well:

- ☐ Synthesizes – summarizes and explains cause and effect
- ☐ Infers
  - ▪ Makes logical predictions
  - ▪ Discusses characters feelings, motivations, and points of view
  - ▪ Gives insight into underlying themes, author's message
- ☑ Makes connections
  - ▪ Text to self
  - ▪ Text to text
  - ▪ Text to world
- ☑ Details images – shows ability to place self within the context
  - ▪ Describes visual images, other sensory reactions (e.g. sounds, smells, tastes)
  - ▪ Discusses feelings, experiences
- ☐ Questions
  - ▪ Poses questions about events, characters actions / feelings, author's decisions
  - ▪ Discusses areas of confusion
- ☐ Reflects & Responds
  - ▪ Gives opinions, reactions with some support (tells why, refers to sections of text)
  - ▪ Talks about personal impact on feelings, values, beliefs, knowledge

What You Need to Work On:

- ☐ Synthesizes
- ☑ Infers
- ☐ Makes connections
- ☐ Details images
- ☑ Questions
- ☐ Reflects & Responds

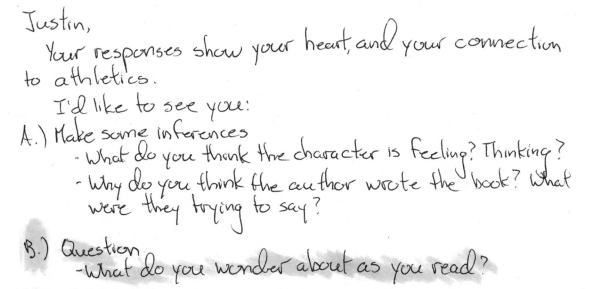

Justin,
   Your responses show your heart, and your connection to athletics.
   I'd like to see you:
A.) Make some inferences
   - What do you think the character is feeling? Thinking?
   - Why do you think the author wrote the book? What were they trying to say?

B.) Question
   - What do you wonder about as you read?

Figure 4.13 Teacher feedback on Double-Entry journal

Although the reading-writing connection is important, students should not be led to think that every time they read, they also have to write. Vary the approach: put the journals away and do role-plays or artistic representations. One activity that I learned at a workshop is called "Literature Response Centres," where students, as a club, had five options for responding to their book:

The Theatre
Students choose an important scene from the book, and act it out. Make materials for props (chart paper for backdrop, paper plates for masks, and so on) available.

The Dinner Club
Students sit and discuss the book—no writing required. Like an adult book club, with a table, chairs, and a snack.

The Artists' Studio
Students represent major scenes or characters through any medium of art they choose. Could be either a group project or an individual one.

The Writers' Den
Students write a sequel, a parody, a letter to the author, or something similar. These pieces are displayed in the centre, so others can read and get ideas.

Cabaret
Students turn the book into a musical—so much fun! Provide musical instruments, or a computer with GarageBand or other music making program. You can also provide materials for props as in the theatre.

Teachers can use varied literature-response resources or programs for ideas about how to mix up such activities. Whether you choose a similar program or not, be sure it fits the following UDL criteria:

1. Use heterogeneous groupings.

Ignore the myth in the literacy field that children have to read at their instructional level. Books or textbooks that are "ability grouped" or "levelled" can be incredibly destructive. The pressure to group students according to ability for reading, combined with early intervention programs, creates a self-fulfilling prophecy. As a resource teacher, I had students in grade one or two who were referred to me come into my room and tell me "I'm stupid. I suck at reading." Once students decide they are dumb because they cannot read, they are much less likely to look at books or read during leisure time, and so the gap grows.

When we look at other developmental milestones such as walking, we place no such emphasis on the age at which the child achieves them. That capability does not determine whether they're an athlete or not. When the children are 18, we cannot tell who was able to walk at 8 months, 10 months, or 14 months. The same is true for toilet training, speaking sentences, and even using mathematics. Such extreme pressure seems to be attached only to reading. If there were no such pressure and we just facilitated the development of reading skills as we do for all other skills, would we know which student at age 18 had learned to read in grade one and which in grade two? Current research tells us that "late" readers tend to struggle their whole academic career, but is that struggle related to a neurological imperative to read by age 6 or the stress imposed on the student to become an "early reader" at an early age—which created the "I'm dumb" identity? I think it is the latter, and global explorations support me. Some countries do not start formal schooling until age 8, and yet their students become literate by age 18, which suggests that children do not require intervention if they are not reading at age 6 or grade one.

None of us read only at our instructional level. Sometimes we just want a light read, other times we slog our way through a really difficult text because we are really interested in it. Why shouldn't students do the same? Why do we tell students, "That book is too easy for you?" Do you want someone to say that when you're reading a magazine or novel? Why do we tell students, "That book is too hard for you?" I recently read a philosophy text that had many words I didn't know and referred to authors and theories I didn't know. I had to search the dictionary, or google the authors, or ask someone else. I would not have been pleased if their response to me was, "That book is too hard for you, Jen. Here, try this one."

2. Use multi-levelled texts

Novel studies, by definition, are not inclusive. Expecting diverse learners to all read the same book, at the same pace, is just not reasonable—the assumption that all students can comprehend, and enjoy, the same text at the same pace is unrealistic. Instead of buying 30 copies of one novel, buy 5 copies of 6 different novels around a theme or genre but at different reading levels and with different text sizes, features, and lengths. For example, you could buy six different mysteries, some with pictures, some shorter, some longer, at varying reading levels, and still have whole class discussions about the features of a mystery. You can buy six different books about immigration, again, at different reading levels, perhaps some fiction and some nonfiction, and still discuss the challenges new immigrants faced arriving in North America. It doesn't cost more money, and you will be able both to challenge your strong readers and to support your struggling readers, while still having deep and inspiring discussions.

3. Use multiple formats.

Use different types of texts—magazines, videos, websites, blogs, newspapers—to honour the diversity of the students in your class. Some of us have seen a movie and then been motivated, and perhaps scaffolded in our understanding, to read the book. Others might have read the book first and then gone to the movie. Why not vary it for your students—reluctant readers might be more willing to engage with the text if they have seen the movie first and feel more confident they can make sense of the book when they are told, "There is more detail in the book." Do you think "But then they won't have to interpret the book themselves"? Wrong! They will have seen one perspective, heard others, and considered their own. How rich is that? Audiobooks also open up a whole other world for readers who lack fluency. Download them onto a student's iPod and let them listen as they read along. No one has to know they're not listening to music, and in the meantime, they are getting multi-sensory input: hearing it and seeing it at the same time, which will help develop sight words and fluency.

Portage & Main Press, 2012, *Teaching to Diversity*, ISBN: 978-1-55379-353-3

4. Vary the response formats.

Students get tired of always responding to reading through writing. I wouldn't want to have to write a summary of everything I read either. So sometimes just let the students read, other times let them have a book club and bring in a bit of food and drink, act out scenes, turn it into a musical, paint portraits of the characters…be creative!

5. Directly teach strategies, not interpretations.

In far too many English Language Arts classes I have seen, the focus is on the interpretation of the text, rather than on *how* we make sense of text. All students need to develop *comprehension* strategies (see Figure 4.9), especially students who are struggling readers. Take time to teach and model how to infer, to make connections, to ask quality questions, to visualize, to determine importance, and to synthesize, as well as decoding strategies. Time also needs to be spent exploring different types of texts, and their features—how to navigate websites; how to use contents outlines, an index, a list of references; how to interpret the value-added of captions and headings.

6. Talk.

Students cannot develop critical thinking skills alone. When an individual interprets a text, they cannot critically analyze their interpretation until they hear other perspectives and alternative interpretations. It is only when I hear a different interpretation of the same text that I am forced to think, "Oh, I never thought of it that way," and decide whether my perspective has changed or not, and justify that change.

7. Use flexible groupings.

Some students tune out whether in whole-class or independent work structures. Research shows that using partner and small-group structures creates higher engagement levels and helps students maintain attention. So use book clubs, partner talk, and other co-operative formats, in addition to whole-class discussions and independent response.

Reading is about learning—it is about thinking, and listening, considering, and inferring. Even very young children can learn to think about why the author wrote this, what the character is feeling and why, and what message we have learned from the text. Whatever reading program you choose, engage the students in rich dialogue, with varied texts, teach strategically, and—most importantly—don't group students by ability, and they will thank you.

Writing as a Means of Expression

Writing is another means of communicating thoughts, feelings, ideas, and beliefs to an intended audience. Writing is about the ability to express oneself articulately, passionately, eloquently. It is parallel to speaking, except that writing lacks the additional information that non-verbal language provides. A speaker's gestures, tone, and facial expression add information for the listener. They can also add

Portage & Main Press, 2012, *Teaching to Diversity*, ISBN: 978-1-55379-353-3

power—a hearty laugh or a tear slipping down the cheek add emotional impact to the words. When writing, we do not have the advantage of these additional communication modes, so we use punctuation, format, rhythm, and descriptive vocabulary to provide that power. These are significantly more difficult techniques for students to acquire because they are symbolic, not natural. A tear is natural and instinctive, as is a yell, but an exclamation mark is a symbol.

Writing is one of the most difficult tasks we ask of students, not only because of its symbolic nature but also because of the amount of memory and processing the act of writing requires. By definition, writing is verbal-linguistic and bodily-kinesthetic, requiring proficiency with language and fine motor skills, and thus is the most neurologically demanding task in school. It's important that teachers understand the demands that writing places on students: In order to write, the message has to be sent from the frontal lobe (the thinking/idea centre) to the language centres (the words), to the hippocampus (where memory is located for the spelling and formation), to the motor cortex (to send the message to the muscles), and out the hand. This process places a tremendous load on working memory, and some students simply do not have such capacity.

Working memory is like the RAM on your computer: the more programs you run at once, the slower the processing. Writing requires RAM to run the ideas program, the spelling program, and the letter formation program. For some children, by the time they get to the formation, they are out of memory and lose what they had wanted to say. The child who says, "I forget what I wanted to say" or "I can't think of anything to say" is struggling with an overloaded working memory.

Keyboarding can sometimes be helpful for some students because it requires only letter recognition, not recall and formation and, therefore, less memory. To lessen the demands on memory, some students might find working with a partner, using word banks, or spellchecking and prediction programs, webbing/brainstorming helpful.

Some students' struggles may stem from grapho-motor or expressive language issues. Drawing, in contrast, runs from the frontal lobe to the visual cortex rather than the language centres, to the motor cortex, and out the hand. Thus a student may be very good at drawing, but have difficulty printing, or vice versa. The two actions use different pathways in the brain. Knowing these neurological processes, we can design a writing program for a diverse class of students by offering them some ramps.

Technology Spotlight

Technology can be invaluable in supporting students with writing. Keyboarding only requires recognition, not recall — thus it has less memory demand than printing/handwriting. There are many supportive software programs, including brainstorming programs like Inspiration, prediction programs like co-writer, and of course, voice-operated software.

Writing in the UDL Classroom

As with reading, when we connect writing to the learning in the thematic unit, we provide students with their best opportunity to achieve success. Because students have talked about a topic, drawn elements of it, constructed models, or participated in role plays, they are more likely to have something to say, and they have acquired greater background knowledge and vocabulary related to the subject.

In the first-term unit, we have wrestled with some very powerful issues—diversity, interdependence, human rights, exploitation, harmony. Such issues provide incentive for meaningful writing—poems, newspaper articles, letters, and reports. Students might choose to write in the role of someone living in Afghanistan during the rule of the Taliban, or living on a First Nations reserve in Canada.

In a similar unit exploring the history of Steveston, B.C., and the issues of internment during the world wars, of the residential schools, and of other discriminatory practices, my students in grade 6/7 were horrified to realize Canada's history includes such racism. The opportunities they had to explore this emotion in depth led to some phenomenal writing (Figure 4.14) by students who had not previously shown strength in this area. Students can also write to respond to what they are reading, keep reflection journals, create scripts for role plays, lyrics for songs—the possibilities are endless.

MEANINGS OF EVERYDAY QUESTIONS IN STEVESTON

I thought about the meaning of life, but all that came to my mind was death
I thought about the meaning of love, but not a single answer came to my mind
I thought about the meaning of reality, but could it just be an illusion all this time?
I thought about the meaning of dreams, but all that came to my mind was to achieve it

I thought about the meaning of agony, but surely the answer lies within myself
I thought about the meaning of sorrow, but all I could see was tears
I thought about the meaning of happiness, but could it be that we were faking our
   smiles all this time?
I thought about the meaning of anxiety, but all that came to my mind was to surpass it

I thought about the meaning of the past, but all the memories are deep inside my heart
I thought about the meaning of the present, but as every second goes by it becomes the past
I thought about the meaning of the future, but is it just a maze with no way out
I thought about the meaning of lies, but why do we need that when we have the truth?

Figure 4.14 Poem created by a Grade 7 student for first term unit of study

The Writing Process and Writer's Workshop

Most teachers use a form of the writing process to teach writing skills. The Writing Process is a stage-like approach to developing a piece of writing:

1. pre-writing: brainstorming and planning
2. drafting: writing the first draft to focus on ideas, not structure
3. editing: revising the first draft to improve the content
4. proofreading: revising the writing to improve the structure
5. publishing: creating a final product

However, it's my experience that teachers too often skip over the crucial first stage in which brainstorming and planning should include reading examples of powerful writing that can help students develop the ideas, vocabulary, and skills that they need to write well.

Portage & Main Press, 2012, *Teaching to Diversity*, ISBN: 978-1-55379-353-3

Current research mentions Writer's Workshop, a constructive approach considered a "best practice" for teaching writing. Of the many versions of this approach, most include the following basic structure:

1. teacher-led mini-lessons
2. student-shared writing; independent writing
3. conferencing
4. publishing, that is, sharing with a wider audience

As with reading instruction, writing instruction in my classroom involved some whole-class mini-lessons focused on a particular aspect of writing (e.g., opening sentences, powerful vocabulary, or voice). We followed up with guided practice, usually with students working with a partner either to write a brief new piece that reflected the lesson or to look for good examples in the class library. Then, students might share with the class how they thought either the book or their written work illustrated that particular aspect of writing.

If they were learning about writing an opening sentence to engage the reader, for example, in my mini-lesson, I would read aloud what I considered the powerful beginning of a book or two, and talk about the purpose of an opening sentence. Then, I might ask students to partner and write an opening sentence that they could use for their next piece of writing; alternatively, to hunt in the class library for another book with what they considered a great opening line. When they had finished, the class would listen to other students read the opening line of their piece or book and explain why they chose it. Finally, in independent application, students engaged in the writing process.

My students kept a portfolio of their writing and, during writers' workshop, students had some "required" pieces, but they also had options for what they created and included in their portfolio. They would go to their portfolio, look at their current piece, and assess their opening line, perhaps changing it, perhaps not. Then all students would continue with their writing. These mini-lessons took no more than 15 minutes; my observations of what students needed to work on came from conferencing with students and assessing their portfolios.

This predictable structure—mini-lesson, practice, then independent writing—helped students feel confident that by the time they were expected to write independently, they would have some ideas and skills to work with. Such mini-lessons in writing should teach students a new tool or concept that they can use in their writing. Teachers can also show students when and why they might use what they have learned using the following process: a) demonstration; b) direct instruction with examples; c) inquiry; d) guided practice.

Fostering a passion for writing is critical. Research shows that specifying a regular time for writing, preferably at the same time of day is best. Give students freedom to choose their topic, because that freedom leads to increased engagement, investment, and passion. Authors write about what they know and care about, and they write in their own style. When we oblige students to write about topics they don't know much about or don't care about, and we focus on conventional styles, we shut down their creativity and interest. Also let children draw—it is the first symbolic representation of thinking. For some students, drawing helps spark ideas, images, and vocabulary for their writing.

Criteria	Student Evaluation	Teacher Evaluation
Intriguing title		
Interesting character and setting		
Exciting problem and solution		
Uses powerful words and sentences		
Characters talk to each other (dialogue)		
Awesome illustrations		
Sentence beginnings are not all the same		

Figure 4.15 Primary Years: Criteria for student/teacher evaluation of a piece of writing

4 = Excellent 2 = So-so, OK 3 = Very Good 1 = Forgot, not yet	Student Evaluation	Teacher Evaluation
Story is original, unique.		
Opening introduces the characters and the problem, and is enticing.		
Has a logical sequence *from beginning to an ending that solves the problem.*		
Has supporting details and descriptions; *creates an image for the reader.*		
Shows a sense of audience — *language, topic, and mood are appropriate*		
Uses language for mood, purpose and to create an impact; *makes it exciting, sad, powerful.*		
Varies vocabulary — *uses sensory detail, figurative and sophisticated language*		
Well-developed characters and situations — *portrays people's inner characteristics through actions and description*		

Figure 4.16 Middle Years: Criteria for student/teacher evaluation of a piece of writing

Portage & Main Press, 2012, *Teaching to Diversity*, ISBN: 978-1-55379-353-3

When my students began writing independently, I took the time to conference one-on-one with them, seeing it as an important opportunity to individualize instruction. I could not only assess students' writing, I could provide instruction, witness them self-assess, and learn what they understood about the writing process—insights from which we could derive criteria for the elements that make a good piece of writing. We could read professional writing and the student's own piece, talk about what the author did well, and create a list of criteria for a powerful piece (see Figures 4.15 and 4.16).

When students came to conference with me, we discussed how they were doing relative to the criteria. Following are my typical questions that led to teacher-student conferences:

1. *How's it going?*
2. *How may I help you?*
3. *Tell me about your writing*
4. *What are you working on?*
5. *What do you have so far?*
6. *What part can I help you with?*

These are my typical questions focused on information, direction, reflection, and purpose:

1. *Why are you writing this?*
2. *Where are you going with this?*
3. *What are you trying to do here?*
4. *Tell me more about X*
5. *I don't understand Y*
6. *Does this make sense?*
7. *What's this piece of writing really about?*
8. *How did you feel or what did you think when X happened? Are there other places where a reader will wonder about your thoughts and feelings?*
9. *As a reader, I cannot feel, see, or hear X. What can you do to help me create an image?*
10. *Is the pace too fast here? Can you make a movie, then expand this part?*
11. *What would happen if you tried to do X here?*
12. *What will you do next?*

Publication/Sharing

Teachers provide opportunities for students to share their writing with an audience, and they need a response to their writing—responses help clarify their work, generate new ideas, and most importantly validate the piece of writing. Varying the audience allows your students to learn about voice and perspective in their writing, and they learn to write for different audiences.

There are many ways for a student to share a piece of writing:

Author's chair

Students sit on a designated chair for "authors" and read their writing to the class. Students in the audience learn listening and responding skills, and get ideas for their next piece.

Other forums:

- class newsletter
- class book
- bulletin board
- young authors night

- record story
- performance art
- read to an adult
- contests

- personal blog
- club website
- music video
- graphic story

It's important to show a genuine interest in what the students write. Take the time to let them share with others, not just edit and proofread it, then file it in their portfolio or hand it in. When students realize they have spent weeks writing and editing a piece, only to have no one read it except the teacher, they lose interest in the next writing assignment.

Writing is not only challenging neurologically, sharing our writing is also challenging emotionally. A good writer exposes their feelings and experiences, which creates a vulnerability as they share what makes them sad or what makes them happy in the life journey they have travelled thus far. If we want more than narratives like "One day John went to the store…," it's crucial that we establish a safe environment. Students need to know that they can take risks with their writing, and that they should focus on content. When we emphasize spelling and neatness over content, students choose the easiest words and sentence structures so they won't have to make too many "corrections." Be careful about what you call the "good copy." If your students take it to mean "Recopy it to be neat and have perfect spelling," then your message is that "good" means "neatness and accurate spelling," not content.

In the social-emotional sphere, we should help students learn how to respond to each other's writing when they share their writing. Without a sense of community, students will never write to the depth they are capable of. Sharing from-the-heart pieces of writing, your own and from other authors, provides models for students to take risks in writing.

Peer conferencing

Peer conferencing has always been somewhat controversial. Fears exist around whether peers will be too critical, whether students who struggle will feel humiliated by showing their work to others, and whether peers can give constructive criticism that will truly advance the quality of their writing. I believe that peers can be taught to scaffold each other's learning; when you have established the necessary compassionate classroom climate, peer conferencing can be a powerful tool in building a team approach to learning. Having said that, I never force my students to share their writing. Instead, I offer a peer-conferencing space where students can go to conference if they choose to.

Portage & Main Press, 2012, *Teaching to Diversity*, ISBN: 978-1-55379-353-3

Look for discussions from published authors about how many times they revised their manuscript before it was published. *Hooray for Diffendoofer Day!* by Dr. Seuss with help from Jack Prelutsky and Lane Smith (1998) is one example. In a section entitled "How this book came to be" at the back of the book, editor Janet Schulman presents the changes in content that Dr. Seuss made while working on the manuscript. Another excellent source is the book, *Dear Genius: The Letters of Ursula Nordstrom*, collected and edited by Leonard S. Marcus (1998), which chronicles the letters between legendary editor Ursula Nordstrom and some of her authors. Make it clear that every author revises, just as every athlete practises.

The Reading/Writing Connection

Reading and writing are not really separate. Reading teaches us about story grammar, about structures for nonfiction texts, about language and imagery. We also learn to spell through reading. You know when you write something down and then think, "That doesn't look right?" That's because you have a visual image of the word in your head—from reading it. I do not mean that word structure and phonemics don't matter. Quite the contrary. They matter, but more for decoding than for encoding. It's more complex than this, I know, but this is not a literacy text.

My point here is simply that the more we read, the better writer we become. As authors, we come to know the process of writing, and we struggle with how to describe, to create images and engagement for our readers. In doing so, we develop an appreciation for authors who can do this skillfully. Just as an artist sees things in art that those of us who don't paint will never see, and a musician hears things in music that those of us who don't play an instrument will never hear, an author appreciates great literature in a way non-writers never will. Giving our students experience with reading many different genres and authors will make them better writers. Giving them experience writing in many different forms and genres will make them better readers. This is true not only in terms of skills but also in terms of emotional investment and appreciation. If you want your students to love literature and language, immerse them in literature and language.

Numeracy and Integration

Integrating numeracy with thematic studies supports learners' ability to make sense of the concepts being introduced. Whatever concept or skill we teach, students' interest increases when they see how it is applied in the real world through exploring issues, through assuming the roles of particular professions, and through problem solving. The applications help explain mathematical concepts that students often find difficult when presented out of a real-world context.

When I was consulting with a grade 4/5 teacher who was teaching a unit on Canada's North, the unit's essential understandings related to the diversity of Aboriginal peoples in the North, and the cultural differences of the three northern territories (Nunavut, Northwest Territories, and Yukon). When she said to me one day, "OK, I have to teach fractions. Tell me how I'm supposed to integrate that," I laughed because, on the surface, she was right. If we think of numerators and denominators, it seems impossible to integrate adding and subtracting fractions without being artificial. However, when you consider how anthropologists and statisticians might use fractions to explore the cultural diversity of the North, it becomes clearer.

After some research for statistics about the cultural diversity in the territories, I walked through the process with the teacher. First, we talked about the *concept* of fractions:

What are the essential understandings about fractions?

How do we turn those understandings into questions as we did with science and social studies?

Figure 4.17 shows what we decided for this class.

MATHEMATICS
Unit Planner

Essential Understandings

1. Fractions represent a piece, or pieces, of a whole.
2. There are many mathematical ways to indicate a piece, or pieces, of a whole (decimals, fractions, per cents), and they can be represented in a variety of ways (concretely, pictorially, symbolically, MI).
3. Fractions show how many pieces there are in the whole.
4. We use fractions in our daily lives.

Essential Questions

1. How can a whole be divided?
2. What is the best way to represent a piece, or pieces of a whole? What are your reasons for thinking this?
3. How do you know how many pieces there are, and which are larger?
4. Why and when do you use fractions?

Figure 4.17 Planning the "essential understandings" of the concept of fractions and linking "essential questions" to them for assessment

Then we created a rubric (Figure 4.18) for assessing the students' work.

Beginning	Approaching	Fully Meeting	Exceeding
Names basic fractions (halves, quarters, wholes)	Understands that fractions are "pieces"	Explains how fractions represent a piece, or pieces, of a whole	Compares different fractions
Names basic fractions (halves, quarters, wholes)	Identifies different ways to represent pieces of a whole	Describes the uses of differing mathematical ways to represent pieces of a whole	Compares and contrasts differing mathematical ways to represent pieces of a whole
Orders fractions when given pictorial or concrete representations	Explains how common fractions can be ordered ($\frac{1}{2}$, $\frac{1}{4}$, $\frac{1}{1}$)	Explains how fractions can be ordered in a variety of ways	Compares similar fractions of different wholes
Identifies common uses of fractions (time, money, measurement)	Understands the utility of fractions as a measurement tool	Applies fractions to problem based learning depicting real life scenarios	Compares and contrasts fractions and decimals as tools for representing pieces of a whole in daily life situations

Figure 4.18 Developing a rubric for assessing students' grasp of concept of fractions

Portage & Main Press, 2012, *Teaching to Diversity*, ISBN: 978-1-55379-353-3

Finally, we looked at two options for how the students could engage with fractions during the numeracy block that was related to the theme we were studying.

Option #1: Create an inquiry problem for student teams to address. We put the students in heterogeneous groups of four, and presented them with the problem in Figure 4.19.

Option #2: Run through a series of MI centres related to fractions and the North (see Figure 4.20).

The fractions in Figure 4.19 are based on the statistics found on the Internet, with the numbers rounded off, and expressed as a fraction. One of the student groups had four students, two of whom were "typical" learners, one whose disorder was on the autism spectrum, and one whose great strength was in mathematics. This group chose to represent their understandings with icons representing the fractions on a map of the three territories (Figure 4.21).

All four students were able to work together. Initially, they wanted to just write a number sentence $7/10 + 1/10 + 1/10 + 1/10 = 10/10$. It was clear this was what they were used to. I wanted them to back up and think about what $7/10$ represented—that it meant "7 of every 10 people in Nunavut are Inuit" was new to them. They got excited when they realized it was not 7 people in Nunavut, but rather 7 for every 10, which Jeff (the student with strength in numeracy) quickly said was "$7 \times 2,950$." They had known how to calculate, but did not.

After this, they discussed how they could show 7 people out of 10, and decided to use icons. The student with autism, who was learning to count to 10, started by counting out 7 pictures (icons) of Inuit children, and continued on. Two students began arranging the maps and icons. What to do about Jeff, who needed some challenging enrichment work? We asked him to create the symbolic representation for his group, including a table showing the actual populations. In other words, he had to determine each population—for example how many Inuit people lived in Nunavut, which required him to find $7/10$ of 29,500. Although the team worked together, the level of complexity was differentiated for each member, and no one was excluded or held back from their potential.

Territory	Total Population	First Nations	Métis	Inuit	Other
Yukon	30, 000	2/10	1/10	1/10	6/10
Northwest Territories	41,000	3/10	1/10	1/10	5/10
Nunavut	29,500	1/10	1/10	7/10	1/10
With your group, create a concrete, pictorial, and symbolic representation of the population of the Canadian North. Explain how your project shows the different people in the North, how many there are, and what the differences are between the territories.					

Figure 4.19 Data for inquiry on the population makeup of the three territories

Portage & Main Press, 2012, *Teaching to Diversity*, ISBN: 978-1-55379-353-3

Instructional Planner with Nine Multiple Intelligences in Mind

Verbal-Linguistic 1. Write a problem using fractions. 2. Debate the merits of fractions versus decimals.	**Musical-Rhythmic** 1. Fractions and beat 2. Compose a song about life in the North, using a particular beat or rhythm
Logical-Mathematical 1. Ordering fractions—Business deals 2. Problem solving using fractions	**Visual-Spatial** 1. Pictorial representations 2. Artistic representations to scale
Bodily-Kinesthetic 1. Fraction Body Boggle 2. Role play: Fractions in the North	**Naturalistic** 1. Fractions related to species endangerment 2. Fractions related to temperature change
Intrapersonal 1. Math Journal: "When I use fractions in my life" 2. My diet in the North (fraction of food groups)	**Interpersonal** 1. European and Aboriginal fractions of the population 2. How fractions communicate
Existential 1. Why do we divide things into pieces? 2. Is time different in the North?	

Figure 4.20 Multiple Intelligences instructional planner for fractions (Math activity)

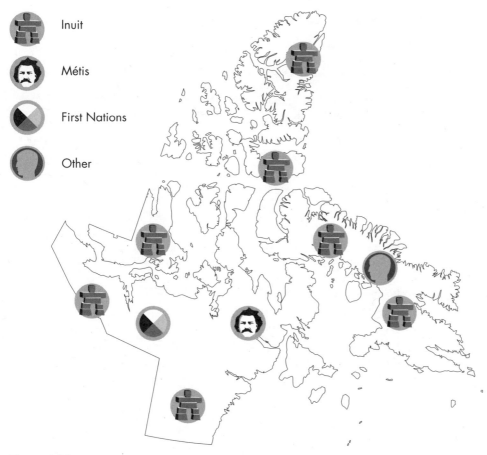

Inuit

Métis

First Nations

Other

Figure 4.21

Essential Understandings and Related Activities

For each of the grade 7 units that we planned earlier in this chapter, I wanted to select several math strands, not just one or two. From Manitoba Education's 2008 Mathematics curriculum (Western and Northern Canadian Protocol, WNCP 2006), we saw that our Diversity and Interdependence unit could incorporate the following essential understandings (from the grade 7 learning outcomes) and activities (see Figure 4.22):

1. Numbers allow us to organize and order things.
2. Numbers and operations allow us to make comparisons.
3. Data provide us with important information about real-life situations.
4. Data can be represented in a variety of ways.
5. By looking at patterns in data, we can predict whether something is likely, or unlikely to occur.
6. Equality is a complex idea, and mathematical equality is not necessarily the same as social equality.

Portage & Main Press, 2012, *Teaching to Diversity*, ISBN: 978-1-55379-353-3

Diversity and Interdependence

Essential Math Understandings

MATHEMATICS STRAND	GLOBAL QUALITY OF LIFE + WAYS OF LIFE IN ASIA FOCUS: AFGHANISTAN AND CANADA	PARTICLE THEORY OF MATTER
Number	• ordering population by size • ordering countries by area • representing populations as fractions, decimals, and percents	• comparing temperatures (integers) • ordering boiling and melting points for various chemicals/ materials
Operations	• population density, dividing populations by area • comparing currency, value of goods, and standard of living • determining distances and travel times between worldwide locations (rate)	• calculating differences in temperatures (integers) • calculating the speed of particles in different states (rate)
Shape and Space	• population density, dividing populations by area, representing population size on maps • volume of water consumed daily and annually by peoples in different countries	• modelling the size of particles in different states • modelling the speed of particles in different states
Statistics and Probability	• researching, illustrating, and presenting data from other countries with tables, graphs, and charts	• based on a certain rate of temperature change, predict when a chemical will change states • identify probable and impossible situations
Algebra (Patterns and Relations)	• growth patterns over time patterns in cultures, such as local art, music, and story telling • equality in mathematical terms and human ways of life	• tables with consistent rates of change in temperature • (Increase of 2° every five minutes. • How long until boiling?)

Figure 4.22 Strands of mathematics for unit of study "Diversity and Interdependence" (Glenys MacLeod, 2011)

Numeracy and Its Parallels to Literacy

Numeracy parallels literacy in that it goes beyond rote skills such as adding and subtracting (like decoding and encoding in literacy) to focus on comprehension, response, metacognition, and affective engagement. The term *numeracy* has connotations of real-life applications and the use of mathematics throughout the curriculum rather than as a discipline set apart. Like literacy, then, numeracy becomes part of every teacher's job. Discipline-specific teachers must take into consideration the types of numeracy required for a professional in their field, and

Portage & Main Press, 2012, *Teaching to Diversity*, ISBN: 978-1-55379-353-3

teach it to their students. Numeracy is used differently by a physicist, a chemist, a cartographer, a librarian, an historian, and a mechanic, but all require specific aspects of numeracy in their work—and in their lives.

Numeracy encompasses the knowledge, skills, and appreciations needed for students to understand and use mathematical ideas, techniques, and applications. Numerate people are proficient with numbers and are able to understand information that is presented quantitatively—in graphs, charts, and tables—through reference to percentage increase or decrease; and in timelines. They also have an acute perception of shape and space, and can rotate images mentally, see patterns, and understand properties of shape and line. The concept of numeracy has 5 main components:

1. Comprehension: Logical-Mathematical /Problem solving

2. Imagery: Visual-spatial skills and concepts

3. Fluency: Computation

4. Metacognition/Reflection

5. Affective Connection

Each of these must include teaching and learning strategies:

1. Teaching for understanding

2. Sensory stimulation, particularly of the visual-spatial cortex

3. An element of rote learning

4. Reflection on strategies

5. Real-world applications—and fun

1. Comprehension: Logic and problem solving

Students must develop their comprehension of the concepts in numeracy just as they do the concepts in literacy. Problem solving in numeracy is much like reading for meaning. We have to make sense of all facets of the problem, draw inferences, make predictions, then test out or check our solutions. The National Council of Teachers of Mathematics has delineated 12 strategies that most young mathematicians use to solve problems (NCTM <www.nctm.org/>).

A careful review of the NCTM strategies shows that they are naturally based on multiple intelligences. "Act it out" is a bodily-kinesthetic strategy; "draw a diagram" a visual-spatial strategy; "look for a pattern" can be naturalistic, musical, visual-spatial, or logical-mathematical. By teaching our students these strategies, we teach diverse learners how to approach problem solving in a variety of ways and through their learning strengths.

We also teach flexible and critical thinking because not all strategies work for all problems. At first, a teacher should model the use of a strategy and have

NCTM Strategies for problem solving

1. Act it out.
2. Draw a diagram.
3. Make a model.
4. Look for a pattern.
5. Guess and check.
6. Number sentences
7. Classify information.
8. Make a list, a table, a graph.
9. Break the problem into parts.
10. Work backwards.
11. Use logic.
12. Simplify the problem.

students try them out with simple problems. Gradually, give students more complex problems, and ask them to choose which strategy they think will work best, and why. As in literacy, direct instruction of strategies for comprehending and solving logical-mathematical problems is much more valuable than rote memorization. In a UDL classroom, we want much higher level thinking than that.

2. Imagery: Visual spatial skills and concepts

The main idea here is to develop students' ability to visualize, rotate images, and work with shapes, angles, and lines as an engineer, architect, carpenter, or similar professional might. Start with 3-D hands-on activities, for example, build models of 3-D shapes or structures using both 2-D and 3-D shapes. Ask students to visualize the model they have built from multiple angles, and sketch it out. Play games where students, working with a partner, look at an object from different angles and describe what they see to each other. Have partner A try to draw what partner B describes, and vice versa. This teaches children that objects look different from different angles, a first step toward their being able to rotate images in their minds.

Have the partners build replicas of their model out of folded paper, using only tape to secure it. Ask them to draw what they think it will look like flattened out (e.g., going from 3-D to 2-D). Then have them undo the tape, flatten out the paper, and compare it to their drawing. Exchange models between students, and have other students sketch what they think this model will look like when it's assembled (e.g., go from 2-D to 3-D). Again, this can be integrated within your thematic units: look at architecture and design in the cultures or civilizations chosen for study; examine how angles and geometry are used in athletic and scientific applications; watch for the imagery in what they are reading and writing.

3. Fluency in computation

Computation, like encoding and decoding in literacy, is a base skill for numeracy— the ability to move fluidly through numerate activities. Students have to learn the vocabulary for and the skills of manipulating numbers, but in contexts that give them meaning and life. Computation practice should occur daily, but for a short period of time. Embed the practice in inquiry projects or work centre activities that are fun and differentiated. Using games makes it fun, but have children compete with themselves, not others, and use multilevel criteria for team games (e.g., in an addition game, give children questions or dice of different complexity—what counts is how many of your questions you get right, so all the children can contribute, and no one becomes the kid you don't want on your team because the points add up to a team total).

4. Metacognition and reflection

In literacy, we want students to comprehend, reflect, and engage passionately with literature, not just decode words and sentences without thinking about meaning, or encode without thinking up creative ideas. Similarly, students develop their logical-mathematical intelligence—and numeracy—as they strengthen their ability to think deductively, to plan strategies for organizing information, and to reflect on what makes sense when considering all elements of the problem. Thus, students must think about their own thinking, about how are they are approaching the problem, asking "*Does this way make sense?*" "*But is it the best way?*"

It is imperative then, in teaching numeracy, that we teach students not to be robotic computers, but rather to be creative, aware, and deliberate in their approaches to problem solving, indeed, all aspects of numeracy. We must ask the question "*How did you approach this, and why?*" rather than "*What's the answer?*" We should encourage children when they say, "*Well, at first I tried___, but then I realized that every time I tried ___, this happened, so I _____.*" This is truly numerate thinking, rather like reading for meaning, but with numbers.

5. Affective connection

Historically, many children, especially girls, have been turned off by mathematics, which seemed out of context and unrelated to their lives; the emphasis on right answers, computation, and competition did not help. Teachers need to search out the ways of acquiring mathematical knowledge and skills in a way that is cooperative, fun, open-ended, and linked to their students' life experiences. By linking the mathematics learned in the classroom to themes and real-life situations, and by making connections between the mathematical knowledge they already possess and what they learn at school, students develop self-confidence bit by bit. It's helpful to use real-life materials, like money, video games, score sheets, and similar materials to enhance connections and generate informal mathematical knowledge. Ask students to bring the materials to class themselves. Challenge them to collect all the ways in which they used math one weekend, and bring it in to class. They will be surprised by how much they use it on a daily basis.

Teaching and learning strategies

Instructionally, you can link mathematical and real-world knowledge and applications by taking a realistic example or situation as your point of departure. Turn this into a mathematical model, leading to mathematical solutions, which may then be reinterpreted as a realistic solution. For example, imagine we were teaching symmetry. Think of a time/place when symmetry would be useful or needed, and use that as a starting point. Pose a problem to students, as we did with the cultural distribution of the Northern territories, like "an architect wants to design a building with a symmetrical entrance using two archways." Have students design a building to meet the criteria, giving different students varying levels of criteria (in terms of complexity). This also helps the many students who have difficulty with the abstract nature of mathematical knowledge. In algebra, when teaching how to solve for x, make it real.

> "You are saving up to buy a new iPod. It costs $240. You have $65 more to go before you can buy it."
>
> If you ask them "How much have you saved?" students will simply subtract, because that's what they have been taught to do.

Portage & Main Press, 2012, *Teaching to Diversity*, ISBN: 978-1-55379-353-3

So ask them "What information do you need that you do not have?" Upon their response, ask how they can find what they need. When they say that they would subtract, ask "Why?"

You may have to show them: "We represent missing information with a symbol, usually x." If so, tell them the symbol x represents the missing information about how much has been saved.

Then give them the opposite, that is, an equation like $x + 17 = 39$, and ask them to write a problem for it. Exchange the problems, and ask students *not* to solve it, but rather, to state what information is missing. *"What does x stand for?"*

Once students understand this, you can move on to teaching balanced equations, and why we solve for x by using opposite operations. As the students begin to see that algebra and symmetry and problem solving are part of their daily lives, they gain confidence and interest in numeracy. When numeracy involves building models, solving puzzles, playing games, drawing, and teamwork, the "math anxiety" is replaced by engagement.

Numeracy and Multiple Intelligences

In my Math Block on Figure 4.8, I follow a gradual release model as in the Literacy Block. I begin with a mini-lesson like the algebra one, then have the students engage in guided practice through the Math Centres in the classroom, cooperative games, or inquiry projects in teams. The gradual release model provides the same flexibility as in the other subjects: I can circulate, pose questions, assess, or pull small groups aside for further instruction.

Numeracy is much easier to differentiate for the learners in my classroom than is literacy. Mathematics is naturally an applied science, which means the applications include those appealing to logical-mathematical, visual-spatial, bodily-kinesthetic, musical-rhythmic, naturalistic, and verbal-linguistic profiles. Numeracy also plays a role in visual development, as we have discussed. Most kinesthetic activities, from construction to athletics, require all kinds of numeracy. Music has beats in measured time, and dance steps are often choreographed in a patterned sequence. Our natural world is filled with math — patterns, measurements, angles, shapes, and problems to be solved.

Math manipulatives, too, can help to differentiate instruction. I use materials that appeal to learners of different intelligences in all grades. Math is supposed to be hands-on and applied at all levels. The manipulatives that appeal to different intelligences include:

1. **Visual-Spatial:** tangrams, pentominoes
2. **Bodily-Kinesthetic:** dice, cooperative games, unifix cubes, constructing models to scale, geoboards
3. **Musical-Rhythmic:** instruments, scores, metronomes
4. **Verbal-Linguistic:** math books, word problems
5. **Naturalistic:** animals and plants for sorting, categorizing, and patterning

Portage & Main Press, 2012, *Teaching to Diversity*, ISBN: 978-1-55379-353-3

For example, if we are working on patterning, students can use beads on a string, unifix cubes, musical instruments, dominoes, tangrams, and their own bodies to make patterns (e.g., clapping or snapping patterns, boy/girl/boy/girl,). Depending on the grade level, I expect more complex patterns, tessellations, and so on, but the materials can be the same. Once or twice a week, I ask students to record in their Math Journals what they have done at the centres. In the illustration below, you can see that the first student was able to make a simple ABAB pattern, while the second student does not yet understand patterns. This allows me to target small groups for further instruction.

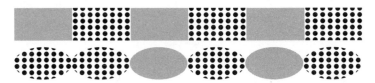

Math Journals

My students use their Math Journals not just for recording activities at the Math Centre. Sometimes I ask them to write their reflections on what they learned that day. Other times, I give students a prompt; for example, to encourage metacognitive reflection, I might ask them which problem-solving strategies they like to use, and why (Figure 4.23). To explore their conceptual understanding, I might ask them

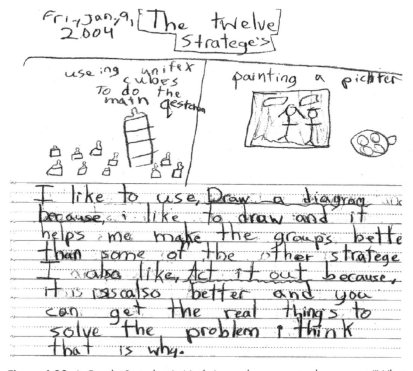

Figure 4.23 A Grade 2 student's Math Journal reponse to the prompt "What problem-solving strategies do you use?"

what they understand about "subtraction," and receive revealing responses. I had not taught the students that counting backwards was related to subtraction, so the response in Figure 4.24 showed a generalization and application of the concept that was advanced for a student in grade 2.

To find out how your students feel about numeracy, ask questions like "*What are you proud of?*" "*What is the most challenging part of...?*" I have collected prompts from the Internet, from colleagues, and from students themselves. My favourite is: "Draw a math monster, and tell all about it." If the student draws a monster who eats people, you know how the child feels about math. But when their monster is like the one in Figure 4.25, you know they are enjoying numeracy.

We have created our class climate, planned our units, and organized our literacy and numeracy approaches. Now, how does this all flow together? How do we manage all this, assess our students, and come up with evaluations for accountability? We are ready to talk about Block Two: Teaching to Diversity in chapter 5.

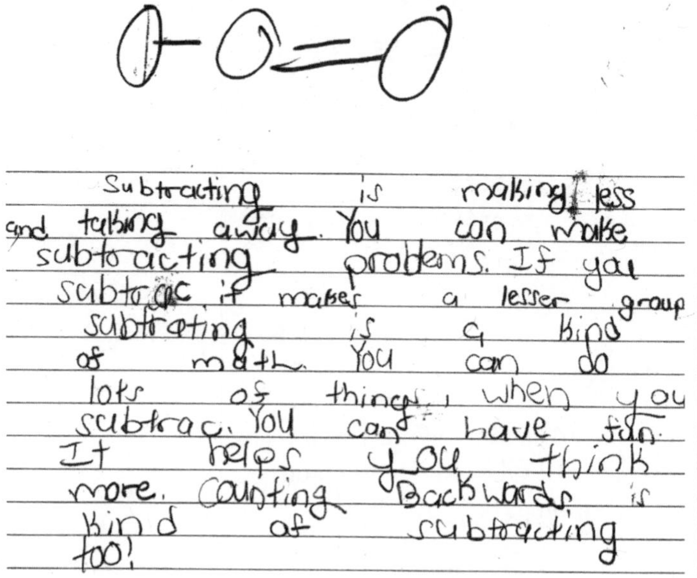

0-0=0
Subtracting is making less
and taking away. You can make
subtracting problems. If you
subtrac it makes a lesser group
subtrating is a kind
of math. You can do
lots of things when you
subtrac. You can have fun.
It helps you think
more. Counting Backwards is
kind of subtracting
too!

Figure 4.24 Grade 2 student's response to the prompt "What is subtraction?"

If a prsn in ask
my maonstour. He wind
cunt by tows like this
2 4 6 8 10 12 13 14 16 18 20
22 24 an tat wind
be the asar.
He like math

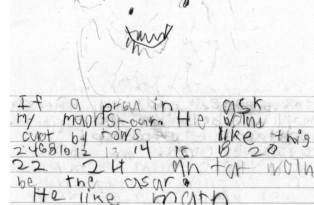

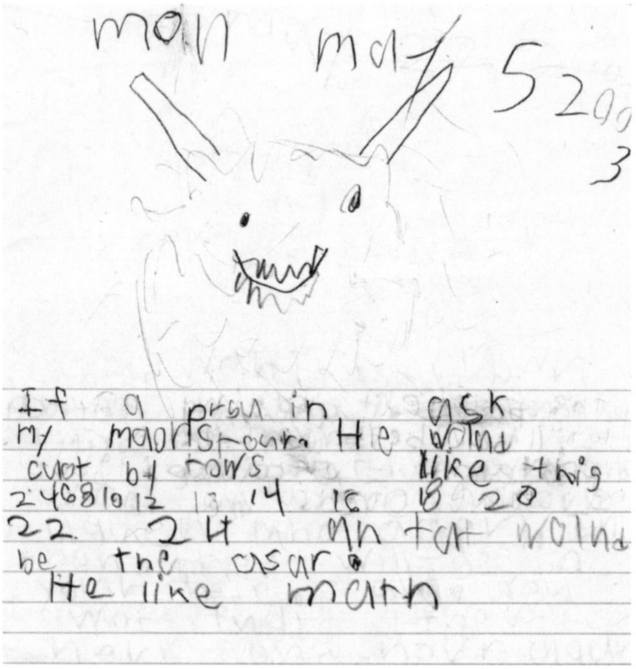

Figure 4.25 Grade 2 student's response to the prompt "Draw a math monster and tell us about it."

Chapter 5

Teaching in the Classroom—Block Two: Inclusive Instructional Practice

With the planning continuum well in hand, it is time to set up our classroom, and create our home for the next ten months. Of course, it will change when the children arrive and we have class meetings, but first impressions are important—colours, arrangement, materials, and resources—there is much to consider, and everything in UDL has meaning.

Classroom Ecology

The word *ecology* is usually associated with nature, but classrooms are ecological systems, too. The environment of the classroom and the inhabitants of that environment—students and teachers—are constantly interacting. Each aspect of the system affects all others. The characteristics of classrooms, the tasks of teaching, and the needs of students all influence those living in the environment. So does the climate, which is based primarily on the relationships and interactions that take place in the room. However, to carry the metaphor over, the abiotic features of this environment affect the inhabitants too.

Spaces for learning should invite and support both the students and the activities planned. The arrangement of the resources and features sends a message to your students. A classroom with desks in rows that face one way toward the teacher's desk sends a clear message about who is in power, and who students are to focus on and interact with. A classroom with round tables that allow students to face each other sends a message about expecting and accepting peer interactions, about cooperation and teamwork. In such a setting, it's not cheating to learn from each other, and it's not disruptive to talk with your team. Of course, students unfamiliar with such a setting have to learn to work within it in appropriate ways—a vital lesson for them to learn.

Teachers must not only plan their approach to the curriculum—the goals, the learning outcomes, and the lessons—with an underlying pedagogical philosophy in mind, they must also plan the classroom and decide what kind of interactions, activities, and power structure will work best to implement that philosophy. I have several goals in planning my set-up:

Portage & Main Press, 2012, *Teaching to Diversity*, ISBN: 978-1-55379-353-3

1. Student autonomy

I want my students to become independent learners who take charge of who they are as a person and as a learner. I focus on helping them build an internal locus of control, and on empowering them to think about whether their behaviour reflects who they want to be, both as a person and as a learner. Research (Reeve 2006) shows that traditional schools and classrooms actually create dependent children, passive learners, and obedient children incapable of critical thinking or passionate engagement. I want the climate in my classroom to encourage students to be insightful and engaged, and confident enough to take or show initiative.

2. Learning community

I want my students to see every member of their community, not just me, as a resource for their growth and learning. So I place tables and desks in ways that support collaboration and discussion with each other.

3. Accessibility

All students must have equal access. The student in a wheelchair should not have to ask for help reaching something that none of the other students have to ask for. They must be able to access every part of the room, and every activity, too. Materials should be placed out in the open, and at students' eye level or within reach to invite independent use. Materials locked away in a teacher's cupboard do not promote student autonomy. Fit your classroom ecology to your philosophy, and to your students.

Interest areas and personal territories are two basic concerns when organizing classroom space:

1. **Interest areas:** First decide what activities the classroom should accommodate, and create spaces for them. If plans include having students construct models, create artistic representations, or hold meetings, consider what space is needed and how quickly your students can transition to that space.

2. **Personal territories:** Consider the ways in which to seat your students and how to arrange that seating and define what "belongs" to whom. Desks become territorial and give rise to irritating little conflicts. I place a common bucket with basic supplies in the middle of the table, which reduces the need to search for a pencil or rummage through desks. It also prevents students whose families cannot afford material resources from being singled out, and sends a message about sharing and community instead of territoriality and showing off parental economic status. We nevertheless have to teach students to be responsible with materials and to share.

Each year and to the best of my ability, I consider my incoming group of students. For example, when a student in a wheelchair cannot get around to other parts of the classroom, we lose the whole point of equal access, and send the message that the student has to be on the periphery. As well, students with behavioural and attentional needs must have quiet spaces, that is, areas of the classroom with minimal distractions. But it should be a place where any student who wants some quiet time can go—the intrapersonal-existential centre, a space for reflection, not a punitive or "time out" space.

I place great importance on creating independent learners, so I want students to access all the materials themselves. I will teach them to be responsible about it, but they cannot learn if I control it all. Too many teachers control all the materials, and then get upset when students sit there because they don't have a pencil.

Figure 5.1 Classroom organization

Pedagogy and Classroom Management

"Management" implies an external locus of control, a top-down version of authority, which does not fit into the principles of universal design for learning. I don't want to "manage" children, I want to teach them. We have to be thoughtful about the messages we send. Teachers who act as if "might makes right" and punish students who do not do as the teacher says wonder later why some kids do the same to younger or less powerful students—punishment is an aggressive act. The teachers who control their classrooms (and then complain to others that, as soon as they leave, the kids act out) have created an external locus of control and, in doing so, have sent the message that behaviour is about not getting

As you can see from Figure 5.1, my students sit at round tables if I can get them, otherwise we push desks together. My desk is at the back and I can see everyone from there, but I am not the central focus. There may still be a sense of my presence as a source of energy in the room, however, the dominant energy should be coming from the kids, not me. It is their learning world, and I am there to support them.

This picture was taken in the summer, as I set up an Early Years classroom. In all grades, I place basic materials on the tables, and notebooks in bins with easy access. Projects line the walls and bulletin boards. I label the centres based on multiple intelligences, but there really isn't much that most classes don't have. Art supplies are visual-spatial, blocks and building materials are kinesthetic, and so on. Regardless of the grade level, I put these things in my room — thanks to dollar stores and garage sales. If older students are going to build a model of a molecule or a Roman aqueduct, they still need construction materials!

caught, rather than about personal integrity. I tell my students that they should act the same way when I'm in the room as when I'm not. They should be who they are, be true to themselves. If something happens while I'm away, my first question to them is "Would you have done that if I had been here? If not, why not?" "Is this who you are, or isn't it—because if it isn't, then why act that way?

Portage & Main Press, 2012, *Teaching to Diversity*, ISBN: 978-1-55379-353-3

Following up with Derrick

When Derrick, the student with ADHD, is seen leaning over the railing of the second floor and throwing paper balls at kids below, I yelled at his friends. Why? Derrick, by definition, is impulsive. He cannot think before he acts; his brain's wiring won't let him. His friends, however, sat there knowing full well that what he was doing was wrong, and that he was bound to get caught and get in trouble.

What kind of friend is that? All they had to do was say something like "C'mon D — chill out," and he'd have come down. I believe it is the community's responsibility to support each other. If we teach the kids that Derrick's behaviour is their responsibility as well as his, they will help him control his impulses and stay out of trouble. They will also be more likely to speak up against a bully or a bad decision from one of their peers. The paper-throwing incident with Derrick happened during the second week of school. In later times, the students had no problem speaking up.

If it is you, why not act that way when I'm here?" I want them to reflect on the idea that their behaviour should match their idea of who they are, not who else is around. Some teachers also send students the message that behaviour is individual, that the community plays no role or has no responsibility. They hold students accountable only for themselves, asking them if they "did it" or asking victims who the perpetrators were—as if students who did not actively participate have no responsibility for what others do.

I disagree. I want my students to show leadership, not to be bystanders; I want them to support each other in doing the right thing. The most dangerous message of all is to say: "Do what you're told." Such teaching does not help children to develop a sense of autonomy and responsibility for self and peers. We must help our students to stand up for others rather than hold back in fear and remain bystanders to bullying, or go along with gang leaders.

Dealing with Challenging Behaviour

I ran my class as a democracy. Running your classroom as a democracy still allows room for a "government" and a "police force." I told my students explicitly that I went to school to become a teacher, not a police officer, and I would be very unhappy if they put me in the role of policing them—although I would play that role if I had to. When students sense that you are not trying to exert power or control over them every day in every way, they resist much less when your doing so is necessary. In fact, they need to know that you will do so when you have to—because they can sense that, when such action is necessary, it is also fair. Early on in the school year, we held class meetings to discuss rules and, because the students and their peers decided on the rules, they all generally tended to buy in.

To work with challenging students, one must step out of ego and step out of power. When Derrick said, "I'm not doing this, it's stupid," I took his cue. Something about the task didn't work for him. That didn't make me a bad teacher or him a bad kid. So I said, "OK. What's wrong with it? What would you rather

Portage & Main Press, 2012, *Teaching to Diversity*, ISBN: 978-1-55379-353-3

do?" This deflated the power struggle immediately. His reply "Well, it's dumb. How the hell am I supposed to..." revealed what part of the task he did not understand. He hadn't wanted to look stupid, so he covered his lack of knowledge with bad behaviour. In most classes, the demand of either "Well, you'll do it now or at recess!" or removing the student from the classroom would result in a power struggle, in mistrust, and in loss of enjoyment for both teacher and student. The true sign of a powerful teacher is to step back, be the grown-up, and empower the student with compassion and strength.

I have worked in special education classes for many years, and I have been called every name you can think of. I've been hit, kicked, bitten, and head-butted. But I try never to make the situation about me or about the students. When something isn't working for them, we figure it out together—and the behaviour diminishes. Students with ankle bracelets (i.e., on house arrest), students with records, students who have assaulted teachers—I've had them all, but once I learned to let go and work from relationship instead of power, I never had a problem with violence again. Ever.

Humans are pack animals. The young of pack animals instinctively try to get along with the alpha leaders. A wolf cub will only growl at a grown wolf if it thinks it's about to be eaten. When a student growls at you, they are afraid. Find out why, and you'll resolve it. Growling back at the student is a "not yet meeting expectations" response.

The term "oppositional" implies that we teachers have the right to control, and the students should passively accept. Most children grant it to us, but they really should not. They should be critical thinkers who ask why the rules are this way and whether they are reasonable, and then judge whether they respect them or not. For our students to learn to oppose discriminatory laws, we have to teach them that they have the right to question rules and laws, and the duty to speak up if they consider them unjust. Explain to a student why you are asking them to do something, and negotiate possible alternatives for their learning and enjoyment, within reason.

My guidelines are simple and clear: Think, and be nice. That's it. You can have trouble sitting still, staying quiet, or finishing your work. You can be silly or off task, or you can have grumpy days. The trick is to learn how to bring yourself back. Someone has to say "OK, guys, we've only got an hour left. We had better get back to it." The students cannot learn that, if we don't give them the opportunity.

No one likes to feel powerless. Students, especially preteens, will resist you if they feel dominated and controlled, which results in a cycle of power struggles:

> Teacher feels that students are oppositional and defiant. ➔ The more the teacher tries to exert control, the more the students fight it. ➔ Children who have histories that involve violence are, in particular, very hesitant to grant power to anyone, because granting someone power in the past has proven dangerous for them. ➔ Whether they were victims or witnesses, they have seen what can happen when power is surrendered so they become "oppositional," and no consequence you impose can match what they have already faced.

You cannot assume that, because a child has nice parents, that child would not have been abused or victimized. Most abusers appear on the surface to be nice, normal people. Of course, the parents might have no idea — the abuser could be a camp counsellor, a babysitter, a cousin, or someone in the neighbourhood.

Portage & Main Press, 2012, *Teaching to Diversity*, ISBN: 978-1-55379-353-3

We all have our bad days and our distractions. What they cannot do is make someone else not want to be there; they cannot assault people emotionally or physically. In the wider society, a person goes to jail for that, losing the right to be a part of the community.

In my class, children learn that they will be segregated from the community until they can be present without hurting others. A teacher can segregate them simply by having the student work on their own, by moving them to a separate part of the classroom, or in extreme cases, arranging in-school suspension. When the only rule is "Don't be mean," boys like Jason and Derrick, who struggled with anger, can focus on one thing and try to exercise control.

Rules for everything overwhelm children. It's not neurologically possible to follow all rules at once, and pretending it is possible just sets them up for failure. Students with ADHD have a disorder that does not allow them to manage impulsivity and multiple demands at once. Asking them to sit still, stay focused, organize their materials, and interact positively means asking them to cope with multiple challenges all at once, which leads to stress and agitation. If you ask them to focus on one thing—not attacking people—and give them your support and the support of their friends, they can manage that. Derrick could attack the task that I assigned because the math sheet has no ego and doesn't bruise easily.

When a classroom is a positive place to be, students don't want to get kicked out, and don't think they have to for their own safety. When it's OK for students to face challenges in some aspect of their learning, they don't have to cover up their struggles with bad behaviour—as the class clown or as the tough guy. When a student's effort to be positive is what gets attention and respect from their teacher and their peers, things change, and they realize this classroom is different. Students are very adaptable and maybe, just maybe, we can plant seeds that then carry over to other places and other people. When Derrick's parents aren't constantly being called into the school for his negative behaviour and instead they hear what a great sense of humour he has, they respond to him differently. When the other students see the vulnerable side, the humanity, of one of their peers, they respond to him differently.

It is a different matter when dealing with students who have mental illness, brain damage, and other neurological conditions. With them, the rules, the program, and the expectations have to be different. One of my students, whose behaviour fell within the autism spectrum, pulled another student's hair—but without malicious intent. The act was simply a tactile stimulation for her and, at times, a way of seeking attention. Clearly, suspending her or even removing her would not be productive; she would learn only that, when she wants to leave the room, all she has to do is pull hair. We taught her other ways she could get the attention of her peers, or ask for a break, and we provided her with sensory toys she could hold in her hands. When we did that, the hair-pulling stopped.

Another student, who was severely mentally ill, hallucinated, heard voices, and had flashbacks to childhood abuse. Trying to reason with him was not an option, and we had to put a safety plan into place. Nevertheless, he was able to

Portage & Main Press, 2012, *Teaching to Diversity*, ISBN: 978-1-55379-353-3

spend 95 per cent of his time with us in the classroom; he worked on the same curriculum, developed literacy and numeracy skills, and learned to the best of his ability how to live in community. His classmates learned how to support him when they could and to be compassionate when they could not—because he needed intensive intervention.

People often ask me: "But is that fair to the other kids? Don't we have to ensure their safety, too?" My answer seems harsh, but it is reality: "Children who have mental illnesses, who are abuse victims, or who are otherwise disadvantaged live in our neighbourhoods. They require emotional support and financial assistance from their whole community, not just from the education system."

So how do we get the best results? If we expel these children or home-school them, we guarantee that they will not learn how to get along with others, and that the other kids will not know how to relate to them. But they will still live in the neighbourhood, and they will be hanging around the street when the other kids walk home from school—where there may not be a teacher or another adult to supervise. This might lead to a situation far more dangerous than having them in school.

We cannot protect some children by expelling others. We are much better off with them in school where we can mediate their interactions and teach them coping skills and strategies. Every child benefits. Healthy children learn to be grateful for how fortunate they are, and they learn to be compassionate toward those not so fortunate. Children with severe neurological trauma can still learn, with the right expertise and support, and learning in a regular classroom costs less than incarceration 24/7.

My years with these kids have been some of the most fulfilling of my career, truly. They were hard—it is hard to see children suffer and struggle like that, and I cried many nights. But seeing such children overcome, make a friend, read their first book, that's what it's all about. So fit your ecology to your philosophy and your kids—and make sure everyone's included.

Following up with Derrick

ST-V 4

Three years later, and Derrick is in high school, and doing well — not perfectly, but well. He proudly emails me his marks (he passes), his attendance record, and a note from his mom testifying to the fact that he has not been suspended for four years running now. There have been blips. He has texted me a couple of times when he is stuck in a bad situation, but the police in the area no longer know his name.

Portage & Main Press, 2012, *Teaching to Diversity*, ISBN: 978-1-55379-353-3

Starting the Year

So how do we get all this started? How do we create a supportive learning community? As the school year begins, I have two main goals for my teaching in September:

1. Teaching my class how to work cooperatively in groups.
2. Teaching my students how to represent complex concepts in a variety of ways.

My students have to learn both how to work together and how to show what they know. Then they will be ready to take charge of their own learning, and I will be able to step back.

Introducing Partnering and Group Work

We want to turn our classrooms into cooperative, compassionate learning communities, but if the students have come from very different classrooms, they may not have much experience with true group work or with the skills of collaboration, compromise, and teamwork. Just as a coach has to teach the players how to work together as a team, we have to teach our students how to learn together. Introducing the Respecting Diversity (RD) program (chapter 3) is the first step to building community and trust, and to sharing who we are as learners.

However, we still need to directly teach cooperative skills. I used lessons like the following to teach some of the basics, starting with partnering, because working with one other person is easier than working with three.

Lesson 1— Building Partnering Criteria

1. Introduction: Initiate discussion on what *partner* means.
   - Define *partnering:*
     - equal status (one does not dominate the other)
     - supportive: "two heads are better than one" attitude
2. Brainstorm, noting students' ideas on a T Chart:
   - Make a T-Chart with "Looks like" on one side and "Sounds like" on the other.
     - Ask *"If I walk up to two partners who are working well together, what would I see?"* After you have listed their ideas in the "Looks like" column, ask *"What would I hear?"*
     - Use both their positive statements and their *not* statements, for instance, "I would hear... 'That's a great idea. How about if we....' "I would *not* hear 'No, that's stupid. We should...'."
     - You can do this with all students, regardless of age, as a good reminder, if not a full lesson.

Portage & Main Press, 2012, *Teaching to Diversity*, ISBN: 978-1-55379-353-3

3. Have students role-play:
   - scenes of being a good partner
   - scenes of not being a good partner (like one partner is talking, and the other starts fooling around in their desk)

Lesson 2 — Developing Listening Criteria

1. Reflect on Lesson 1 and the criteria for partnering. Ask "Anything to add?"

2. Have students define "listening," and suggest criteria for what makes a good listener; for example:
   - Eyes on speaker; minds on speaker.
   - Focuses on partner; not distracted by others, or by own thoughts.
   - Listens, rather than thinking about own response or experience.
   - Nonverbal—makes eye contact; facial expression shows interest.

   Reflect on the partnering criteria, and stress the idea that partners really listen to each other. They focus their attention, and think about what their partner is saying. It's the exchange of ideas, the building on each other's thoughts, and showing respect for another point of view that makes for good partners.

3. Have partners role-play telling their partner about a really happy experience they had:
   - Partner A tells B (3 minutes); B reports out what A said.
   - Partner B tells A (3 minutes); A reports out what B said.

   The partners ask one another how they did. This allows students to give each other feedback on how they felt about being heard and on whether their partner really listened. It's important to directly teach these actions because they are often not modelled.

4. Reflection
   - What did you do to help your partner?
   - What did your partner do to help you?

   Note: Lessons 1 and 2 could be combined in one day. In all grades, listening is key.

Lesson 3 — Developing Skill in Questioning and Coaching

1. Reflect on Lesson 2 and the criteria for listening. "Anything to add?"
   We add "Partners ask good questions to clarify their understanding of their partner's ideas."

2. Discuss what makes a good question. "How does questioning help you clarify your ideas and your ability to communicate?" Develop criteria for good questioning; for example:
   - Extends your partner's thinking.

- Doesn't change the topic.
- Focuses on what's important.
- Partners are supportive, not critical.

3. Discuss what else makes any question a good one:
   - Does it clarify or extend thinking? Is it respectful?

4. Role-play partner work:
   - Have partners sit back to back, with one partner facing a teacher and the other facing away. Show an artifact (such as a painting, vase, cushion or something colourful or detailed). Ask the student who can see the artifact to describe it to their partner, who must ask questions in order to draw it.
     - Partner A has their back to the artifact.
     - Partner B describes artifact to partner A.
     - Partner A questions partner B "Could you say more about...", and draws artifact.
   - After a period of time (7–10 minutes), have the partners turn together, look at the drawing, and discuss how well they communicated. What did they miss? What could they have said or asked that would have clarified what they meant? Repeat with roles reversed.
     - Look at a second artifact.
     - Partner A describes artifact to partner B.
     - Partner B questions partner A "Could you say more about..."; draws artifact.
     - Partners tell each other how they did.
   - Reflection: "What did you do to help your partner? What did your partner do to help you?"

Lesson 4 — Developing Skills for Reporting Out

Rationale: Reporting is a key skill for two reasons: All year long, students will share their group's thinking, so they need to know how to share the group consensus, not just their own ideas. As well, by creating accountability, reporting out improves listening skills—every member of each group has to be prepared to be the reporter. When we come back together after group work, I use random criteria to decide on the reporter (e.g., "Whoever has the most pets in your group, stand up.") All students have to have listened and participated, or all members will be held accountable for not having worked together.

Of course, if a student is learning English or has a cognitive disability, a group mate may need to help. Nevertheless, all group members have to participate; it is not OK to allow one member of the group to take over. The "reporter" must share their partner's or group's ideas in a summary or synthesis, not just give their own, even if they disagree with ideas of others.

Portage & Main Press, 2012, *Teaching to Diversity*, ISBN: 978-1-55379-353-3

1. Introduction: Reflect on the criteria for questioning. "Anything to add?"
2. Discuss: "What makes a good reporter?" Set out students' criteria:
   - Summarizes what partner said.
   - Doesn't change what partner said, or give own opinion.
   - Is supportive and positive.
3. Role-play partner work: What does being a good friend mean to you?
   - Partner A tells B; B reports out.
   - Partner B tells A; A reports out
   - Each partner tells their partner how they did.
4. Have students reflect on the role-playing:
   - What did you do to help your partner?
   - What did your partner do to help you?

Lesson 5 — Criteria for Small-Group Work

1. Review the criteria for partner work. "Anything to add?"
2. Discuss: "How is working in a group the same as, or different from, working in a partnership?" "Would the criteria have to change? How?"
3. Group Activity: Record on the T-Chart what you hear and see when a group is working well together.

Organize the students in groups of four, and give each group a T-Chart with two columns "Looks like" and "Sounds like" on it. Ask them to think about what would be the same and what would be different for being a good group member, and what criteria describe a good group member. Expand the students' discussion along the following lines.

Every member of a group, small or large, has to be prepared to be the reporter. When students come back together as a class after group work, the teacher will use random criteria to decide on the reporter.

Each member of each group must have listened and participated, or the whole group will be held accountable for not having worked together. Allowance can be made for students just learning English, or a teammate may need to help one who has a cognitive disability. Nevertheless, all group members have to participate; it is not acceptable for one member to take over.

Discuss the idea that the student chosen to report out for a group shares everyone's ideas, not just their own, in a summary or synthesis; similarly, in a partnership, their partner's ideas.

Again as a class, have students share out and create a combined T-chart of students' criteria for what group work looks like, sounds like, and feels like (the social-emotional piece).

Post it in the classroom for students' reference during subsequent group work on essential understandings. It will serve as a reminder to the students of what a teacher expects to see and hear while moving around through the groups, and can be used for reminders.

If I have noticed that individuals are dominating in some groups, I say something like "Let's remember when we get in our groups today that we are trying to think about what quality of life means, and every member of your group should be contributing to the thinking. I'll be watching and listening to see good leadership—which doesn't mean taking over—it means inviting others in and finding every team member's strengths."

Introducing Work Centres

After working through the Respecting Diversity (RD) program in the first two weeks of September, followed by the preceding lessons on partnering and small groups, I move on to lessons that require group work. For this, I introduce our first unit of study in the curriculum that I set out for the first term of the school year.

As a teacher-led introduction, this unit provides lots of opportunity to introduce a concept, then group the kids as partners to discuss it and practise their partner work. Once they have developed some skill with partner work, I describe how I will assign groups of students to different centres. Each centre addresses some of the unit's "essential understandings" through the lens of one of the multiple intelligences, so it doesn't matter what centre they start with, because every group will work through every centre.

Steps in the process:

1. Form the groups and assign their starting centre.
2. One member of the group reads the instruction card.
3. The group members discuss the concepts and understandings, but don't start work right away. Give them the time to think and discuss.
4. Next, they start a discussion of a plan for carrying out the task; for example: "What should be in the final product? How can we be creative? How can the product we create show our thinking?"
5. Group members discuss plans for how they can work together and who will do what (e.g., divide labour, partner, timeline).
6. Members gather the materials needed.
7. Begin the assigned task.

Note that this process is very different for students. They are used to teacher expectations that they "get to work" immediately. I want students to be thinking and process oriented—focusing on concepts and learning how to learn. The idea that they should discuss first, research what information is missing, consider creativity and process—all before starting—will take some getting used to. The teacher should circulate to ensure that the groups at each centre share their understandings, plan the process of the task, and get organized.

Portage & Main Press, 2012, *Teaching to Diversity*, ISBN: 978-1-55379-353-3

Proton Symphony

(Musical-Rhythmic)

Using Garage Band or musical instruments, create a musical piece that reflects the sounds of solids, liquids, and gases. Think of the sounds you, as a person, hear from them (e.g., running water, air coming out of a balloon), or the sounds you would hear if you were a proton living inside a solid, liquid, or gas!

Figure 5.2 Sample MI instructions for the group tables in a Grade 7 classroom. First theme, Diversity and Interdependence, focused on Canada and Afghanistan, Musical-Rhythmic centre.

For instance, if the task is to create a role-play depicting the differences in gender roles between Canada and Afghanistan, the students would begin with a discussion about gender roles. What do they know about the roles of females and males in each country? Do they have to gather more information before they begin writing the role-play? What information and understandings must be included? All of this requires review of their rubric, which outlines what they are expected to learn and how to show their learning.

Then the students have to start outlining the process: Who will gather the information? Who will write the role-play? Who will act out the roles? With younger students, it's necessary to walk through the process of group work at a centre: organize the students in groups, explain that when they go to the centres, they read the instruction card and talk about the task, and they do one centre per afternoon.

We planned nine centres, and we have three weeks (fifteen afternoons) for the groups to rotate through them. A class of 30 students would have no more than seven groups, which leaves two centres free on any given afternoon. The task outlined at each centre is planned to be completed in one afternoon, but if students need more time, we can be flexible enough to accommodate that. If one group finishes early, the students can go to a free centre and begin that new task; if another group needs a second day at a centre, the groups should be able to accommodate that.

Before starting the first round of group work at centres, take time for whole-class discussion of your behavioural expectations. Students can move about and talk, but they must be thinking and discussing—what matters is that they are on task and thinking. All students must show self-respect and respect for others for teamwork to be successful.

Portage & Main Press, 2012, *Teaching to Diversity*, ISBN: 978-1-55379-353-3

Explain how assessment will be done for group work at centres. Explain that you as the teacher will move around from group to group, and that what matters is their own thinking, whether they show that through discussions, teacher/student individual conferences, or various products of the groups. Remind students of the criteria (the rubric of the essential understandings). Make clear that the group does not receive a penalty for work by, or reporting by, students who are learning English, or by those who face challenges in particular tasks. However, it is vital that the group support and involve all members.

Barriers to inclusion

I conducted a research study asking students what the barriers to and facilitators of inclusion are, from their viewpoint. I gave them a scenario in which David, a student with Down syndrome, is at the back of the classroom working with his educational assistant. He gets up, approaches a group of students, and says, "I want to work with you guys, OK?" Then we asked the students what they thought David was thinking and feeling, what the group should do, and what they thought the group would do, and why. Students were eloquent in their expression of empathy and compassion for David:

> He's sort of feeling left out because of his disability and he has to work with this guy, Mr. Brown. He really, really wants to work with the other kids that don't have disabilities. I guess he sort of feels like, even though I have a disability why should I be working with this guy? I'm like the same species as you guys, I'm not a dog, I'm not a monkey, why shouldn't I be able to work with you?

Most students expressed an understanding that the right thing to do would be to include David. However, they outlined three barriers that might prevent them from saying yes.

1. **Grades:** Students were concerned that if they included David in their project, it would affect their final mark. This is why it is critical to explicitly state that group grades are not penalized because the group includes students who are learning the language or who face challenges doing their part in the activities. While there is much discussion in the literature about differentiating instruction (Lawrence-Brown 2004), the differentiation of assessment is more rarely addressed (Brighton, Hertberg, Moon, Tomlinson, and Callahan 2005). If the group were allowed to present their grasp of the understandings in a way other than writing, David might be better able to contribute to the group, and therefore be more welcome.

2. **Pace:** Students expressed concern that including David would affect their ability to get the task done in the time allotted ("Maybe they don't want to include him because he might slow them down—because they would have to explain everything to him"). Again, the students responding in the research assumed that they would face time pressures on the task, which likely reflected their experiences in other classrooms, but the scenario they were given did not state a timeframe. For that reason, ensure that students know you will check with the groups and give flex time as needed.

3. **Educational assistants and aides:** Assigning educational assistants to support students with disabilities in inclusive classrooms is widespread. However, "the professional literature is nearly devoid of student outcome data as it pertains to the utilization of paraprofessionals" (Giangreco and Doyle 2002, 3). Social inclusion requires that students with disabilities interact with and develop friendships with students without disabilities; at times, they will also have conflicts and have to solve problems with other students, as all do.

However, the preponderance of interference by educational assistants in these interactions comes into question. In one study exploring this issue, excessive proximity of educational assistants resulted in a series of problems such as:

- interference with teacher ownership and responsibility
- separation from classmates
- dependence on adults
- interference with peer interactions
- loss of personal control
- limitations on receiving competent instruction
- interference with the instruction of the other students (Giangreco et al. 1997).

In the David scenario, for example, the students appeared to be profoundly, and negatively, affected by the existence of an aide (Mr. Brown). For some students, the presence of the aide marked David as so different that they did not believe he "belonged" with other kids:

> People with special aides shouldn't be working with normal people. Sandi's normal, and David has an aide.

Many of those who were willing to include David did so partially in reaction to the presence of the aide, assuming David wished he didn't have one:

> I think they should let David be in the group because maybe they could learn stuff from him and understand how he's feeling. Maybe he will tell them what he is feeling about being with an aide, that he's telling them I'm a normal person.
>
> Say yes and kind of work with him, and then they might become friends after; then he will feel better in class, instead of working with Mr. Brown.

Interestingly, not a single student commented in a positive light about the presence of Mr. Brown. No student considered that by including David, the whole group would have the additional help of Mr. Brown; they did not see the aide as a positive addition to the class. It appears, therefore, that the assignment of one-to-one aides to students with disabilities interferes with social and academic inclusion rather than facilitating it (chapter 6). It is vital that all staff in a classroom work with all students, and that they see their role as facilitating the social and academic inclusion of all students.

Portage & Main Press, 2012, *Teaching to Diversity*, ISBN: 978-1-55379-353-3

Teachers in the UDL Classroom

Our role is to facilitate children's learning. While they are working in their groups at the centres, I circulate, observe, and conduct formative assessment. Which students understand the concept? Which ones are struggling? Who needs enrichment?

I use my class profiles and rubrics. I give students feedback on a rubric showing them where they have done well, and what they need to work on, or I do it orally. I record my observations on my class profile. When I notice a few students struggling, I can pull them aside the next day while the groups are at centres, and do some direct instruction with them, before sending them back to rejoin their groups. I can also pull aside the students who have mastered the concept and provide them with an enrichment challenge. This freedom is what allows me to meet the needs of diverse learners.

I also facilitate discussions as I move from group to group, posing higher order questions to scaffold the learning, giving feedback and providing the resources that students may need as I see where their learning is taking them. As a teacher circulates, it's important to stop and draw attention to groups that are working well together, to their creative ideas, and to the depth of the students' thinking. I break into the group work, asking the class to stop, look, and listen for a minute. When they are all focused and listening, I ask the student who expressed a great idea to share it out; or I mention someone's great leadership in teamwork. When the students turn back to work, they can build on the ideas they just heard or just be reminded of their social goals.

Collaborative Practice

Learning communities and teamwork are not just for the students. A true learning community involves students, teachers, staff, administration, and families in collaborative, democratic decision-making and practice. When teachers tell me "Co-teaching will only work if you share the same philosophy and style," I think, "Really? If we expect eight-year-olds to learn how to work together, shouldn't we?"

Portage & Main Press, 2012, *Teaching to Diversity*, ISBN: 978-1-55379-353-3

Cory

Cory, a student in my grade 3 class, was cooperative, friendly, and well-liked by the other kids, but Cory could not read. At all. He struggled even with a pre-primer word list. After going through the Respecting Diversity program, Cory had shared with the class his goal of learning to read. Because he was not the only struggling reader in the class, we had talked about how the other students could support a group member in achieving this goal.

However, the school had decided to conduct a school-wide reading assessment in order to determine the number of students not "meeting expectations" in reading and to target the supports that the school could offer. To conduct the assessment, resource teachers called students one at a time to have them read aloud, to record the students' level of fluency, then to ask oral questions about the passage to assess the student's comprehension. I had approached my resource teacher about Cory, because we both knew that he could not read a grade 3 passage, so there was no point in taking him for this assessment since he would only feel bad. I asked her to just record that he was "not yet meeting expectations" and leave him be, which she agreed to do.

Unfortunately, a different resource teacher came to my room and, while I was busy working with a small group, led some of my students, including Cory, out for the assessment. When I turned around to see that Cory was gone, the other students told me he had left with the resource teacher. I ran down the hall to try to stop Cory's assessment. At the doorway, I saw a group of my students sitting at a table reading. Cory was standing beside the resource teacher's desk, and I heard her say, "OK, can you read this for me, please." "Nope," he replied. She looked a little taken aback, and asked, "Why not?" Cory, with no hesitation answered, "Because I suck at verbal-linguistic." In that moment, Mary, a grade 2 student in the class, jumped up and went over to the desk. She reached across and took the story from Cory and proceeded to read it to him. When she had finished, she handed the story back to Cory, turned to the teacher, and said, "You can ask him the questions now," and returned to her work.

This was one of my favourite moments in teaching, because Cory felt no hesitation or humiliation in acknowledging his challenge, and because my students did not respond with giggling or making fun of him. Instead, they did what was normal for us, they backed him up. The RD program had worked. Cory understood his strengths and his challenges, was OK with who he was, and was unafraid to share his challenge. Above all, my kids knew the expectation was that they would support each other. If Cory had had an educational assistant, the kids most likely would have thought it was the EA's job to help Cory, would have ignored him during class, and not known what to do in a scene like this. When we as adults step back, we create space for the kids to step forward.

Cory's acceptance of his challenges should not be mistaken for complacency. He was involved in intensive reading intervention, and our team was working hard to support him in developing his reading skills. However, in the meantime, we were determined not to have his reading interfere with his ability to learn and participate in the academic life of the classroom, or damage his self-esteem. He knew what he was good at, and what he was working to develop, and so did the other students. They knew how to work together to support each other, and we did the same.

Portage & Main Press, 2012, *Teaching to Diversity*, ISBN: 978-1-55379-353-3

The collaborative model usually involves a resource teacher and classroom teacher in a team approach to meeting the needs of all students, not just the students with exceptional needs. Research (Cook 1995; Little and Dieker 2009) has shown the teaching team is a powerful model for supporting inclusive education because a team:

- reduces territoriality;
- combines talents, knowledge, and energy;
- reduces stigma and normalizes differentiation;
- creates a family and a community atmosphere;
- helps teachers engage in more active instruction, learn new strategies, and more easily differentiate (one teacher can supervise one task, while another teacher implements a different version);
- helps students show improved academic achievement (including reading levels and higher order thinking), become more engaged, and have better self-esteem and social relationships (Cook and Friend 1995).

Co-teaching has traditionally been defined as the interaction between professionals who offer different areas of expertise, yet share responsibilities and goals. However, co-teaching can also happen between two colleagues, as when two math teachers or two grade 7 teachers choose to work together. Co-teaching requires that hierarchies and divisive role descriptions be done away with, and that partners work together as equals. Co-teaching involves co-planning, co-instruction, and co-assessing. When classroom and resource teachers are teaming, classroom teachers bring subject knowledge while resource teachers bring specialized knowledge about learners with differences to the team. One way of framing this work is through a tiered model.

Response to Intervention

The three-tiered response to intervention (RTI) model works well in inclusive education. Each year all students begin as general education students, and teachers use evidence-based practices to meet the needs of all learners. Resource and classroom teachers work together in the classroom. They begin the year by implementing the Respecting Diversity program and group work pieces without immediately worrying about individual education plans and interventions, except for students' health and safety, of course.

Every year, students get a chance to start the year as part of the community, joining in and developing relationships, focusing on their strengths, and having a fresh, new experience of school. We begin our units of study, implement the principles of universal design for learning, and assess all students to see how they are doing.

When students appear to be struggling to learn in spite of universally designed classrooms, curricula, and co-teaching support, they are moved to Tier 2, where short-term, intensive intervention is provided. At this stage, with appropriate

Spotlight

For more information on RTI, visit the website: www.rti4success.org/

Portage & Main Press, 2012, *Teaching to Diversity*, ISBN: 978-1-55379-353-3

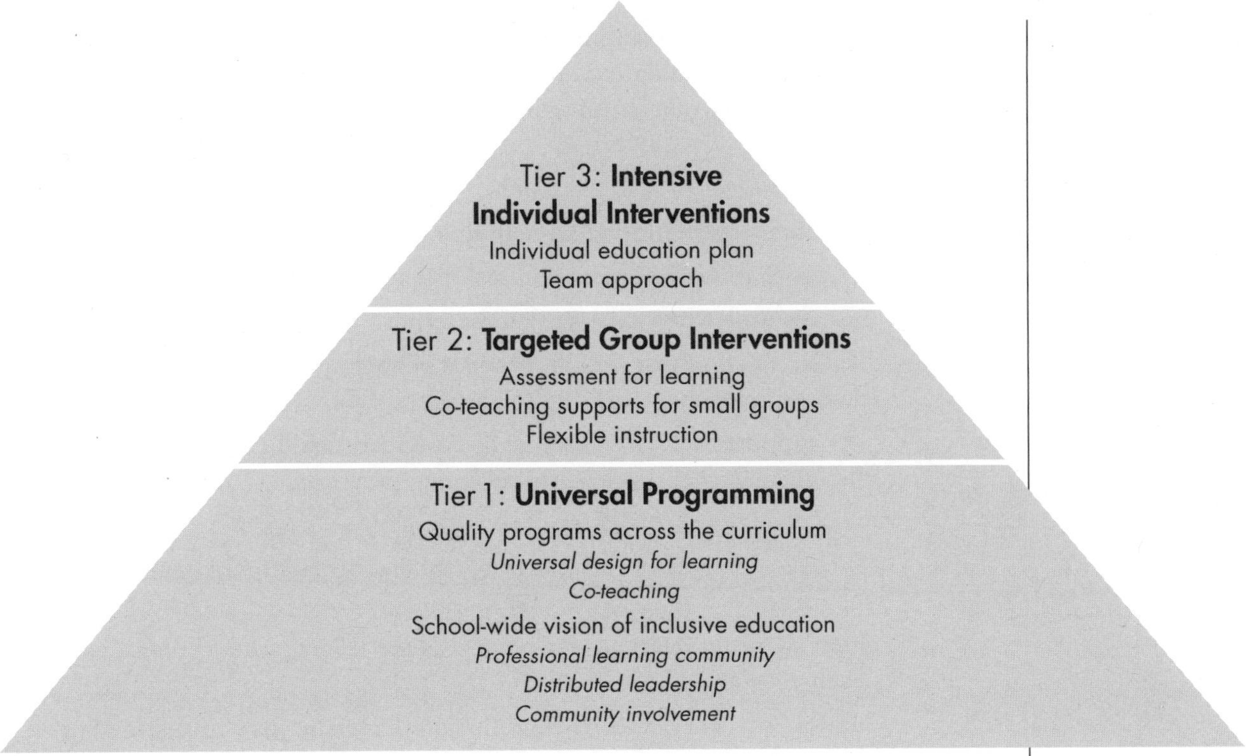

Tier 3: **Intensive
Individual Interventions**
Individual education plan
Team approach

Tier 2: **Targeted Group Interventions**
Assessment for learning
Co-teaching supports for small groups
Flexible instruction

Tier 1: **Universal Programming**
Quality programs across the curriculum
Universal design for learning
Co-teaching
School-wide vision of inclusive education
Professional learning community
Distributed leadership
Community involvement

Figure 5.3 Response to Intervention pyramid

assessment using class profiles (see Figure 5.4, p. 147), interventions can be planned for small groups of students having difficulty with specific concepts and skills. This does not mean pulling students out of the classroom and into the resource room; instead the interventions take place in the original classroom, maybe over a set period of time, with different students involved, depending on the skill or concept being addressed.

If significant knowledge or skill gaps persist over time for some students, they are moved to Tier 3 where long-term interventions are considered. An IEP may be considered or developed again, but students are rarely removed from their classrooms. Instead, the teachers recognize the need for some concentrated teamwork to support this student's learning.

Teachers work together fluidly through both Tier 1 and Tier 2 and, possibly, Tier 3. Collaborative practice requires that instruction be evidence-based, meet the needs of diverse learners, ensure access to curriculum for all students, gather data for programming purposes, and allow for specialized and individualized instruction for students in Tier 2 and Tier 3.

Co-Teaching

There are many different models for co-teaching, depending on the particular concept or skill being taught and on the strengths of the teachers involved and the students. A good co-teaching team flows back and forth through different strategies; Friend and Cook (2010) identified several formats:

Portage & Main Press, 2012, *Teaching to Diversity*, ISBN: 978-1-55379-353-3

1. **One Teaching, One Drifting:** With this model, one teacher has the primary responsibility for planning and teaching, while the other teacher moves around the classroom helping individuals and observing particular behaviours.

    Some advantages of this approach:

    - Students receive individual help in a timely manner.
    - It's easier to keep students on task because one teacher is usually nearby.
    - It saves time when distributing materials.
    - The supporting teacher can observe behaviour not seen by the classroom teacher directing the lesson.
    - The supporting teacher can walk around and still continue to observe the other teacher model good teaching practices.

    Some challenges of this approach:

    - Through the eyes of the students, one teacher has more control than the other.
    - Students often relate to one person as the teacher and to the other as a teacher's aide.
    - Having a teacher walk around during the lesson may be distracting to some students.
    - Students begin to expect immediate one-on-one assistance.

2. **Parallel Teaching:** The teachers plan jointly, but split the classroom into two groups to teach the same information at the same time.

    Some advantages of this approach:

    - Preplanning provides better teaching.
    - Teachers can work with smaller groups.
    - Each teacher has the comfort level of working separately to teach the same lesson.
    - Splitting the class allows teachers to separate some students.

    Some challenges of this approach:

    - Both teachers have to be competent in the content so the students will learn equally.
    - It is difficult to pace the work so that both groups end at the same time.
    - There must be enough flexible space in the classroom to accommodate two groups.
    - The noise level must be controlled.

3. **Alternative Teaching:** One teacher manages most of the class while the other teacher works with a small group inside or outside the classroom. The small group does not have to integrate with the current lesson.

Portage & Main Press, 2012, *Teaching to Diversity*, ISBN: 978-1-55379-353-3

Some advantages of this approach:

- Working with small groups or with individuals helps meet the personal needs of students.
- Both teachers can remain in the classroom, so one teacher can informally observe the other.

Some challenges of this approach:

- Groups must vary with purpose and composition or the students in the group will quickly become labelled (the "smart" group).
- The students might view the teacher working with the larger group as the teacher in control.
- Noise level must be controlled if both teachers are working in the classroom.
- There must be adequate space.

4. **Station Teaching:** Both teachers divide the instructional content, and each takes responsibility for planning and teaching part of it. In station teaching, the classroom is divided into various teaching centres. Each teacher plans, and facilitates, one or more of the centres.

Some advantages of this approach:

- Easier to differentiate instruction and take advantage of strengths. For instance, one can run a musical activity, the other a visual or kinesthetic one.
- Each teacher has a clear teaching responsibility.
- Students have the benefit of working in small groups.
- Teachers can cover more material in a shorter period of time.
- Fewer discipline problems occur because students are engaged in active, hands-on learning.
- It is possible to separate students.
- This approach maximizes the use of volunteers or extra adults in the room.

Some challenges of this approach:

- To work effectively, this approach requires a lot of preplanning.
- All materials must be prepared and organized in advance.
- The noise level will be at a maximum.
- Sometimes it is difficult to pace the teaching to end at the same time.

5. **Team Teaching:** Both teachers are responsible for planning, and they share the instruction of all students. Lessons are taught by both teachers who actively engage in conversation, not lecture, to encourage discussion by students. Both teachers are actively involved in the management of the lesson and discipline. This is the ideal of co-teaching when whole class structures are being used.

Portage & Main Press, 2012, *Teaching to Diversity*, ISBN: 978-1-55379-353-3

Some advantages of this approach:

- Each teacher has an active role.
- Students view both teachers as equals.
- Both teachers are actively involved in classroom organization and management.
- This approach encourages risk-taking. Teachers may try things in pairs that they wouldn't try alone.
- Teachers model how to work cooperatively and disagree respectfully, which creates a sense of family.
- "Two heads are better than one" leads to creativity.

Some challenges of this approach:

- Preplanning takes a considerable amount of time.
- Teachers' roles need to be clearly defined for shared responsibility.

Working with Educational Assistants

The job of an educational assistant (EA) is to support students' engagement in the academic and social activities of their classroom and school. They do not plan those activities, nor even implement them; they facilitate all students' engagement in them. I ask my EAs to circulate, helping students stay on task and facilitating peer interactions. If they are busy with a group of students, and one of the students with disabilities needs support, then I will provide that support and vice versa. In other words, they are assigned to the classroom, not to an individual student.

One-to-one EA supports stigmatize the children being supported and interfere with peer interactions; the supported students develop learned helplessness, and it actually decreases student engagement (Giangreco 2010). Like resource teachers and classroom teachers, educational assistants should understand that, in a UDL classroom, all staff work with all students. It is like a family, where different parents and extended family members all contribute something different to the raising of the child.

However, treating EAs with respect as collaborative team members does not mean that they can take on all the roles of a teacher. They have significant contributions to make and each individual's strengths are different. Some have significant strengths in organizational skills, behaviour management, art and music, or kinesthetic and athletic activities. In a classroom based on multiple intelligences, these strengths provide rich experiences for students that the classroom teacher might not. The job of an educational assistant is to develop independence in students, not to own and protect them, holding them back from growth and development. Respect, collaboration, and an understanding of the roles is key.

Teaching Conceptual Representation

When I first started working with teachers on this model of UDL, they said that the responses of students, given opportunities to represent their thinking in a variety of ways, were superficial. Just as students often have little experience with group work, so too students often have little or no experience with alternative means of representation; they have only been taught to write. I had always done some modelling lessons for students about various ways of showing their understanding at the beginning of the school year.

In one grade 8 classroom studying the novel *Island of the Blue Dolphins*, the teacher asked students to represent the characteristics of the protagonist, Karana. They automatically started to write a character sketch. But I stopped them and said the catch to this activity was that they had to represent what kind of person Karana was without words. The students looked at me, stunned. One of the students asked, "How are we supposed to do that?" I explained they could draw, paint, sculpt, play an instrument, sing, or act out (like charades) their perception.

The students were grouped into teams and began brainstorming. Asked to describe one characteristic they believed described Karana, one student said, "Brave." Asked how they could visually represent the concept of bravery, they insisted at first that the only way was to draw a scene where she was being brave. I pushed them to think symbolically, a much higher order, more complex kind of thinking. "What is a symbol of bravery?" I asked. One student said, "In the military, you can get a medal for bravery." I agreed that a medal was a perfect symbol of bravery. "So if we were creating a collage of symbols representing Karana, we could include a medal. What else?"

Soon the students were throwing out answers: a brain for intelligence, a teardrop for sad. Next, we talked about music: "What tone or beat would you use to show bravery? Would it be a slow or fast? What about sad? How would you act out that characteristic? After we discussed these ideas, I set the students back to work. They were excited, engaged, and in the end they did a great job for a first effort of representing their interpretations of Karana's personality in a variety of ways.

At the beginning of the year, it's important to teach students how to represent complex concepts in sophisticated ways, for example:

1. Do some whole-class demonstrations or show videos/images (e.g., show a painting in which the artist has depicted concepts such as poverty, love, bravery). Discuss why the artist chose the particular colors, images, and style they did.

2. Play music without lyrics that evokes particular moods or experiences such as Rimsky-Korsakov's "Flight of the Bumble Bee."

3. Play charades; show video clips of mimes; build models.

4. Take a written piece, and ask students to transfer the ideas into other formats, for example, a poem about freedom. How could you represent freedom in images, musical tone, acting, or dance? I have used Salvador Dali's painting "Persistence of Memory" to model a visual representation of concepts such as time, memory, and history.

Portage & Main Press, 2012, *Teaching to Diversity*, ISBN: 978-1-55379-353-3

Moving Forward

Once you have prepared the students to work together and to represent complex thinking in a variety of ways, move into the real academic content for the year. After being introduced to some of the concepts in the first unit, the students are ready to move into the group centres. At this point I know my students well enough to assert control and choose the members for each group. I need to surround certain students with supportive group members, or I will be setting them up for failure.

As the year goes on and the kids learn to self-manage their learning and behaviour, I can offer them the choice of putting themselves in groups. When I do, I set the criteria: we need groups of four or five; everyone has to be included; they need to consider who works well with whom, including who has complementary skill sets. The students may ask the teacher to pick group members, but other times, they do very well at organizing these groups in second and third term of the school year, when they know each other better and also know the learning expectations for the term.

It's usually October by the time the class starts the first round of working in centres, and this step can be challenging. My whole system and approach to universal design is all still pretty new to the students. They are excited and engaged, but still need a fair bit of support with how to manage their own learning. Younger students struggle with compromise and communication. Older students struggle with taking risks with their learning, and wanting teachers to just tell them what to do (they have been "schooled" through prior experience). Both younger and older sometimes struggle with the freedom—they can go too far when they first break the chains. It takes strength and faith not to intervene with them, either by solving the social problems or by giving directions on the task, or not to rein them in.

You have to be willing to let students struggle a bit in order to work it out for themselves, and find the strengths that lie within themselves and their peers. When you see a group off-task, don't give in to the temptation to step in and get them back on task. Let them learn the natural consequence (they don't finish), otherwise they do not learn to self-regulate or to develop time-management skills. Sometimes, kids have to fail, not the grade, but they have to realize it's Friday and they didn't finish, which gives you the opportunity to have the conversation: "What went wrong? What should the group have done?" Next time, you will hear them say, "Come on, guys. We gotta get this done."

It is a judgment call for the teacher. There are times to give a gentle reminder of expectations or timelines, and times to step back and let the kids figure it out. I'm far from perfect, but somehow we always figured it out, and by November we were sailing. I spent the rest of the year loving my time with them, learning and teaching, laughing and debating. There were heavy times, to be sure. Kids who disclosed abuse, family tragedies, first loves and broken hearts, incidents of cyber bullying and of serious illness. Teaching is not for the faint of heart, not if you truly care for your kids and build a relationship in which they will share their lives with you. It is, however, for those who truly want to make a difference in the life of a child.

Portage & Main Press, 2012, *Teaching to Diversity*, ISBN: 978-1-55379-353-3

Assessment for, of, and as Learning with Diverse Learners

At various times in my career I have had to write anecdotal reports, give grades, give percentages, or place students on a continuum. It seemed to change every other year. I want the best for my kids, so I strive to make the system work for them. When it comes to assessment and evaluation, there are three key terms:

1. **Assessment:** The ongoing process of gathering evidence of what a student is able to do and identifying his or her learning needs. Assessment can be informal or formal, but almost all assessment serves to guide teaching and learning.

2. **Evaluation:** A snapshot of where students are in their development relative to a standard. We use all the information gathered through the term to determine what level of mastery students have achieved relative to the standards set for them (rubrics of essential understandings).

3. **Reporting:** Communicating to the students and their parents information about their progress in learning content and skills. The reports can be informal as when commenting on a response during a discussion or conference, or formal as in writing feedback on a product the student has created or writing marks with comments on report cards.

The assessment process begins when planning the unit, selecting the essential understandings, creating the rubric, and designing the first diagnostic assessment. You have to know your goal—what does mastery look like?

Formative Assessment: Use formative assessment to determine what students already know, can do, or are in process of mastering in order to guide both teaching and learning.

Summative Assessment: Use summative assessments to gather the information needed to determine the level of mastery that students have reached.

Differentiating Assessment

To truly honour diversity, we differentiate the types of assessment as much as we differentiate instruction. We must give kids a chance to show, through their strengths, what they know. The assessment in a UDL classroom, therefore, becomes process-oriented, and multi-modal. Many teachers have to cope with mandatory exams, but probably only 25 per cent of the mark has to come from a paper-and-pencil test. If students have talked about the concept/topic, sung about it, role-played it, built it and more, they are much more likely to have something to write about it. Your students do not have to learn through paper and pencil in order to prepare for a paper and pencil exam.

In a UDL classroom, assessment takes place on an ongoing basis. Students work as a group in their centres and discuss the concepts presented; the teacher circulates, listening and asking questions and highlighting the outline of objectives on the rubric. I carried a clipboard with rubrics for each student, with their names at the top. As they talked/worked, I highlighted the rubric based on what I noticed.

When they began creating their products (whether through dance, song, art, role-play, written, or other representation), I circulated and observed. I also had the final products and presentations, and their individual projects at the end of term. So I had lots of data to work with, and the kids had the chance to show what they know in a variety of ways.

Methods of Assessment

1. **Observation:** Observation is the most common form of assessment in my room. The students understand that I am always listening and observing to determine their level of understanding. I do not base all my assessment on what they produce—everything counts. For instance, if a student makes a comment during a class discussion that shows a deep level of understanding, I'll note that and count it as a demonstration of fully meeting the expectations. If I approach a group creating a role play about the life of a plant, and Jason is directing his group members "OK, Steve, you kneel down, you're the seed. Sonya, you kneel and put your arms up like this, you're the seedling." I'll note that Jason knows the stages. I can't assess the others, because they may or may not know the stages, so I move on to observing another group, and will catch Jason's other group members on another day.

2. **Conferencing:** Conferencing means having an individual conversation with a student about their learning. These conferences may be brief, as when we lean over a student's desk to check in with them; or they can be more structured in a longer discussion with a specific intent, for instance, a reading or writing conference, or a review of a particular product. Sometimes, when I have overlooked a particular student, I say "I haven't had a chance to talk with you lately; we've been learning about the particle theory of matter, how's it going for you?" After our discussion, the student returns to his or her group, and I record where they are at on my rubric.

3. **Portfolio assessment:** A student's work in a portfolio is meant to show process. It should include drafts and reflections in addition to final products. When I look at the portfolio, I look for the ways he or she demonstrates a grasp of the essential understandings. Whether the student chose a written product, a visual representation, or any other format, the product is treated equally.

Assessment for Learning: Creating Class Profiles

Assessment for learning is assessment for the purposes of guiding teacher instruction. We gather data on what our students understand, and what they have not yet mastered to help us decide what to teach and when. I use a class profile or checklist for each discipline, which helps me see patterns for the group. Each one-page document has student names down the left side and the phrasing for "fully meets" the essential understandings in the study unit for each term in each discipline in the top row. Figure 5.4 is an example of my grade 7 students' class profile rubric for writing.

Portage & Main Press, 2012, *Teaching to Diversity*, ISBN: 978-1-55379-353-3

Name/Class	Understands that vocabulary and sentence structures enhance clarity	Understands that particular forms are appropriate for selected audiences	Selects language for mood, purpose — has an impact	Composes with detail and descriptions
Julie	✓		✓	✓
Sam	✓		✓	✓
Tanya	✓	✓	✓	✓
Pho		✓	✓	
Lani	✓		✓	
Shota	✓			
Mary			✓	
David	✓	✓	✓	✓
Sara			✓	

Figure 5.4 Class Profile for Writing

I place a check mark for the students who "fully meet" or "exceed" for each criterion. Such a profile gives me the language for a report card, for instance: "Julie understands that vocabulary…, selects language for mood…, and composes with supporting details. Julie is working on considering form and audience for her writing" (so her goal is in her blank column, because the lack of a check mark means she has not yet met expectations). The profile also shows that most students are doing well. However, Tanya and David, having check marks in each column, may need enrichment, while Shota, Mary, and Sara are struggling.

- From these observations, I get together with my resource teacher and educational assistant to discuss how to meet their needs.

- To target my whole-class instruction, I scan vertically down the columns. I see that few of the students consider form and audience in their writing, so that will be my target for mini-lessons for a while.

- To determine small group or individualized instruction, I see that a few students don't know how to select appropriate words and sentence patterns to enhance clarity and artistry. So while the class is working on their writer's workshop, I take these few aside and do a mini-lesson with them on this topic.

- My goal is to fill the class profile with check marks—it will mean that all my students fully meet the expectations.

- Whether it is writing, or reading, or science, my process is the same. I use the class profile and the rubric to guide my instruction—and that is assessment for learning.

Portage & Main Press, 2012, *Teaching to Diversity*, ISBN: 978-1-55379-353-3

Assessment as Learning: Student Self-Assessment

Student self-assessment involves their development of metacognitive awareness that can guide their own learning. Our purpose is to involve students in their own learning, which gives them ownership, empowers them to take initiative, and develops their autonomy. When we teach students to self-assess, we guide them to become reflective learners, to deepen their understanding of the criteria and essential understandings in each discipline, and to develop metacognitive skills, strategies, and awareness.

Students have to understand what it is they are trying to learn, and what a good example of success looks like, for this to be a possibility. By giving rubrics to students and discussing them before they begin a task, not after, they know what our expectations are. Mini-lessons allow us to clarify those expectations.

For the criterion "uses language for mood and purpose" in writing, we can select a poem or story that represents this skill, and guide the students to a discussion of the poet's use of words, and how the vocabulary made them feel. Then we can ask students to look at their own drafts, and think about whether they selected powerful words to create the mood they wanted. Such review and comparison brings students to see the criteria, understand what we are looking for, and then reflect on whether they have applied that understanding to their own learning. The actual process of assessing their own writing serves as a learning opportunity for them, helping them see what's working, what's not working, and what's next.

When we conference with students, we also have an opportunity to promote assessment as learning. For instance, my students have the criteria for what makes a good story (age-dependent) in their writer's workshop folders. When they believe they have met the criteria, they sign up for a conference with me. They bring an assessment page, along with their draft (Figure 5.5).

4 = Excellent 3 = Very Good 2 = So-so, OK 1 = Forgot, not yet	Student Evaluation	Teacher Evaluation
Understands that vocabulary and sentence structures enhance clarity		
Understands particular forms are appropriate for selected audiences		
Selects language for mood, purpose — has an impact		
Composes with detail and descriptions		

Figure 5.5 Mini version of rubric: Criteria for Writer's Workshop conferencing with student

Portage & Main Press, 2012, *Teaching to Diversity*, ISBN: 978-1-55379-353-3

I ask the students to self-evaluate first. We use the numerical code in the top row left above the four criteria. After the students have self-assessed their piece, I assess it. If we agree on the scores, then we move on to the next step. If we don't agree, then we have a discussion. Remember the scenario discussed earlier, where a student gave her own work "4 Excellent" for "Selects language for mood and purpose," and then circled "nice" when I asked her to show me the example in her work? That scenario represents assessment as learning, because now the student has a chance to learn what we mean by "Powerful language that creates a mood." No matter the subject, the process is the same.

Assessment of Learning: Evaluation and Mastery Learning

The most controversial part of assessment in a UDL classroom is the stage of *evaluation of learning* and *mastery learning*. We need to be clear about what we want to achieve with different assessments, especially end-of-unit evaluation. The kids have the rubrics that state what learning outcomes are expected by the end of the unit. If we continue to give marks at stages throughout the unit and average them, we have contradicted ourselves—why should a mark from two weeks into the unit count for the same amount as a mark at the end of a unit? Who are we marking two weeks into the unit? We are not marking the student because we haven't taught the full unit yet. We are marking the work of last year's teacher, or of their parents, in other words, we are marking their background knowledge and cultural capital. We are punishing the kids who came into the unit with less background knowledge and skills than others did. This is not *inclusive education*.

We can and we must assess progress all through the unit, but we should not evaluate early in a unit. All through the unit, I observe, conference with my students, and assess products from them. I highlight on the rubric what level of understanding they have demonstrated. I watch to see whether they are moving from "Beginning," to "Approaching" to "Fully meeting" the expectations. I give the students constant feedback about what I have seen them demonstrate, what they are doing well, and what I would like to see them improve, (just as we did in the reading and writing sections in chapter 4). However, I do not give them a mark. I assign marks only at the end of the unit. That does not mean that their mark is based on one end product. Everything they have done throughout the term helps me to determine their level of understanding. For example, in the second week of the unit, we have watched and talked to Sandy, and her progress is shown in Figure 5.6.

In the sixth week, Sandy is at the visual-spatial centre, and her strength is shown in Figure 5.7.

However, in her final project, Sandy challenges herself to try writing an essay about this, and her scores are evident in Figure 5.8.

When we average these findings, Sandy's achievement is somewhere in between "Approaching" and "Fully meeting" range. But we would be punishing her for having taken a risk in trying something that challenges her, and we would be marking her writing proficiency instead of her understanding of science. Truly, if Sandy has shown that she can explain how matter can be classified in a variety of

Subjects	Beginning to Develop (C-)	Approaching Expectations (C)	Fully Meeting Expectations (B)	Exceeding Expectations (A)
Science	Understands that all things are made of matter	Defines states of matter, solutions	Explains how matter can be classified in a variety of ways, with supporting examples	Compare and contrast classification systems
	Understands that scientists study how the world works	Explains why scientists postulate theories (they are trying to figure out how the world works)	Explains the connection between wondering, theory, and experimentation	Argues the role of science in "progress" (ie the pros and cons)
	Recognizes states of matter (solid, liquid, gas)	Gives examples of changes of state	Explains The Particle Theory of Matter (PTOM) as a theory of how things (matter) exist in and change states	Connects the PTOM with environmental issues such as global warming and desertification

Figure 5.6 Rubric showing teacher's impression of student (Sandy's) work

Subjects	Beginning to Develop (C-)	Approaching Expectations (C)	Fully Meeting Expectations (B)	Exceeding Expectations (A)
Science	Understands that all things are made of matter	Defines states of matter, solutions	Explains how matter can be classified in a variety of ways, with supporting examples	Compare and contrast classification systems
	Understands that scientists study how the world works	Explains why scientists postulate theories (they are trying to figure out how the world works)	Explains the connection between wondering, theory, and experimentation	Argues the role of science in "progress" (ie the pros and cons)
	Recognizes states of matter (solid, liquid, gas)	Gives examples of changes of state	Explains The Particle Theory of Matter (PTOM) as a theory of how things (matter) exist in and change states	Connects the PTOM with environmental issues such as global warming and desertification

Figure 5.7 Rubric showing Sandy's strength in visual-spatial intelligence

Portage & Main Press, 2012, *Teaching to Diversity*, ISBN: 978-1-55379-353-3

Subjects	Beginning to Develop (C-)	Approaching Expectations (C)	Fully Meeting Expectations (B)	Exceeding Expectations (A)
Science	Understands that all things are made of matter	Defines states of matter, solutions	Explains how Matter can be classified in a variety of ways, with supporting examples	Compare and contrast classification systems
	Understands that scientists study how the world works	Explains why scientists postulate theories (they are trying to figure out how the world works)	Explains the connection between wondering, theory, and experimentation	Argues the role of science in "progress" (ie the pros and cons)
	Recognizes states of matter (solid, liquid, gas)	Gives examples of changes of state	Explains The Particle Theory of Matter (PTOM) as a theory of how things (matter) exist in and change states	Connects the PTOM with environmental issues such as global warming and desertification

Figure 5.8 Rubric showing Sandy's evaluation (shading) for an essay in Science

ways; the connection between wondering, theory, and experimentation; and the connection between PTOM and environmental issues visually, then she deserves a mark that reflects that stage of understanding—she is fully meeting expectations. The fact that she did not demonstrate it in writing is not the point. However, Sandy did not demonstrate that she could compare and contrast classification systems or discuss the concept of "progress," so she does not get marks for that—she is not exceeding expectations. We are not gifting kids such marks; in fact, my standards are high and I demand a lot, but we are also not punishing kids for not having a lot of prior knowledge, or for not being good at writing it down.

Grading diverse learners

How do we come up with a mark or grade that is fair to diverse learners? The key is to maintain high standards but provide multiple opportunities and methods of learning for students. Even at the university, my rubrics have grades and percentages at the bottom of each column as in Figure 5.9.

In this case, Sandy, is slightly more than "Fully meeting" so I would give her a B+. Remember, an A means exceptional, exceeding what the teacher asked. Sandy did not achieve that, but she did do a very good job on the EUs as I had set them out. When I have to give a percent, I take the middle of the range so all students who get a B+ get an 87. After all, what is the difference between 86 and 87? So Sandy, after moving through the group centres, conferencing, and completing her independent project, showed she had fully met the expectations, and received a B+ or 87 per cent.

Portage & Main Press, 2012, *Teaching to Diversity*, ISBN: 978-1-55379-353-3

Subjects	Beginning to Develop (C-)	Approaching Expectations (C)	Fully Meeting Expectations (B)	Exceeding Expectations (A)
Science	Understands that all things are made of matter	Defines states of matter, solutions	Explains how matter can be classified in a variety of ways, with supporting examples	Compare and contrast classification systems
	Understands that scientists study how the world works	Explains why scientists postulate theories (they are trying to figure out how the world works)	Explains the connection between wondering, theory, and experimentation	Argues the role of science in "progress" (ie the pros and cons)
	Recognizes states of matter (solid, liquid, gas)	Gives examples of changes of state	Explains The Particle Theory of Matter (PTOM) as a theory of how things (matter) exist in and change states	Connects the PTOM with environmental issues such as global warming and desertification
	D 60–69 F Below 60	C+ 75–79 C 70–74	B+ 85–89 B 80–84	A+ 95–100 A 90–94

Figure 5.9 Rubric with additional row to show alpha-numeric information

Reporting to and about Diverse Learners

Reporting requires consideration of many things. Why do we report? "Because I have to" is true. The education system requires reporting as a measure of the whole system's accountability. We have a responsibility to inform parents about their children's progress and development. In general, most systems require teachers to report on what a student has done well, what the challenges or goals are for the student, and what parents can do to support their child. These are reasonable expectations, but the process often becomes ridiculously detailed and stressful. You may be given a template you must follow, but how you communicate is more important than what you communicate.

The tone of a report card can be overly positive and unrealistic, which sets a student up for a fall or it can also be too negative, and punitive. Stop and ask yourself: What is the purpose of reporting? What is my goal? Why and to whom is this important? I believe the purpose of reporting, whether formal or informal, is to involve and empower students and their families in their education. It is not meant to punish students, or weed them out. Holding report cards over a student's head as a threat is unprofessional and unethical. Yet I have heard teachers talk like this many times, "Well, when your parents get your report card, we'll see how you feel then," or staffroom talk about "When his parents get his report card, maybe they'll wake up."

Some teachers seem to believe that report cards can help to control behaviour, mistakenly thinking parents will "smarten their kids up." You will never improve

Portage & Main Press, 2012, *Teaching to Diversity*, ISBN: 978-1-55379-353-3

a student's behaviour by causing them conflict at home. That only increases a student's anger, stress, and cortisol levels. Destroying students' relationships with their parents and theirs with you is not productive or helpful. Parents and students need to be supported, to have a positive relationship, to know what they can be proud of, and how they can work together to improve the student's progress. Be truthful, but help students and their families see that everyone has strengths and challenges; tell them what the student is doing well and can be proud of, and what challenges the student is facing and needs support with.

Report cards are not required for job applications, relationships, or attainment of any future life goals. Parents and teachers often place far too much emphasis on marks and report cards, rather than learning. The only person that report card is important to is that child, so be sure it serves to help them grow and learn and be successful. Have students evaluate themselves, and incorporate their comments on the report card. When reports were anecdotal, I wrote a section for each intelligence (see Figure 5.10).

The parents loved these detailed reports because they told them so much more than bulleted lists of learning outcomes. It didn't take more time because the initial sentence was the same for everyone, and the comments come from the class profile, as noted in the previous discussion. At higher grades requiring reports and grades by subject, my reports looked like Figure 5.11.

The student's grades and attendance were recorded on a cover page. It does not matter what format you use; what you say and how you say it sends a very clear message to children and their families about that child.

Portage & Main Press, 2012, *Teaching to Diversity*, ISBN: 978-1-55379-353-3

Intelligence	Student and Teacher comments
Naturalistic	*Steven says:* I learned to respect the environment. I think I am meeting expectations.
	The teachers say: This term, we have studied the natural resources involved in the development of Steveston, particularly the fishing industry and the use of the waterways. Steven is able to understand how communities live off the natural resources of their surroundings, and the balance required for interdependence. Steven is affected by environmental issues and often comments on them.
Interpersonal **Intrapersonal** **Existential**	*Steven says:* I learned to respect others and myself. That's what R3 means... respect for others, respect for self, and respect for the environment. I think I am meeting the expectations.
	The teachers say: Steven is beginning to meet the expectations for social responsibility. Steven has made great progress in his interactions with peers. He has learned how to enter a group, ask someone to play, and seek attention from his peers in more positive ways. When conflict arises, he is usually able to attempt a peaceful solution, though he gets easily frustrated and resorts to blaming others. Steven can now contribute appropriate solutions to issues arising during class meetings, as well. Steven is working on finding ways to meet his needs for attention and movement without disrupting others.
Verbal-Linguistic	*Steven says:* My vocabulary is good. I think I am meeting the expectations.
	The teachers say: Steven is exceeding the expectations for reading literature. He is a confident reader and chooses appropriately challenging texts. He often has great insights to share about his reading , when given the chance to do so orally. In writing, Steven's written output challenges continue to hold him back. We have used a tape recorder, scribe, and computer to support him this term.
Bodily-Kinesthetic	*Steven says:* "I learned to do speed laps. I think I exceeded expectations."
	The teachers say: This term we have participated in gymnastics, tennis, and track and field. Steven has improved his coordination and conditioning for track activities. He still finds the eye hand coordination needed for tennis challenging. Steven should be provided with opportunities to engage in athletic activities at home or in the community — this will allow him to keep healthy and will give him opportunities to interact with peers in cooperative activities.
Visual-Spatial	*Steven says:* "We made 3D maps of Steveston. Some parts were easy, some were challenging, so it's medium."
	The teachers say: Steven prefers working with 3D construction pieces to 2D drawing activities. In 3D, he is able to represent images from memory and scale items to fit the space, something he finds challenging in 2D.
Musical-Rhythmic	*Steven says:* I learned to hate music.
	The teachers say: Steven finds the coordination involved in moving to music very difficult. He therefore does not like dance or instrumental activities, especially where performance is involved.
Logical-Mathematical	*Steven says:* I learned divison...it's too hard!
	The teachers say: Despite what Steven says, Steven is actually exceeding the expectations for numeracy at this grade level. Steven has strong problem solving abilities and excellent visual-spatial perception. His mental math actually exceeds his written computation, as his difficulties with writing seem to interfere with his attention and working memory.

Figure 5.10 Anecdotal report at elementary level, using multiple intelligences with student's input

Portage & Main Press, 2012, *Teaching to Diversity*, ISBN: 978-1-55379-353-3

Subject/ Intelligence strand	Student and Teacher Comments
Health & Career Education/ Interpersonal and Intrapersonal Existentialist	*Sharon says:* I think I have made progress by getting enough sleep and eating a balanced diet. I now understand why eating healthy and getting fit is important. *Ms. Katz says:* This term we have focused on developing our understanding of healthy living. Students have learned about the different types of foods (proteins, carbohydrates, and fats) and their role in the body. They have written meal plans and learned to read nutrition labels. Students have also explored how media and peer influence affect their lifestyle. Sharon is reflective in her consideration of healthy living, and is developing her physical fitness.
Social Studies/ Interpersonal	*Sharon says:* The MLK speech changed how I thought about racism. I learned how Canada/USA has a history of racism when Obama became president it means progress. *Ms. Katz says:* This term we have been studying about the Canadian justice system and human rights, focusing on the Charter of Rights and Freedoms — its history and implementation. We have also compared Canada to Afghanistan to elaborate on issues related to human rights around the world, and Canada's role in this regard. Sharon is able to compare and contrast the UN declaration of Human Rights and the Canadian Charter of rights and freedoms, and can articulate her opinions regarding issues of justice, fairness, and equality. Sharon has good ideas, but often does not share them in discussions — this will be a goal for next term.
Science/ Naturalist Logical-Mathematical	*Sharon says:* I learned about extreme environments and how they affect us. I enjoyed doing the M.I. centers with my group. *Ms. Katz Says:* This term we have studied survival and exploration in extreme environments. Sharon is able to assess how and why extreme environments are places where human survival and exploration face significant challenges. She can describe technology that has been developed to allow such exploration, and understands the role Canadian scientists have played in these innovations.
Mathematics/ Logical-Mathematical	*Sharon says:* I learned that math is everywhere and how it affects our lives. I excelled in the calculating part. Think I need to do more problem solving stuff. *Ms. Katz Says:* We have continued to develop our problem solving skills as we explored the application of decimals, fractions, and percentages to everyday life and science. Sharon understands the relationship between decimals, fractions, and percentages as indicators of parts of a whole, and is able to convert and apply calculations with them to real life problems, and explain her thinking.
English Language Arts/ Verbal-Linguistic	*Sharon says:* I learned how to use tools for my poems, I think I made progress in that. I also learned how to project my voice so it's audible and make eye contact when speaking. *Ms. Katz Says:* This term we have focused on student's ability to recognize and utilize the structures and patterns of language and literary tools such as personification, similes and metaphors, imagery, symbolism, and figurative language to add power to their writing, speaking, and literary interpretations. Sharon is able to recognize some literary structures, and is learning to use them in her own writing. Her poetry includes some imagery and similes, as does her stories. To make her writing more powerful, Sharon will need to add more detail and begin to use some symbolism and figurative language. This will be a goal for next term.

Figure 5.11 Anecdotal report at secondary level, using multiple intelligences with student's input

Portage & Main Press, 2012, *Teaching to Diversity*, ISBN: 978-1-55379-353-3

Subject/ Intelligence strand	Student and Teacher Comments
Physical Education/ Bodily-Kinesthetic	*Sharon says:* I think I gained more stamina. My skill to play basketball is better, and during free time I think I can play badminton better as well. *Ms. Katz Says:* This term students have learned about the difference between cardiovascular health / exercise and strength training, and have participated in daily "workouts" to develop both! Sharon is developing her strength and stamina, and has joined the basketball team where she has improved her skills and is a cooperative team player. ☺
Fine Arts/ Visual-Spatial Musical-Rhythmic	*Sharon says:* I think I got better in drawing. Doing surrealist art made me improve my imagination. I really liked doing the two pieces of art. *Ms. Katz says:* This term the focus has been on Visual Arts. Students have been exposed to and explored techniques related to a variety of genres, including Impressionist, Realist, Surrealist, Abstract, and Cubist art, compared images created in these styles, and developed and defended personal preferences within them.

Figure 5.11 (continued)

My Teaching in the UDL Classroom

For over 16 years, I have loved teaching students—from year one to year sixteen, but I never enjoyed teaching as much as in the last few years while I was implementing this pedagogy. September was always a challenge—helping the kids find themselves as learners and as people was intense, but so incredibly powerful, too. My days in these years were filled with wonder, with energy, and with laughter. As a teacher with a PhD in Special Education, I worked with a lot of the most challenged learners who were placed in my classroom. In one of my last classes, I had 31 students, 11 of whom were on individual education plans. They had learning and behavioural challenges significant enough that an individualized program had been deemed necessary. That's one-third of the class, not including the 11 students (35%) who were learning English as a second language. It was the best year of teaching I had.

We began the year with my Respecting Diversity (RD) program followed by an introduction to group work and the multiple ways in which to represent information. These pedagogical approaches served to build a learning community that was very supportive for all, including myself. I was able to teach the way I had always wanted to—circulating among the students and facilitating their learning, posing questions, supporting aha moments, celebrating the kids and their phenomenal ability to grow and give back. We did service projects in the community, raised money for a homeless shelter for teens, trained me for my first athletic competition (yes, the kids lunged and squatted around the school with me daily) and, in the end, formed a family that continues, four years later, to communicate via social media. In the end, the cliché really is true—teaching is all about relationships.

Portage & Main Press, 2012, *Teaching to Diversity*, ISBN: 978-1-55379-353-3

Chapter 6
Leadership, Policy, and Practice—Block Three: Systems and Structures

My years of experience have shown what the principals and the school divisions in which I worked could have done to support me as a teacher in my struggles to meet the needs of the diverse learners in my classes. As a teacher in a segregated class for students with autism and cognitive disabilities, I struggled to get my students integrated into the "mainstream classes." Later, as both a resource teacher and classroom teacher in inclusive schools, I worked closely with school and district-based administrators. Then, as a board office consultant and as a presenter of professional development workshops, I collaborated with school leaders, divisional personnel, supervisors in the Ministry, and leaders of teacher unions. My current work as an assistant professor in the education faculty of the University of Manitoba has led me to collaborate as a professional developer with several school divisions, dozens of schools, and the Manitoba First Nations Education Resource Centre, which consults to over 60 band-operated schools.

From such personal experience, I know the effort required to develop capacity in teachers and to effect system change in schools and in school divisions/boards. However, I write first and foremost as a teacher and as a collaborator in implementing system change for inclusive education. Although I have consulted with several administrators while developing this chapter, I cannot claim personal experience in those roles. With that proviso, I describe in the following sections how systems and roles could be changed over a short period of time to support all students and the varied members of the teaching staff in schools.

Policy and Practice in Ministries of Education

When examining the role of systems and structures in inclusive education, it is useful to consider historical and sociological perspectives on the inclusion and exclusion of children facing the challenges of disabilities. Debate continues on whether our schools should reflect society or create it. I believe it is a choice—we can choose to follow social practices at large or we can choose to be leaders for change.

Although some curricula and policies have changed, the essence of the system continues; for instance, grouping children by chronological age, physical plants that isolate groups, and standardized testing. The current education system was designed post-World War II, when inclusive education was not a goal. Although

Portage & Main Press, 2012, *Teaching to Diversity*, ISBN: 978-1-55379-353-3

education systems have updated their policies and curricula over the decades, the curricula with specific learning outcomes (whether core, general, or distinctive) and assessment standards still privilege some students over others.

While it's true that families endow their children with cultural, economic, and social capital, the education system can either help to narrow the gaps between socioeconomic groups or serve to enlarge them. When some groups of children are segregated in separate classrooms, however, that separation prevents the exchange of cultural capital, knowledge, and understanding between groups. As a result, all students, whether in regular classes or in segregated classes, lose out on the opportunity to learn from each other and to transfer different forms of human capital to each other.

In an inclusive school system based on the principles of UDL, respect is given to diverse forms of cultural capital, and all students have access to all forms. If students grow up living and learning in relationships with diverse others, they are more likely to promote an inclusive society when they become adults. As educators we have a tremendous opportunity, and responsibility, to be leaders for change. In fact, I think we are, whether we like it or not. The question is: What kind of change are we going to inspire?

In 1994, more than 300 representatives of 92 nations gathered in Salamanca, Spain, for four days to discuss inclusive education under the umbrella of the United Nations Educational, Scientific and Cultural Organization (UNESCO).

To read the entire Salamanca Statement, visit the UNESCO website at www.unesco.org

The document, *Salamanca Statement on Principles, Policy and Practice in Special Needs Education and a Framework for Action* (UNESCO 1994), issued at the end of the conference, described the philosophy of the nations gathered there on the right to "education for all" children. The guiding principle of the framework adopted was that schools:

> should accommodate all children regardless of their physical, intellectual, social, emotional, linguistic or other conditions. This should include disabled and gifted children, street and working children, children from remote or nomadic populations, children from linguistic, ethnic or cultural minorities and children from other disadvantaged or marginalized areas or groups.

The statement recognized:

> the necessity and urgency of providing education for children, youth and adults with special educational needs within the regular education system.

The delegates to the conference created an action plan to address this need, stating that:

> those [children] with special educational needs must have access to regular schools which should accommodate them within a child-centred pedagogy capable of meeting these needs." *They further asserted that* "regular schools with this inclusive orientation are the most effective means of combating discriminatory attitudes, creating welcoming communities, building an inclusive society and achieving education for all; moreover, they provide an effective education to the majority of children and improve the efficiency and ultimately the cost effectiveness of the entire education system.

Well said. If we are to become a peaceful society and heal our people and our planet, we must begin to celebrate and respect the human and natural diversity of our global village.

Portage & Main Press, 2012, *Teaching to Diversity*, ISBN: 978-1-55379-353-3

Policy on Inclusive Education

The *Salamanca Statement* committed the signatory nations to creating laws and policies that promote inclusive education, to developing financing arrangements that support inclusive school systems, and to monitoring progress toward these aims. The governments of the signatory nations were called on to assume an important role in this process.

Seventeen years later, the education systems of the provinces and territories have made some progress toward the goal of inclusive education. Several documents available on the website of the Council of Ministers of Education, Canada (CMEC, the national voice in Canada and abroad for the provincial and territorial ministries of education) describe the policies established and the progress made since 1994 toward inclusive education in the individual jurisdictions, but there is still a long way to go.

Every province in Canada has policy related to inclusive education. For instance, in Ontario, the Ministry of Education's *Equity and Inclusive Education Strategy* envisions an inclusive school system in which:

- all students, parents, and other members of the school community are welcomed and respected;
- every student is supported and inspired to succeed in a culture of high expectations for learning.

The strategy defines inclusive education as "education that is based on the principles of acceptance and inclusion of all students." It calls on schools to create systems in which:

> students see themselves reflected in their curriculum, their physical surroundings, and the broader environment, in which diversity is honoured and all individuals are respected.

In British Columbia, inclusive policy is far less inclusive, as the policy states:

> A board must provide a student with special needs with an educational program in a classroom where that student is integrated with other students who do not have special needs, unless the educational needs of the student with special needs or other students indicate that the educational program for the student with special needs should be provided otherwise.

The policy does not indicate who decides whether or not to segregate, but goes further:

> British Columbia promotes an inclusive education system in which students with special needs are fully participating members of a community of learners. Inclusion describes the principle that all students are entitled to equitable access to learning, achievement and the pursuit of excellence in all aspects of their educational programs. The practice of inclusion is not necessarily synonymous with full integration in regular classrooms, and goes beyond placement to include meaningful participation and the promotion of interaction with others.

Inclusion is not synonymous with integration? How can you be included if you're segregated? If you're not present, or welcome? That is an oxymoron. What does "meaningful" mean?

Portage & Main Press, 2012, *Teaching to Diversity*, ISBN: 978-1-55379-353-3

In Manitoba, the *Appropriate Educational Programming Act* sets out policy for inclusive education.

> Inclusion is a way of thinking and acting that allows every individual to feel accepted, valued and safe. An inclusive community consciously evolves to meet the changing needs of its members. Through recognition and support, an inclusive community provides meaningful involvement and equal access to the benefits of citizenship. In Manitoba, we embrace inclusion as a means of enhancing the well-being of every member of the community. By working together, we strengthen our capacity to provide the foundation for a richer future for all of us.
>
> The *Public Schools Amendment Act* (Appropriate Educational Programming), S.M. 2004, c.9, proclaimed on October 28, 2005, reflects Manitoba's commitment to providing all students with appropriate programming that supports student participation in both the academic and social life of schools.

Other provinces and territories have similar policies. The policies are not perfect, but all indicate that the first choice is that students should live and learn together. Despite this, it is still common practice for schools to segregate based on language, origin, disability, and emotional or mental well-being (Canadian Council on Learning 2007). The schools set aside classrooms for students with a range of disabilities, for students learning English as a second language, and for students with emotional or behavioural disorders. Even when students with disabilities are placed in regular classrooms, they are frequently given a separate space and a separate program; they work solely with an educational assistant and do not participate in the academic or social life of the classroom (Giangreco 2010; Giangreco and Doyle 2002).

Research studies show that inclusive classrooms benefit both the students with disabilities and those without disabilities—socially and academically (Katz and Mirenda 2002). Academic outcomes for both the typical and the gifted learners in these inclusive classrooms indicate they have at least equivalent literacy rates, scores on standardized exams, and college entrance rates. In fact, in some studies, typical students in inclusive classrooms made significantly greater gains in reading and math than did typical students in traditional non-inclusive classrooms (Cole, Waldron, and Majd 2004). It is clear that the presence in class of students with disabilities does not negatively impact the learning of others. As for social interaction, both typical and gifted learners have been shown to benefit from classrooms that include students with disabilities. All students' communication skills, leadership, and self-concept are better in inclusive classrooms than in non-inclusive classrooms. Students who do not have disabilities but who have previously struggled in school, or had poor attendance, or demonstrated social and behavioural problems show the greatest improvements when in classrooms that include students with disabilities (Ruijs and Peetsma 2009).

Scores for low-achieving students on all kinds of academic measures, as well as for attendance, self-concept, and behavioural indexes are significantly better for these students when they are in classrooms that include students with disabilities than when they are in non-inclusive classrooms. Perhaps this is because in classrooms that include students with disabilities, teachers differentiate instruction,

Portage & Main Press, 2012, *Teaching to Diversity*, ISBN: 978-1-55379-353-3

and may have additional personnel present; the range of understanding is broader, which means that they incorporate all students within their instructional planning. Students with disabilities, of course, also show academic and social improvements in inclusive classrooms, including improved health, learning, and love for school (Timmons and Wagner 2008). They are exposed to far more curricular objectives, language, and literacy or numeracy levels in a regular classroom than they ever would be in a segregated classroom.

However, in spite of mounting research attesting to the positive effects of inclusion for all students and of the demonstrable willingness of teachers to include students with disabilities in their classrooms, real concerns remain over lack of training, classroom management, general and special education collaboration, and a perceived lack of support and resources (Bennett 2009). The result is the segregation of students with exceptional needs, negative classroom climates and peer interactions, increases in alienation and bullying, and a reduction in educational achievement for all students (Symes and Humphrey 2010). Clearly, more needs to be done to equip and empower educators with the competence and confidence required to teach all students, including those with exceptionalities, in the same classroom.

Manitoba policy (*Appropriate Educational Programming*, 2005) specifically states that UDL should be an underlying framework for our public schools.

> Inclusive schools provide a learning environment that is accessible to all students as a place to learn, grow, be accepted and enjoy all the benefits of citizenship. Inclusive schools should be aware of the concept of universal design.
>
> When applied to the field of education, the concept of universal design means that school communities, including teachers, develop plans for the full diversity of their student population. In education, universally designed schools, classrooms, curricula and materials provide all students with access to the resources they require, regardless of their diverse learning needs.

Despite this law being place for six years, few teachers in Manitoba have yet received training in universal design for learning, and the principles are taught only sporadically in teacher training, whether faculties of education or professional development programs across the country. Some of the courses purporting to teach UDL are actually based on the architectural, not the educational, paradigm of universal design, and are limited to technology or differentiation of instruction as the intervention (Specht and Katz, forthcoming).

The *Salamanca Statement* on inclusive education was adopted by the nations, Canada included, that participated in the UNESCO conference, and has been interpreted by the provincial and territorial ministries of education. However, the language used in official documents, such as "appropriate" education or "when indicated." leaves open the door to segregation. Were residential schools for Aboriginal children appropriate or indicated? The federal government of the time thought so. In order to be truly inclusive, revised policies must not leave room for exceptions, loopholes, and subjective decisions about segregation and exclusion, or what is "appropriate" or "indicated."

Portage & Main Press, 2012, *Teaching to Diversity*, ISBN: 978-1-55379-353-3

Curriculum Development and Assessment

Provincial and territorial curricula are developed by educators drawn from school divisions after a need for an update, a revision, or a new strand or discipline has been identified. Sometimes a major revision is undertaken collaboratively through a pan-Canadian organization like the CMEC, sometimes through regional education organizations like the Council of Atlantic Ministers of Education and Training (CAMET) or the Western and Northern Canadian Protocol (WNCP), and sometimes by individual provinces. Generally, the curriculum director, sometimes a deputy minister, assembles or assigns a team of teachers known for their work in one or more particular disciplines. They collaborate to develop the scope and sequence of topics and learning outcomes or expectations for the range of grades they have been asked to update or revise. At times, efforts are made to connect one curricula to another. At other times, curricula are developed in isolation and are not connected well with the curricular content in other disciplines taught at the same level or in ways that support integration and connection. Although teachers may feel pressed to cover the full curriculum, there is usually room for divisions/boards or schools to make choices among the abundance of topics and learning outcomes.

More inclusive curricula require that developers take into consideration a developmental range that is differentiated for content, process, and product. Such a curriculum requires involvement by diverse stakeholders who reflect the educators and students of the province as well as experts in the discipline. When a cross-subject perspective is brought to these conversations the results could be much richer and more practical for the teachers. Even for subject-specific teachers, the redundancy of learning outcomes in all the curricula leaves many teachers feeling overloaded, and their students end up with too many assignments and demands at the same time.

When I was working with a group of secondary school teachers discussing what each other teaches, they were horrified at how much time was being spent on the same topics. As an example, multiple subjects include outcomes related to safe handling of sharp or hot objects (e.g., chemistry, auto-mechanics, cooking), sustainability (social studies, vocational courses, science, or economics), and research skills. These teachers were distressed by how much time and how many assignments students were doing on the same subjects or skills. Working together provided the opportunity for teachers to co-teach, reduce the number of redundant assignments, and provide opportunities for students to generalize understandings and skills across disciplines.

Assessments at the provincial level respond to the public demands for accountability from the education system in terms of academic achievement and graduation results. However, it is impossible to consider regional concerns, ethnic influences, and diversity issues when creating one assessment for an entire province. Much has been written about the issues surrounding standardized testing and so-called "accountability" agendas. For now, suffice to say here they have been proven over and over again to be socially, and academically, exclusive (Froese-Germain 1999).

Portage & Main Press, 2012, *Teaching to Diversity*, ISBN: 978-1-55379-353-3

I suggest that the money invested in developing, implementing, and marking assessments instead be put into professional development for teachers, particularly on how to develop essential understandings and rubrics for authentic assessment. A rubric outlining levels of essential understandings is based on students' thinking as well as skills or specific outcomes, and can be used differentially across regions. For instance, a rubric that concisely describes progressive levels of students' understanding of the interdependence of organisms in an ecosystem can be used by teachers in varying regions to study a local ecosystem. It is possible to create common rubrics and achieve the goal of consistent measures without removing a teacher's discretion to make them place-based and relevant to their learners.

The *BC Performance Standards*, for example, are set out in rubrics that assess reading, writing, and numeracy. Yet teachers can choose which texts, materials, and formats their students will use to demonstrate their mastery.

Community Education and Involvement

For schools to be inclusive and to truly celebrate diversity, they should operate in collaboration with their community so that teachers and parents come to view each other as allies, not adversaries. Schools should be careful not to place expectations on families that may be impossible for them to meet, leaving parents feeling judged and disrespected. For example, often when I read the individual education plan (IEP) for a student with reading challenges, I see the support strategies include both pull-out remedial instruction and home reading. What do these recommendations say to the parents? The classroom teacher has difficulty teaching this child to read, so the responsibility is being shifted to the resource teacher—and the parents? But if a trained teacher finds the task challenging, how much more challenged might the parents be? They might themselves be struggling with language and literacy, which sets up conflict in the home, with parents fighting to get their children to read, children resisting, and learning to hate reading because it has become a source of strife in their family. The situation only increases the anxiety all round. Some families are simply not capable of supporting their children with literacy, or homework in general, either because of language differences, poor skills, job schedules, lack of space, or their own school experiences. Instead, take a strengths-based approach, assessing what our families and communities could bring to the learning.

In past generations, parents sent their children to school hoping they would have a better life. Many were immigrants with limited education or ability in English. How many of those parents could help their children with their homework? But they nevertheless supported their children's education. Expecting parents to oversee homework, which almost always requires a high degree of literacy and numeracy, is a very class-based and ethnicity-based definition of support.

Inclusive schools celebrate the diversity of their surrounding community, and find ways to involve families and community members in the learning process of their children. Inviting guest speakers into the classroom, asking parents who have expertise in music or art to share their gifts, contacting an Aboriginal Elder or

Portage & Main Press, 2012, *Teaching to Diversity*, ISBN: 978-1-55379-353-3

ST-V 12

José

For José, a student with a significant reading disability, I decided to try a program called Rebus. It involves the use of a light box that shines through a set of word cards to reveal images that cue the student as they read. The light box is similar to the old slide viewers — a piece of plastic that the cards sit on with a light bulb underneath. I asked the kids in my class if anyone had a parent who liked to build things. One raised his hand and said that his dad "was always building something or other" (obviously quoting his mom)!

I asked him to bring his dad in to school the next day. When his father came in, I explained what I needed and why — a simple wooden box with a plastic top and a light bulb underneath. I told him I would pay for it, gladly. The next day, he brought the box in, built perfectly to my specifications, refused my payment, and said "I wish they'd had something like this when I went to school — I hope it works."

Some time later, when José was successfully reading with his light box, I called the father in to see what his work had done. He came and watched and began to cry, telling me how much he had struggled with reading, and still did. I asked him if he would be willing to mentor José. I explained that reading with him would make José feel less alone in his challenges, and teaching him to build light boxes for other struggling readers would give him a sense of empowerment and of making a difference. He agreed.

This man and José spent the year reading and building together (not just light boxes, they moved on to other service projects as well). I facilitated the reading program for both of them, and José not only gained three grade levels in reading that year, he also developed expertise in carpentry and a greater sense of self.

---

storyteller—these are all ways to involve parents and others in our communities in the children's education. As adults enter schools and see the respect they are granted or hear from their children about these experiences, they begin to see the school as a welcoming and inclusive space. Aboriginal children who go home and tell their parents about the weekly visit of an Elder send a message to these parents that their culture is respected and that they are safe and welcome. Such inclusion cannot be tokenism; it must be genuine and it must, consistently and regularly, be part of what we do in schools. Community feasts, parent-child reading programs, arts festivals—there are many ways to reach out to the community, and enrich our curriculum. Nothing makes people feel more included and valued than being asked for their support or their participation by sharing their talents.

Parent education, in addition to parent involvement, is critical to the success of any educational reform. As we move toward more inclusive schools and universal design for learning, we must be willing to explain to parents what the changes are and why they are being implemented. Just as you wouldn't want to be the guinea pig for some newfound medical procedure without knowing exactly what it involves and why it's being recommended, parents don't want their children to be guinea pigs either. We need to take the time to have a good bedside manner and explain, with confidence and compassion, the educational principles involved in what we profess.

Portage & Main Press, 2012, *Teaching to Diversity*, ISBN: 978-1-55379-353-3

In my first few years of teaching this way, I took a lot of flack from parents. They did not understand the lack of math worksheets or spelling words, and the seeming chaos of students singing, painting, and building rather than sitting silently in rows filling out their worksheets. They feared that their children were not learning, and would be behind in the next school year—as they told my principal and me. When I talked to my vice-principal one day, exasperated at having to constantly explain myself, she looked at me intently and said "Jen, if you don't like blowing snow, don't blaze new trails." After that, I realized it was my responsibility to help parents see the beauty of fresh powder.

Every September, I held a parent night, and explained the theory of multiple intelligences and my goals for their children to become deep thinkers, compassionate leaders, and respectful community members. I explained my "No homework" policy and why I emphasized thinking rather than rote memorization. I involved the parents in playing some of the math games, building a model of a molecule or another structure, and making up a song with their children about the life of an early settler or new immigrant to this country. I talked about how their children would be developing the thinking skills to become architects and engineers, project managers, or service professionals. I asked when the last time was that someone asked them for their grade 6 report card—and emphasized that learning, growing, and feeling good about themselves and what they had to contribute was what mattered more than grades. I'm sure not everyone was immediately convinced, but they didn't call my principal again. As the year wore on and their children came home happy and excited about their learning, the parents would come in and express their support—they had just needed to see for themselves, and that's fair.

If we really want policy and practice to change, we must educate the public— because they vote, and the politicians will follow.

School Divisions: Supporting Inclusive Education

The schools within each division or board of a province implement the policies advanced by the ministry of education in each provincial/territorial government (e.g., www.edu.gov.mb.ca/edu/mandate.html). The divisions or boards handle the multiple aspects of administration: financing, staffing, purchasing of resources, building and personnel management—and implementation of the curriculum. Personnel in the school divisions act as translators who interpret provincial policy, consider regional needs, and determine methods of implementation.

Creating a Vision for Inclusion

School divisions or boards steer the changes in educational direction. When a division creates segregated classrooms, they send a clear message to their teachers: "You are not responsible for teaching these children. There are specialists for that." Whenever I enter a division with a lot of segregated classes, I know it almost instantly because the first thing the teachers say to me is: "Well, I don't feel like I have the training for that. He/she needs someone who is a specialist." In the

Portage & Main Press, 2012, *Teaching to Diversity*, ISBN: 978-1-55379-353-3

divisions that have closed down the segregated programs, the teachers who are struggling to meet the needs of the kids don't see it as someone else's job. They say to me: "I've tried strategy X and Y, but they're not working. Any ideas?"

Just as we teachers send subtle messages to our students about what we believe they are capable of, divisional policies and personnel send subtle messages to teachers. Teachers in the divisions committed to inclusive classrooms have received the message that these children, like all children in their classroom, can learn, deserve to learn, and are their responsibility. The teachers don't question whether the kids should be there, they question the how, which is a fair question and the reason for this book. Research tells us that, to successfully implement change, school divisions or boards must:

1. have an uncompromising commitment to and belief in inclusion.
2. perceive differences among students and staff as a resource.
3. encourage teaming and a collaborative interaction style among staff and children.
4. nurture a willingness of staff to struggle to sustain practice.
5. ensure inclusion is understood as a social/political and academic issue.
6. demonstrate a commitment to inclusive ideals that is communicated across the school and into the community. (Kugelmass 2006)

A division that is truly dedicated to inclusive education will close down segregated classes, and provide support through professional development, public education, budgeting, staffing, and resources to make inclusive education work.

They persevere through challenges, and they hold to a vision and a consistent message that the path they are on is the right one, if not an easy one.

Professional Development and Capacity-Building

Just as students cannot learn when they are stressed and feel incapable and devalued, teachers, too, require a nurturing environment and the assurance of support in the high expectation that they and the students will experience success. Racing through the curriculum does not promote deep learning and internalization of the essential understandings. Racing through one initiative after another with one-off professional development days and no consistent follow-up is destructive to teachers' feelings of self-confidence.

I was a pretty competent and confident teacher, but even I became overwhelmed when my division and school administrators kept switching priorities from literacy to assessment to social responsibility. Attending workshops on differentiating instruction, assessment for learning, inquiry, performance standards, reading comprehension, reading assessment, character education, promoting moral development, and more in just a few years was too much. Speaker after speaker came in, all with great ideas, but one day's exposure left no one expert enough to implement anything. And the rare follow-ups were conducted by district consultants who had had the same one-day workshop.

Portage & Main Press, 2012, *Teaching to Diversity*, ISBN: 978-1-55379-353-3

According to Hargreaves (2007), successful inclusive reforms:

- are implemented systematically, throughout the division and school.

- have democratic teacher involvement. Teachers are fully involved in planning and implementation.

- ensure teachers are fully engaged, with time allotted for planning and implementation.

- recognize that roles among staff become blurred as specialization becomes minimized.

- create environments in which teaching, planning, and problem solving are done collaboratively.

- facilitate the heterogeneous grouping of students by the elimination of placement and programming by fixed bureaucratic categories of disability.

- encourage student engagement through interactive models of instruction and classroom organization in which students have authentic choices.

- promote school subjects and skills being integrated in thematic curricula.

- assert that cooperative learning activities are central to classroom instruction.

- insist that student work be assessed and monitored through authentic assessments and portfolios.

The Three-Block Model of UDL will ensure all of these things. However, implementing this model on a divisional or board scale is a major undertaking that requires participants to develop a multi-year plan. My recommendations follow:

1. Choose a big-picture framework. Choosing one small piece of the practice of inclusive learning, like inquiry or differentiating instruction, is ineffective when taken out of context (e.g., having teachers differentiate instruction, but keeping their students seated in rows). Implementing such partial elements of the process are likely to result in more behavioural challenges because students perceive the hypocrisy of it and resist being told to play a role or to draw a response in an emotionally unsafe environment. We can choose to give people the big picture, then break it down into manageable segments; for instance, in the Three-Block Model, we could choose to focus on Block One in Year One, that is, "building learning communities," knowing that even this one step requires interaction with other aspects of the model (e.g., service delivery, instructional practice) because they all impact classroom climate and social and emotional learning.

2. Create some local expertise: Send a team of consultants and teachers to be trained in the selected model and strategy. With that training, have them try planning for their own classrooms, and implement their plans so they can discuss what the process involves—what works and doesn't work.

3. Have a kick-off, a day or two of professional development where you bring in a knowledgeable speaker to give your staff the big picture of where the

division is going over the next few years. Explain the pieces, and how they all fit within your vision.

4. Use your local expertise to follow up on the kick-off. Their classrooms can be demonstration sites for others to visit; they can facilitate professional learning communities, be released to support other teachers through demonstration, co-planning, or co-teaching. Be creative.

Budgeting for Inclusive Education

In one of my segregated classrooms, we had two teachers and three educational assistants for eight kids. Both teachers had master's degrees in special education and were paid high salaries. Added to the salaries were the costs of busing in the kids from all over the city, and to special programs like swimming or work placements. In school divisions with segregated classes, busing is anywhere from 2% to 5% of the budget—amounting to multi-millions of dollars. For instance, in one small school division in Manitoba, busing costs are reported as being over $3,000,000—imagine what could be done with even half of that money.

Segregated special education, as practised, is incredibly detrimental on every level. Because the kids may arrive later and leave earlier than other students, they (the neediest learners) have less time for education. Segregation also means they are unable to make friends in their own neighbourhood, which adds to the social challenges they already face. When they go to their neighbourhood religious or community centre or a summer program, they don't really know nor are they known by any of the neighbourhood kids, who know each other and have formed friendships in school. Such a situation means the children with disabilities are even more on the outside. The same is true for the parents because they have not met the parents of other children in the community, and the parents of the other children have not learned to know and understand the child with disabilities. It is already stressful and isolating to be the parent of a child with disabilities, and these factors only serve to exponentially increase that experience.

Segregated classrooms are expensive economically, socially, and emotionally. Their impact carries over into the community negatively, leading to discrimination and fear. Other costly and inefficient practices include hiring one-to-one educational assistants and purchasing both class sets of textbooks and class sets of novels even though they offer only one level of reading material—and, thus, are not suitable for an inclusive classroom. Even in regular classes, all students in one class cannot read at the same level and at the same pace. If we redistribute the funds allocated in the current budgets, we can:

1. move the funds from the busing category to the line for staffing and technology that supports inclusion in local schools.

2. eliminate segregated classes and reassign personnel to school-based positions in UDL classrooms, or as consultants whose expertise can provide support throughout the whole division.

Portage & Main Press, 2012, *Teaching to Diversity*, ISBN: 978-1-55379-353-3

3. reduce the number of educational assistants and hire co-teachers, so that the neediest learners are being taught by trained personnel.

4. purchase multiple copies of several different trade books offering a range of reading levels in both fiction and non-fiction; for example, "ecosystems" as the topic of one unit of study allows a choice of many different books on relevant topics (deserts, oceans) at a variety of reading levels. With so many books as a resource, all the students could conduct their research on ecosystems simultaneously; they could all learn to use text features such as a book's table of contents and its index, but would be allowed to read at a level and at a pace that is appropriate for them.

> Among the fiction books, one might have five copies of 6 different titles available on the topic (e.g., novels set in different ecosystems) or a theme such as racism or a genre such as mysteries. In contrast, sets of textbooks for a new curriculum for students in a particular grade and subject might require thousands of dollars ($50 x 30 students x 4 classes in grade 7 = $6,000). How many varied literary, visual, and hands-on resources could a school purchase with that money?

5. take professional development budgets and make long-term, focused plans for their allocation. Instead of spending the dollars to send teachers out for training or to pay big-name speakers to present particular talks and training sessions, a school's leadership team could describe their vision and map out the pathways to achieve that vision; that is, set out high expectations, but provide the support to get there.

The research literature shows that inclusive education is not more expensive (Mawdsley 1995; McLaughlin and Hopfengardner Warren 1994). Although training requires some start-up costs, such costs are counterbalanced by the reduced costs of transportation for children who require special education. Of course, the real impetus behind inclusive education is not economics, but those who are responsible for budgets and the allocation of funds have no financial basis for not moving in this direction.

Hiring and Staffing Inclusive Schools

The most significant challenge in developing inclusive education within one board or all boards in a province/territory is selecting the educators to implement it. But before we consider the specific qualities the applicants should possess, we have to consider the tasks for which each position will be responsible. Traditional school systems have operated on a hierarchical basis, usually flowing from a school board to a superintendent to one or more assistant superintendents, to administrators (e.g., curriculum coordinators, student services directors) to school-based administration (principals, vice-principals, and school staff), and eventually to teachers and classroom support staff. Is this the best way? Are there other ways that are more conducive to inclusive education?

Ideally, all stakeholders would contribute to the overall vision and functions of the organization. Although our current structures do not prohibit inclusive education, they do rely on the leaders to distribute that leadership, to be invitational and collaborative in their decision-making process. Leadership at the

Portage & Main Press, 2012, *Teaching to Diversity*, ISBN: 978-1-55379-353-3

divisional level must have visionary thinking, that is, big-picture and long-term thinking. These leaders have to know what is happening in the classrooms and on the ground. They must have a vision of where they want to go, and they must have the skills and patience to listen to stakeholders, to collaborate, to reshape that vision, and to inspire others to join in the journey over extended periods of time without losing momentum or flitting from one initiative to another. Change does take time, but during that extended time, it does take root.

Service delivery models

The process of staffing must take specific considerations into account. Inclusive learning communities must determine how to deliver support to all students with exceptionalities. What types of support services are needed? Who has the skills to provide these supports? What additional qualities should those who fill the positions have? The research outlined below has shown that co-teaching, clustering, and universal design for learning are of paramount importance.

1. **Co-teaching is the most effective model of service delivery.**

   The research into the effects of co-teaching has documented the positive outcomes as to student behaviour and achievement and teacher job satisfaction (Murawski and Hughes 2009). Co-teaching lowers the student-to-teacher ratio and gives the teachers a support system. It also ensures that students are being taught by qualified teaching personnel rather than by assistants, and brings varied teaching talents and expertise to deal with diverse students. Such research demonstrates the need for personnel who are open to and skilled in collaborative practice. Can boards afford to have two teachers in a classroom? Yes, in several ways:

   - One secondary school reduced its educational assistants to only those required for student safety; that is, only those children with physical needs such as suctioning, tube feeding, toileting, and so on are accompanied by assistants. In addition, such classrooms as the chemistry lab and the vocational shop had an assistant in place to provide extra supervision for general student safety. For every 2.5 assistants in its previously budgeted salary line, the school could hire one experienced teacher. The first year, they hired two additional resource teachers and two subject-specific teachers in the mathematics and English language arts classes; the next year, they added two more co-teachers.

   - Schools can assign teacher teams to classrooms with some students whose needs are educational and behavioural; the co-teaching allows teachers to note and provide support to struggling students. The re-allocation to inclusive education of the resources spent on special education (the enormously expensive staffing of segregated classes and bus transportation to and from different locations) means that individual schools can afford school-based personnel such as co-teachers—much more inclusive education for all students, teachers, and the families in the community.

Portage & Main Press, 2012, *Teaching to Diversity*, ISBN: 978-1-55379-353-3

2. Clustering

Clustering of students with specific types of needs has been shown to be effective and efficient. If a school has three students who would benefit from an FM audio system (e.g., those with hearing impairments or auditory processing difficulties), class assignments could place all three in one class together, but with other typical students. These students learn and live with typical students, but can also see that they are not alone in facing their hearing challenge. Such clustering also means that specialty staff resources that were previously spread thinly across several classrooms and special-needs students can focus their efforts more intensely on a small group, and allow more time for co-teaching.

If I, as a resource teacher for a particular board, have students on my caseload in twelve different classrooms, it's complicated to co-plan and co-teach with twelve different teachers. However, if these students are clustered into three or four classes, I can spend significantly more time with them and can truly be a part of the co-teaching classroom. It would not be advisable, however, to cluster either the students with severe behavioural challenges or those diagnosed with autism spectrum disorder. However, students with generalized reading difficulties, sensory disabilities, attentional challenges, or enrichment needs can benefit from being in the same classroom (clustering) as like students and from having personalized support from another teacher. Clustering does require that classroom teachers be prepared to handle a group of students with disabilities in their class.

For cost efficiency, clustering allows a school to purchase one FM system and hire one sign language interpreter; to put one or more computers in a room with read-aloud software, or to set up a classroom with quiet spaces and dimmers on the lights. We can still universally design our interventions. All kids benefit from such things as visual schedules, chunking activities, taking stretch breaks, having access to technology, and other common adaptations.

Let's imagine we have a student in a wheelchair, who requires stretching of her muscles twice a day. Is it necessary for a physiotherapist and an assistant — two adults — to work with one student? Could we not all take a stretch break in the class twice a day, and have the kids and I and perhaps the physio help this student? All too often I have seen educational assistants wheeling or walking a student down to sessions with the speech language pathologist, occupational therapist, physiotherapist, or the teacher for the hearing/visually impaired. A hundred thousand dollars in salaries sitting in some little room with one child. There is sometimes a need for pull-out or one-to-one services, but in many cases, multiple specialists aren't needed. When I have invited clinicians in to my class, they have almost unanimously welcomed it, and 30 children benefited; and the assistant was free to go and provide support elsewhere during that time.

Portage & Main Press, 2012, *Teaching to Diversity*, ISBN: 978-1-55379-353-3

3. **Universal Design for Learning**

   a. UDL allows us to lower the number of students needing specialized support. When teachers taught in the style of "Turn to chapter 4 and answer the questions," a lot of students needed an IEP, pull-out supports, and educational assistants. When co-teachers work with these students in multiple ways, allowing them to express their understandings in multiple ways, and work in teams, we find many of them achieve the learning outcomes or essential understandings without any specialized supports. Thus, resource teachers spend less time on paperwork and pull-out supports and more time co-teaching in classrooms.

   b. In time costs, IEP meetings are expensive. A lot of money is spent in hiring substitute teachers to cover both classroom and resource teachers for the time they meet. Universal education does not, of course, eliminate all IEPs, but it will significantly reduce the number of them and the behaviour plans, too, which means that some extra funds can be spent on resources rather than on meetings. The research of Stuart and Rinaldi (2009) on response to intervention (RTI) documents the reduction in the number of students requiring specialized services after co-teaching and UDL are established in a school.

   The bottom line as we approach staffing is that we have to consider what positions we need and the characteristics we are seeking in the personnel we assign or hire to fill those positions.

Hiring Qualified Personnel: What Are the Qualifications?

1. **Principals/Vice-Principals**

   School-based administrators have a tremendous impact on the success—or the lack thereof—of inclusive education. The research that examines the characteristics, practices, and attitudes of successful leaders of inclusive schools should inform our hiring practices, because we seek educational leaders rather than administrators or managers. According to Leithwood and Riehl (2005), successful leaders of inclusive schools are skilled in three core practices:

   a. **Setting the direction:** Defining the vision, setting high standards, and helping people create a shared set of goals and the strategies for achieving them. The chosen person should have a positive attitude toward diversity, should believe in inclusive education as a matter of moral and social justice, and constantly research and seek out new methodologies and ideas that they model for and share with their staff.

   b. **Developing capacity:** Teaching through modelling, intellectual challenge, and individual and collective support requires a person unafraid of ambiguity, complexity, and conflict. Leaders have to be willing

Portage & Main Press, 2012, *Teaching to Diversity*, ISBN: 978-1-55379-353-3

to challenge traditional views and methodologies, create cognitive dissonance, negotiate conflicts, make educational rather than popular or political decisions, and encourage their staff to be reflective, analytical thinkers. Such persons are not disruptive nor do they create negative climates. They require tremendous interpersonal skills, and the teaching skills to do for staff what teachers do with students—challenge them to grow while ensuring they feel nurtured and supported.

c. **Redesigning the organization:** Having an ability and willingness to reshape school culture and organization through challenging the status quo, introducing new initiatives, and collaborating to achieve new objectives. Changing an organization involves developing the capacity of its workers, but it goes beyond that to working as a facilitator of relationships between divisional initiatives and personnel, school-based initiatives and personnel, and local community, families, and students. Principals who roll up their sleeves and enter classrooms to teach, who sit in on meetings and professional development days, who walk outside at recess and get to know kids, families, and staff are perceived as interested and involved—and are highly respected by all. Those who are pencil-pushers. who hide in their offices behind paperwork and meetings are perceived as lacking knowledge of the reality of their students (whether that perception is accurate or not) and are dismissed by their staff (Jacobson et al. 2005).

More than anything, we need leaders who come from a core of caring, of vision, and of inner strength and resilience. Leaders who try to please everyone, who want to be popular, or who fear conflict are rarely successful in creating a positive school climate, let alone in effecting change. Leaders need to model perseverance, flexibility, and ingenuity, and to hold to a profound and consistent vision of the rightfulness of inclusion and the wrongfulness of segregation and discrimination. This vision should underlie every interaction and decision. Research has shown that teachers, parents, and students consistently nominate such leaders as "excellent," even when they have not always initially agreed with the leader's vision.

The best approach I have ever seen in the interview for a leader was this request and question: "Tell us about one time when you had a vision or a goal for a group you were a part of. What were the challenges you faced, and how did you overcome them?" In the answer, I would be looking for the power of that vision/goal to them, collaborative decision making, creativity, and perseverance.

2. **Resource Teachers**

In the past, we hired resource teachers (RTs) who specialized in planning for students with exceptional needs, but they often did not have much classroom experience. If we ask those teachers to co-plan, co-teach, and co-assess in the general education classroom, they will need to have, or develop, a different skill set.

a. Their knowledge should be related to how to support a student with exceptional needs *in their classroom* rather than through remediation in a segregated setting. One of the contributions resource teachers can make is to help classroom teachers understand the challenges a student's disability poses, what impact it has on learning and behaviour, and what common strategies support the student's needs.

b. Resource teachers and classroom teachers alike should have knowledge of inclusive instructional practice within the framework of universal design for learning, or at least have an openness to learning about it. Both have to be open to teaching to diversity, that is, teaching all students, not dividing children into segregated categories, which may require an attitude shift. Many special educators in the past considered children with disabilities as "my kids," and often took a maternal or paternal attitude toward them, which was detrimental because:

- It tends to create learned helplessness in the students. When allowed to persevere through a challenge many students find a way to overcome, instead of relying on their resource teacher or assistant to do it for them.

- It sends a message to the classroom teachers that they are not responsible for the learning of the students with disabilities in their classroom; they only have to "tolerate" their presence and that of their support teacher.

c. Resource teachers should also have consultative skills and a positive attitude toward teamwork and collaborative practice.

3. **Classroom Teachers**

   Classroom teachers must make similar shifts.

   a. Classroom teachers must have a strong knowledge base in the content of their curricula. If those planning the units and lessons do not have a good grasp of the scope and sequence of the concepts and skills involved, it is very difficult for them to differentiate instruction.

   b. Classroom teachers have to combine knowledge or information about disabilities with their curricula and teaching strategies in order to understand how the disability might affect students' learning in the particular discipline or context.

   c. Classroom teachers must have a sense of responsibility to the community in seeing that all the learners in their class deserve to be there, that they can learn, and that they, the classroom teachers—not the resource teacher or the educational assistant—have the responsibility for teaching them.

   d. Attitude is everything. All teachers should have a general ability to be flexible, to remain calm, and to respond with sensitivity. Such traits come from a sense of efficacy and an understanding of the individual

Portage & Main Press, 2012, *Teaching to Diversity*, ISBN: 978-1-55379-353-3

student, their family, and the context. This means that teachers must take the time necessary to know students and, even in secondary settings, focus on teaching the student rather than the subject. They have to let go of power and ego and focus on developing student autonomy, engagement, and a relationship to the child.

4. **Educational Assistants**

   Educational assistants (EAs) have an important role in an inclusive education system. However, I question the number hired and the duties assigned. In Manitoba, some schools with 200 students have 21 EAs. With only 8 to 10 classrooms, that means there are 2 or 3 EAs and one teacher in most classrooms. In BC, in contrast, my class with 11 students with disabilities did not have a full-time EA. This disparity indicates a lack of understanding and integrity regarding the role of an EA.

   When hiring EAs, we should look for individuals who have collaborative skills, who are willing to work flexibly with a variety of children, and who have the skills and understanding necessary for working with children from diverse backgrounds and abilities.

   We must ensure that educational assistants are provided with training to develop their understanding of inclusive education and universal design for learning, and to develop their skill for facilitating the social and academic inclusion of students with disabilities.

   The job of an EA is to facilitate engagement of *all* the students in the classroom. They need to know how to help a student be an active part of the learning, and when to back away and allow students to interact with their peers and develop independence.

School-Based Administration: Showing Leadership for Inclusive Education

The jobs of the school-based administrators (principals and vice-principals) are highly complex and focused on the many different aspects of a school's operations. The traditional role has been a functional one—keeping the school running smoothly, which has inevitably meant not introducing fundamental change. In addition, preparation and training for administration, as well as the selection criteria for the job, tend to focus on individuals who will fit in to the structure, and maintain it.

Most administrators are not fundamentally oriented toward change. They tend to view the existing social and academic system as legitimate, believe in the values of democracy and meritocracy, and adopt a managerial orientation instead of a socially transformative one (Riehl 2000). Despite all the pessimism, some school-based administrators have demonstrated great leadership in moving their schools toward being a more inclusive learning community. The Professional Development Council of the Australian Principals Associations outlines the characteristics of these leaders in four synthesized categories (Figure 6.1).

Portage & Main Press, 2012, *Teaching to Diversity*, ISBN: 978-1-55379-353-3

Cultural and Wise Leadership

If we want to change the system fundamentally, we must pay close attention to the belief in meritocracy, which holds that if all children receive the same education (*the same* meaning *equal*), then success will be based on *merit* (that is, *ability and effort*). However, as discussed throughout this book, *equal* does not mean *the same*, because of the "knowledge capital" with which some children enter and travel through school. In track and field competitions, the person in an outside lane starts in a forward position at the starting line because he or she has further to run. In contrast, we in education have started all children at the same starting line without making allowances like the "forward position" for those who have further to run.

Those who want to bring about change, whether major or minor, in their provincial or territorial education system have to negotiate longstanding laws, structures, and timelines. Nevertheless, exceptional leaders have persisted with grace and strength and they have succeeded in creating and supporting compassionate learning communities in their schools.

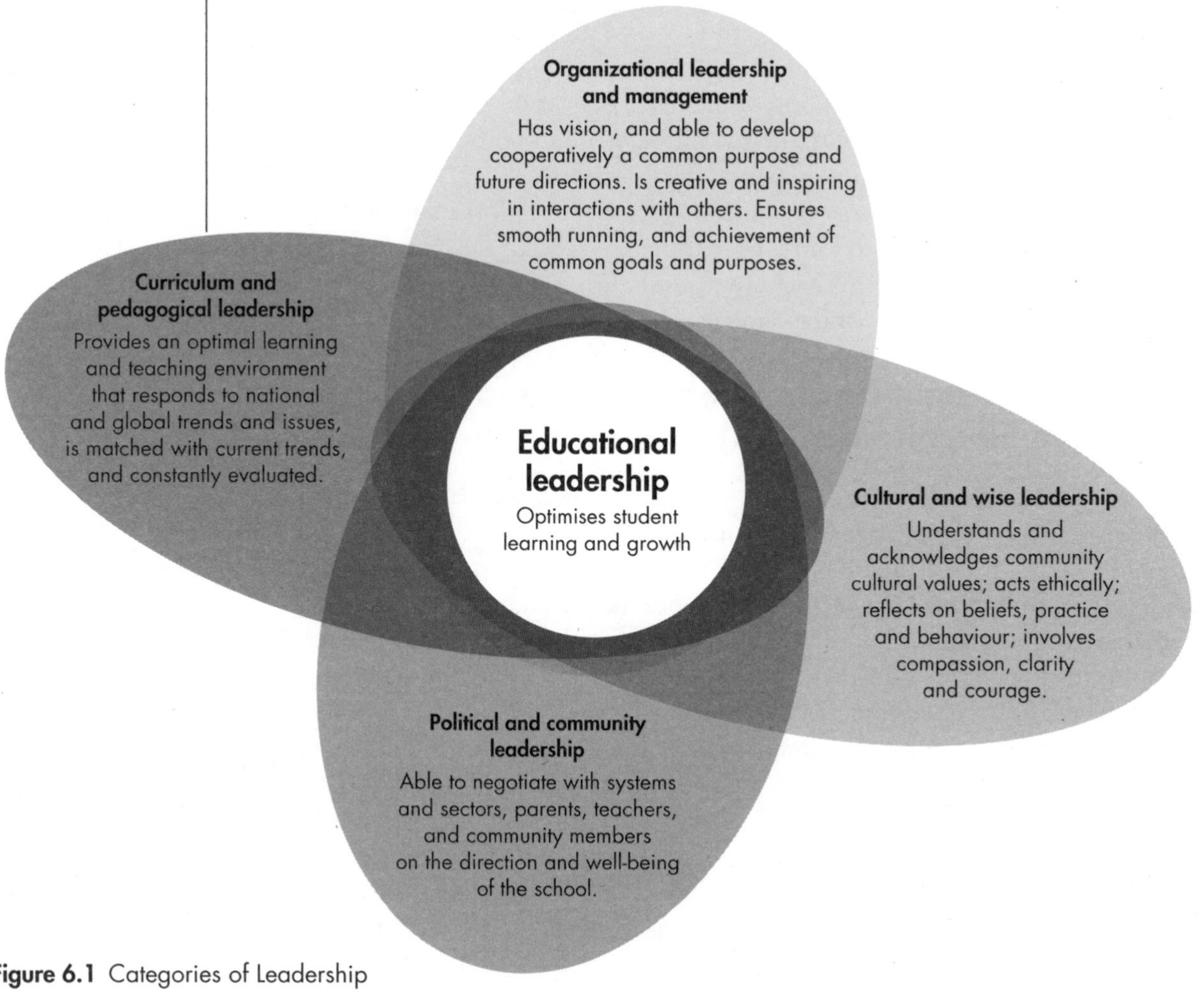

Organizational leadership and management
Has vision, and able to develop cooperatively a common purpose and future directions. Is creative and inspiring in interactions with others. Ensures smooth running, and achievement of common goals and purposes.

Curriculum and pedagogical leadership
Provides an optimal learning and teaching environment that responds to national and global trends and issues, is matched with current trends, and constantly evaluated.

Educational leadership
Optimises student learning and growth

Cultural and wise leadership
Understands and acknowledges community cultural values; acts ethically; reflects on beliefs, practice and behaviour; involves compassion, clarity and courage.

Political and community leadership
Able to negotiate with systems and sectors, parents, teachers, and community members on the direction and well-being of the school.

Figure 6.1 Categories of Leadership

Leaders wise to the varied cultures in their region recognize that an essential skill of leadership is the capacity to weave together the visions, values, beliefs, and dreams of these communities. A leader in a community with a large Aboriginal population, for instance, has to be willing to acknowledge the common void in their knowledge, seek information and understanding, and find ways to involve the Elders of the community. Across the country, leaders find ways to connect and involve communities that have a unique cultural make-up or a majority of one of many different immigrant groups. They find ways to harmoniously blend cultural perspectives with provincial curricula, educational pedagogy, and the beliefs and skills of their staff. Their success in overcoming these challenges is tremendously inspiring.

Organizational Leadership and Management

Organizational leadership involves the ability to develop a shared vision among staff, parents, students, and community. In the educational leadership literature, this is often referred to as "distributed leadership," that is, the democratic involvement of students, teachers, parents, and community.

Research has shown that change rarely if ever takes hold without democratic discourse and meaning-making in transformational learning. If people do not understand and accept the goals for changing their practices or are doing so only because they have been told to, they are likely to discontinue this change when the leader or leaders of the change move on. It is imperative that leaders of the change toward inclusive schools involve all teachers and parents in discussions about how instructional practices can include or exclude particular groups of children, what the vision and goals for an inclusive school entail, and about how they can accommodate diversity.

As in rowing or dragon boating, a principal needs to steer the boat and count aloud while at the same time beating a drum—recognizing that, if she or he does not support the rowers to feel empowered to row with strong strokes and in a shared direction and pace with the other rowers, the boat will go nowhere, or perhaps worse, will go in circles—and we have all been in meetings, and schools, where that is exactly the feeling. Like a good coach, the principal facilitates meetings, helps in the planning, provides training, but recognizes that the teachers and students are the ones who play the game. So it's crucial for that leader to ensure that the players understand and fully accept the goals and values implicit in the proposed changes and, then, that they are consulted, involved in, and empowered to help define the changes.

Curriculum and Pedagogical Leadership

Carolyn Riehl, in her article, "The principal's role in creating inclusive schools for diverse students" (2000), reviews the literature on the practice of educational administration, and stresses the importance of the leaders in educational change. They must know the curricula that their teachers are wrestling with, the challenges of teaching diverse learners, and the current research regarding effective

Portage & Main Press, 2012, *Teaching to Diversity*, ISBN: 978-1-55379-353-3

instructional practice in inclusive classrooms. They must constantly evaluate the progress their school is making toward such ideals. In her description, the principals' effective actions included hiring and socializing new teachers carefully, buffering teachers from intrusions on teaching, providing substantive feedback to teachers on their teaching, and helping to create norms of continuous improvement in the school (Riehl 2000).

Supporting student development

Leaders of inclusive schools must be directly involved with student learning, which means actively teaching in a classroom, working one to one with students, and attending meetings on IEPs; that is, leaders must engage in the trenches. As one teacher put it when discussing why she believed her principal to be exemplary, "You can't ask people to do the things you're not willing to do yourself. If you're not willing to stay after and come in on a Saturday, and if you're not willing to sit in the office and help a kid who's [in] after school, then don't ask anyone else to do it. Leading by example, especially showing a willingness to do the hard work of teaching, is the biggest thing that's made a difference. It's made all the difference in the world" (Jacobson et. al. 2005, 614).

Building learning communities

To create an inclusive culture and sense of community within a school, leaders and their teachers should ensure that students have opportunities for interactions with other students and teachers beyond their classroom. School-wide programming can encompass both academic learning (such as science fairs, math competitions, and school newsletters) and social and emotional learning (such as family multi-age activities focused on respect, diversity, and cultural activities).

Creating professional learning communities

PLCs are also essential to inclusive education (Ainscow and Sandill 2010). Teaching diverse learners is challenging and ever-changing. Teachers and staff require an environment in which there is ongoing professional development supported by a sense of community. It is vital that teachers feel they can raise questions and concerns, share ideas and challenges, and feel supported without judgment by their collegial community. Effective leadership involves giving individual attention to teacher development and fostering networks of professional development on teaching and learning in inclusive schools. Significant topics for both discussion and training should include, but not be limited to:

- school vision and core beliefs
- collaborative practice and co-teaching
- universal design for learning, including instruction on inclusive practices and social and emotional learning
- resources and budgeting
- community involvement

Portage & Main Press, 2012, *Teaching to Diversity*, ISBN: 978-1-55379-353-3

- technology
- wellness

In several schools I worked in, professional development days were set aside to learn about UDL, to co-plan, problem solve, and engage in book clubs. Teachers planned their themes together, and were then involved in allocating the school's budget to purchase multi-levelled, multiple copies of fiction and non-fiction books, videos, models, and other materials that became "resource bins" to support differentiated instruction for each theme.

Planning time, planning time, planning time

In my research, I asked teachers what would provide the most support to them in implementing universal design for learning in their classes and schools. I had listed "coursework, resources, professional development." Their response in the Comments section of the questionnaire, often in very large and underlined print, was almost unanimous: They needed time, time to plan units in a whole new way, time to meet with other teachers to plan collaborative initiatives, time to revise plans based on students' responses in class.

To support teachers in developing a professional learning community in which they collaboratively plan, co-teach, and support each other, the school-based administrators can do several things. They can find innovative ways to offer collaborative planning time. In one secondary school, the principal placed all students in different cohorts per grade, and each cohort was scheduled to take all their core courses together. A team of teachers (one for each of math, science, English language arts, and social studies) was assigned to each cohort of students. These teachers were also given a common preparation and planning schedule so they could meet and discuss their students and curriculum integration.

Another school and principal, along with the parent council, agreed to extend the school day by half an hour from Tuesday to Friday. On Mondays, the students were dismissed two hours early, so that the teachers could use that time to meet and devise integrated co-teaching plans for the week. Still another principal arranged to take all classes from the same grade outside for physical activity for a period of time, or arranged activities with older buddies so that their teachers could plan together for an hour with their grade group. All three principals inspired their teaching staff by their willingness to take on the challenge and find ways to support them. Their teachers were willing to give back, and they spent considerable time meeting after school as well.

A most powerful form of professional development occurs when one educator spends time observing in another educator's class. The teacher-observer has the invaluable opportunity to see an inclusive teaching-learning process in action; the teacher being observed gains insight into their own practice through the feedback and questions from the observer. As Ainscow and Sandill (2010) point out,

> It has been noted, for example, that when researchers report to teachers what has been observed during their lessons they will often express surprise (Ainscow 1999). Much of what teachers do during the intensive encounters that occur in a typical

Portage & Main Press, 2012, *Teaching to Diversity*, ISBN: 978-1-55379-353-3

lesson is carried out at an automatic, intuitive level, involving the use of their tacit knowledge. Furthermore, there is little time to stop and think. This is perhaps why having the opportunity to see colleagues at work is so crucial to the success of attempts to develop practice. It is through such shared experiences that colleagues can help one another to articulate what they currently do and define what they might like to do (Hiebert, Gallimore, and Stigler 2002). It is also the means whereby taken-for-granted assumptions about particular groups of students can be subjected to mutual critique.

Principals can support these opportunities by assigning professional development funds to release teachers for these visits, or by covering classes themselves.

Political and Community Leadership

Political and community leadership is related to, but differs from, leadership of an educational or cultural organization. Political leadership means you know who you represent as an educational leader:

- Do you represent the provincial education system, the education ministry and its various strands? Do you take the values, needs, and concerns of the provincial or territorial government to the teachers, parents, and students?
- Do you represent the local school (the teachers, parents, and students) and take their needs and concerns to the relevant members of the provincial education system?

A school principal who advocates for the staff and for the community creates a team atmosphere because when teachers believe that their leader supports them, they tend to rally together as a team. One principal who was much loved by his staff told us that, when the board had mandated the administration of a particular assessment, he had argued against it, but failed. Subsequently, the teachers met together and figured out how to make the assessment the least negative experience possible for all, and they carried it out without further opposition. Because they believed he had tried his best to explain their preferences, they supported him.

Political leadership, much like parenting, means that you help your students and staff to function in the real world. At times, this means that you advocate within the education system for your students and their families, or for your staff. At other times, it means helping the school staff and students in the community understand the needs and workings of the education system, and how to function successfully within it.

It All Boils Down to Unwavering Commitment

The jobs of school-based administrators are difficult. Principals must balance the demands of the education system with a dogged determination to stay focused on the true depth and meaning of education. They have to remember, as teachers, why they became an educator and who the system exists to serve. As Aboriginal Elder Myra Laramee says (Chapter 7), education is about helping children become "persons of peace," an inner peace, and leaders for peace in their community. If

Following up with Cole and T.

Cole continued to struggle with his sensitivity and anxiety, which compromised his emotional and mental health. But we kept a warm and supportive space for him, focused on his gifts and strengths, and took great joy in his humour. He went on to secondary school, where he found a place for himself in technology and in a peer group with similar interests.

When T. left our school, he handed me a tiny brown bag. Inside was a fridge magnet that read: "If I could sit across the porch from God, I'd thank him for lending me you." For years afterward, he would come to visit, just to help with the younger kids and to talk about issues he was dealing with in his home. School was always a struggle for him, but T. had learned to find places that suited him. In secondary school, both basketball and vocational shops kept him involved. I lost track of him after that, but I never fail to smile when I open my fridge.

---

inclusive education is to work, such unwavering commitment to the ideal of a school and society that welcomes and celebrates all of its children has to be held close to the hearts and minds of all of us—parents, teachers, and administrators alike. With every decision and every action on each and every day, we make the choice—to harm or to heal.

Jody Carr, New Brunswick's Minister of Education and Early Childhood Development since October 2010, discussing inclusive education, said:

> If inclusion has happened in one classroom, anywhere in the world, then it is not a dream. It's possible, and it is a matter of choice.

It has happened in my classroom—by choice—and continues to happen in many others across this country and around the world every day. What is your choice?

Portage & Main Press, 2012, *Teaching to Diversity*, ISBN: 978-1-55379-353-3

Chapter 7

Aboriginal Education and Universal Design for Learning

Co-authored with Myra Laramee, MEd

A book about teaching to diversity in Canada today must make special note of the two population groups identified by the Council of Ministers of Education, Canada as "most at risk for exclusion"—Aboriginal students and students with disabilities (CMEC with CCUNESCO 2008). In earlier chapters, we have discussed how students with disabilities can be included in the social and academic life of the regular classroom, using the Three-Block Model of universal design for learning (UDL). In this chapter we turn our attention to specific concerns about Canada's indigenous populations.

Graduation rates for First Nations, Métis, and Inuit (FNMI) students have fallen significantly short of acceptable (Gunn, Pomahac, Striker, and Tailfeathers, 2011). So the question arises: Can the Three-Block Model of UDL facilitate the inclusion of Aboriginal/FNMI students, culture, and perspectives in the curriculum? As a non-Aboriginal educator, I did not believe I could determine whether this pedagogy fit with Aboriginal beliefs and cultures that are diverse in themselves, but my personal dilemma was the same as what I hear when I teach or conduct professional development workshops. Teachers of non-Aboriginal descent feel unqualified—and fearful of erring—when dealing with a culture that is not their own, especially when teaching students from that culture. But, in truth, we do this all the time, and I have come to believe that the Three-Block Model of UDL can, indeed, serve as a framework for successfully implementing inclusive education in Aboriginal classrooms as in all inclusive classrooms.

Many of the cultures, languages, and family structures of my students are not my own. I do not share the life experience of a refugee, nor of a person with a disability. Nevertheless, I believe I can teach in a way that is inclusive and respectful of all. In this chapter particularly, I want to raise awareness about the issues in Aboriginal education, and to explore how UDL can, perhaps, build a bridge for all educators to the inclusion of Aboriginal students and Aboriginal perspectives in our classrooms and schools. I could not write a book on inclusive education and the necessity of building compassionate learning communities if I did not speak directly to the issues facing First Nations, Métis, and Inuit people, and the children most at risk in our country.

We must begin by recognizing the negative history of Aboriginal education in Canada, and by exploring the continuing challenges and efforts to heal in the present day, because "a broader understanding of what was, and what is, allows an

Portage & Main Press, 2012, *Teaching to Diversity*, ISBN: 978-1-55379-353-3

envisioning of what could be" (Atleo 2009, 455). From such an overview, we look at how we can use UDL and some specific strategies for Aboriginal education that fit within its principles to create inclusive learning communities for both Aboriginal and non-Aboriginal students.

Two years ago, I was approached by the Manitoba First Nations Education Resource Centre to present the Three-Block Model to their consultants. The MFNERC has twelve teams of five educators that serve over sixty band-operated First Nations schools across the province, many in very remote areas. After I met with these educators/consultants and shared the model with them, we agreed that they would provide feedback about its appropriateness within their work and cultural communities. Three days of intensive dialogue and sharing ensued, culminating in an agreement by the Centre that they would like to promote this model in their schools. They also asked me to deliver a keynote address at "Lighting the Fire," the provincial conference for Aboriginal education several months later.

Among those consultants was Myra Laramee, a Cree Elder, long-time educator, and new-found friend. Myra, now retired, has taught in schools, has served as a principal, as a consultant in the board/division office of Winnipeg's largest school division and in the Aboriginal Education Directorate of Manitoba Education. She also authored many resources during her thirty-five years in the public schools of the Inner City Division of Winnipeg. She continues to serve as a consultant to the Manitoba First Nations Education Resource Centre and the Council of Elders. Myra has co-authored this chapter with me, and I am deeply honoured by her willingness to share her wisdom, and the wisdom of her people, with us. Aboriginal youth and Aboriginal education present a unique challenge—and a unique and rich opportunity for our schools and our nation.

Challenges to Social and Academic Inclusion

A History of Racism

Historically, dealings with Aboriginals in Canada have been fraught with deep racism and persecution. European education of Aboriginal children began in the early 1600s in New France in mission schools operated by French religious orders. Since that time, the responsibility has fluctuated back and forth from church to state, that is, the federal government.

From 1763 to 1830 the imperial government in Britain dealt with "Indian Affairs" through the military, but the provision for education of Aboriginal peoples was minimal. After 1830, administration was transferred to the British Secretary of State for the Colonies, and some money was diverted to education by means of donations to church organizations. This funding allowed the building of rudimentary schools in pre-reserve Aboriginal settlements and the beginning of the establishment of residential schools for indigenous peoples. After Confederation in 1867, education for indigenous peoples fell into two categories:

- Education for status Indians became a federal responsibility under the constitution and the treaties.

- Non-status Indians, Métis, and Inuit became a provincial or territorial responsibility.

By 1900, there were 64 residential schools in Canada, and some 226 federally funded day schools on reserve. The majority of teachers were missionaries, and the curriculum included a large proportion of religious instruction. By the 1930s, the curriculum was supposed to be more closely patterned on that of the non-Aboriginal provincial schools. However, little time was devoted to academics.

Following a major review of Aboriginal education in the late 1940s, the federal government, in cooperation with provincial education authorities, established a policy of education integration. Federal funds were provided to enable Aboriginal students to attend provincial elementary and secondary schools, and all reserve schools adhered to the provincial curriculum. Numerous problems became evident in the program, which led to its re-evaluation by Aboriginal parents and political leaders.

In 1972, the National Indian Brotherhood (now known as the Assembly of First Nations) produced its policy on Aboriginal education, "Indian Control of Indian Education," which was subsequently adopted by Aboriginal Affairs and Northern Development (AAND) as federal policy. The policy identified key requisites for improving education on reserve:

- local community control
- more Aboriginal teachers
- development of relevant curricula and teaching resources for Aboriginal students
- instruction in Aboriginal languages and values

Although some Inuit were educated in mission schools in Labrador as early as the 1790s, formal education for Inuit began on a national scale only in the 1950s with the construction of elementary and residential schools throughout major settlements in the Arctic. The decrease in residential schools in the Arctic paralleled the decrease in residential schools for Aboriginal children and led to a school-construction program by the federal government in most Inuit villages by 1970.

Statistics are not available for Métis and non-status Indian students, but studies generally indicate that, owing to poor socioeconomic conditions and the absence of specific provincial or federal responsibility for their education, Métis suffer consequences similar to those of other Aboriginal people in their attempt to receive a formal education (*The Canadian Encyclopedia* 2012; Mendelson 2008).

A great deal has been written about the legacy of the residential schools. The lack of true education and the abuse that the schools represent in the minds and hearts of Aboriginal peoples today have left a lasting distrust of schools and education systems. In 2010, almost two hundred Aboriginal children in Manitoba alone died by their own hand. Suicides among First Nations youth have risen by 45 per cent since 1980, especially among youth up to 14 years of age, a demographic with almost no known suicide rate among non-Aboriginal youth (Manitoba Aboriginal and Northern Affairs 2011).

Spotlight

For more information on residential schools and their impact, visit the Truth and Reconciliation Commission of Canada website at www.trc.ca.

Portage & Main Press, 2012, *Teaching to Diversity*, ISBN: 978-1-55379-353-3

Continued Underfunding and Dehumanization

In the twenty-first century, First Nations youth on federal reserves across Canada attend schools that receive far less funding from the federal government than do the public schools, which are funded by the provinces at significantly higher rates. The First Nations schools find it difficult to attract trained teachers because the pay is lower than in other settings, and the living conditions are not attractive to non-residents. The dedicated educators who do try, however, face significant challenges in the lack of resources (books and computers are often non-existent), of professional development opportunities, and of funding to support students with exceptional needs.

Federal funding under the *Indian Act* is outdated and costs have continued to climb. Even the small amount of money allotted to education is sometimes diverted to bringing in life essentials like food and medicine. In some remote communities, a litre of milk can cost up to $18 because most grocery supplies arrive by air transport. Children on some reserves effectively live as if in refugee camps, in homes with no heat, no running water, no indoor plumbing. Many schools also are not heated, lack supplies, and don't meet safety standards.

When I returned to Manitoba two years ago to teach at the university and became involved with First Nations schools, I began to discover that basic human rights—such as food, safety, health, and shelter—are not provided. First Nations children with disabilities are doubly challenged. For example, more than fifty children in Northern Manitoba living on reserve who are deaf or hard of hearing have no hearing aids, and they have not been taught sign language. Why? The federal government says health is a provincial matter, and the provincial government says First Nations people on reserves are in federal care. This shifting of responsibility is also true for the care of children who are visually impaired, physically disabled, or mentally ill. They are Aboriginal, so they have become invisible.

The parent of one young man with disabilities filed a human rights complaint saying that the lack of care he received on reserve, in comparison to a person with similar disabilities in the local town, amounted to discrimination. The suit was turned down with the justification that a claim of discrimination is valid only when comparing similar cases. In this situation, one person is under federal jurisdiction, and the other under provincial jurisdiction—hence, they are not "comparable." So two Canadian youths, both with disabilities and both living within a kilometre of each other, are not entitled to the same care. Our former auditor general had done much to publicize such issues, but little action has been taken as a result (Mendelson 2008). The bottom line is that we have children, Canadian children, living in third world conditions out of our sight—except when a crisis erupts to capture the attention of the news media.

System Does Not Reflect Aboriginal Experience

Today, there are 518 schools on First Nations reserves across Canada, and funding of the schools on reserves continues to be the responsibility of the federal government. In the First Nation systems of education on reserve communities, many non-Aboriginal teachers come from other places in Canada to teach. A large number of the staff members in some First Nations schools are, thus, not First Nations themselves but they end up having a strong voice in how First Nations schools are run, in spite of their often glaring lack of knowledge about local cultures and issues.

Too few Aboriginal people have teaching degrees to fill staffing positions on or off reserve, or in Inuit communities. Beginning in the 1960s, some teacher training programs designed to educate Aboriginals to teach Aboriginal children were developed with the hope of filling staff positions on reserve, but the number of graduates is insufficient to fulfill the hope of employment equity. This is also a serious issue for postsecondary education (Stonechild 2006).

Although it is absolutely possible for non-Aboriginal educators to create a respectful, inclusive learning community for Aboriginal students, they must recognize their lack of knowledge about Aboriginal culture and the local community, and educate themselves as much as possible. Policies exist in almost every province that support professional development in this area for all educators. It is critical that Aboriginal educators take a leading role in education and that Aboriginal students see some Aboriginal adults who have become teachers, as role models, to reduce the community's distrust of education systems, the legacy of residential schools, and to provide a vision of hope for their own future.

Graduation rates for Aboriginal youth across the country remain significantly lower than those of non-Aboriginal students. The reasons are complex, but of particular significance is the historical difference that Aboriginal cultures and teachings are based on oracy, on mentorship, and on inclusivity. Most large urban and suburban public schools leave few opportunities for such relationships, and pedagogical strategies, curricula, and assessment have been conducted predominantly in written formats, and do not reflect the lives of Aboriginal students. Instead, science curricula appear to denigrate cultural beliefs about our natural world, which creates a sense of alienation. Historical perspectives are those of the dominant majority, and English Language Arts emphasizes "Eurocentric" literature and the written word over oral and visual texts (Sterenberg and Hogue 2011). There are few representations of successful Aboriginal people, literature, or science. Although curricula have recently begun to include Aboriginal peoples' history, cultures, and values, many Aboriginal youth in urban schools continue to struggle with the effects of poverty and social and academic exclusion. As Wotherspoon (2002) says:

> The distance between school and community, and therefore the possibility that students will feel and become excluded, increases when the school "world" is divorced from, and privileged over, the "worlds" that students bring with them and return to outside of school.

Lack of Awareness and Misunderstanding

The report (Haldane, Lafond, and Krause 2011) of the National Panel on First Nation Elementary and Secondary Education for Students on Reserve, commissioned by the federal government, stated that students coming from First

Portage & Main Press, 2012, *Teaching to Diversity*, ISBN: 978-1-55379-353-3

Nations schools into public schools were automatically being placed in special education or alternative placements, without assessment or investigation. This is common practice in many places where Aboriginal students move from remote communities and schools into towns and cities. They might enrol in grade 9, but be reading at a grade 2 level, so they are assumed, or assessed, to have some disability. But such significant learning gaps occur because of the lack of resources and the general underfunding of the schools on reserves. If these students were coming from a refugee camp in a war-torn country, we would not make the assumption that they had a disability just because they had learning gaps. We must recognize that the same is true for many of our Aboriginal students who stop attending or lose years of schooling because of poor educational environments—until their chance to go to a new school leads them to try one more time. These students have been failed by the current system, but we have one last chance—and we must not lose them.

When these students enter a system that makes them feel like strangers and failures, teachers encounter struggles with challenging behaviour or student dropouts. Whether the educational jurisdiction is federal or provincial, the statistics on educational attainment for First Nations students are dismal. Graduation rates of these students in most schools, regardless of whether they are urban or on reserve, show little sign of improvement. Clearly, schools have not yet found a way, whether well-intentioned or not, to meet the needs of Aboriginal youth and engage them in their education. But I believe that if we were to create schools and classrooms in which these children can feel a sense of belonging, can recognize themselves as learners and see that their culture is valued, we could go a long way to retaining these students in school.

Opportunities for Social and Academic Inclusion

Cooperative Learning and Relationship

Despite the many concerns about the education of Aboriginal youth and about Aboriginal/non-Aboriginal relations today, if we step back in history, we see a cooperative model of relationships. When European settlers first came to Canada, they learned a great deal about living in community and living in Canadian settings (climates and landscapes) from Aboriginal peoples. While not perfect by any means, we also exchanged ideas, tools, and cultural beliefs. Treaties were signed by Aboriginal leaders in a spirit of collaboration. The intention of First Nations was to develop a close partnership with European settlers based upon mutual respect and assistance (Stonechild 2012).

I believe we can, once again, learn a great deal about contemporary Canadian issues if we open ourselves to Aboriginal perspectives regarding such topics as sustainability, community, and the role of Elders. These perspectives can enrich the curricula for all our learners, not just those of Aboriginal descent, and in so doing, will make our schools feel more inclusive and recognizable to Aboriginal peoples. For instance, pre-contact, in Aboriginal ways of living, the responsibility

Portage & Main Press, 2012, *Teaching to Diversity*, ISBN: 978-1-55379-353-3

of the collective was to ensure that each member understood that their presence was important and that their potential in the collective was valued (Brendtro, Brokenleg, and Bockern 1990). Reciprocally, the individual made every attempt to learn the ways that would be helpful and contribute to the survival of the collective. So in the past, teachers would engage their learners as relations—in other words, as relatives—and in doing so, would treat this learner with the respect and responsibility of a grandparent (Elder). The education that a child, youth, or adult received was based on learning to contribute to the survival and good health of the collective. Absolutely no one was excluded from an education, and most learning experiences were based on one's individual potential or the gifts they brought to the community. Within this community framework, we also find perspectives regarding inclusion, teaching through relationship, community building, the role of mentoring and multiple intelligences, which fit with the pedagogy of inclusive education and the Three-Block Model of UDL.

Inclusive Philosophy

UDL can help to reconnect our current education system to that of Aboriginal pedagogies of the past and the present. Long before we ever started talking about "integration," "mainstreaming" or "inclusion," Aboriginal elders recognized that all children can learn, that using a model based on strengths and multiple intelligences allows diverse learners to have valued roles in the community, and that learners need to be scaffolded through a continuum of gradual release. Children were naturally drawn to the hunter (bodily-kinesthetic), the shaman (existential), the artist (visual-spatial), and so on, and they were mentored to develop these talents. The focus was on what they could do, and expectations were high. After all, family depended on you, and children took pride in knowing they had importance and value. Assessment happened through interpersonal exchange, observation, and perhaps to a lesser extent, products. Here too, the pedagogy fits within a UDL framework for assessment.

Community Focus

In profound and compassionate ways, Aboriginal education recognized the need for a sense of community, for balancing the development of individual self-concept and pride with a sense of responsibility and respect for the community. In returning to this foundation through UDL, we can create an environment that acknowledges and honours the benefits of Aboriginal educational epistemologies.

Using the RD program helps to introduce these same values: that we all have strengths and challenges; that everyone has something to contribute; that diversity is necessary for the survival of the community. As we teach in integrated and applied ways, learners can see how their education benefits themselves and their communities. When we open our doors to Aboriginal students and their families, they will be able to recognize that the wisdom of their ways are present in the learning environment; perhaps they will also begin to see schools as welcoming, relevant, and safe places.

Portage & Main Press, 2012, *Teaching to Diversity*, ISBN: 978-1-55379-353-3

Facilitating Social and Academic Inclusion

Many devoted educators, both Aboriginal and non-Aboriginal, across systems and provinces/territories, have been working hard to begin the healing. Blair Stonechild, in discussing the controversy over government involvement in Aboriginal education, states that it is a fallacy to believe that Aboriginal peoples should not take or accept input from others (2012). He explains the traditional beliefs of First Nations leaders about good relations and describes how well-established spiritual traditions, which became an essential part of creating diplomatic and trade relations with the Europeans, assumed that both had committed themselves to a mutual life-giving relationship. It is in this spirit of good relations that our efforts must be dedicated.

Connecting Block Three: Systems and Structures

Policy and Systemic Support

Across the country, policies and initiatives have been implemented in an effort to include Aboriginal students, culture, and perspectives into public curricula and schools. Integrating Aboriginal content can improve student self-concept, aid in creating effective learning environments, and build understanding in non-Aboriginal and Aboriginal students alike (Deer 2010). All Canadian provinces and territories have policy related to this, available on their website.

At the national level, the report of the National Panel on First Nation Elementary and Secondary Education for Students on Reserve (Haldane et al. 2011) "Nurturing the Learning Spirit of First Nation Students" suggests that Aboriginal and non-Aboriginal educators work together to co-create a "Child-Centred First Nation Education Act." In Manitoba, for instance, goals related to Aboriginal student development are reflected in the (2004) document *Aboriginal Education Action Plan* produced by Manitoba Advanced Education and Training with Manitoba Education, Citizenship and Youth. In this document, Manitoba Education offers an action plan that includes "Improving the System," "Increasing Parent and Community Involvement, and "Increasing the Number of Aboriginal Teachers."

More recently, Manitoba Education, in the 2011 document "Bridging Two Worlds: Aboriginal Education and Employment Action Plan," sets goals for student engagement and high school completion, and plans initiatives in teacher education, teacher professional learning, and curriculum. The Ministry promises to work with the Manitoba First Nations Education Resource Centre, community leaders and Elders, and Aboriginal and non-Aboriginal educators.

In BC, targeted funding supports students of First Nations descent with specialized programming within public schools. The "Shared Learnings" documents outline strategies for BC educators to integrate Aboriginal content across curricula. Providing policy, resources, and professional development is incumbent on all provincial ministries. This endeavour will take time, face challenges, and require perseverance and dedication, but it can, and must, be done.

Portage & Main Press, 2012, *Teaching to Diversity*, ISBN: 978-1-55379-353-3

Collaboration between Aboriginal and Non-Aboriginal Educators

The complexities of this journey are intricate and numerous. In 2010, I was honoured to be the keynote speaker at Manitoba's Aboriginal education conference called "Light the Fire," sponsored by the Manitoba First Nations Education Resource Centre. The room was filled with over 1,000 Aboriginal educators. Many of these had survived the residential schools, gone to university, completed their teaching degrees, and returned to try to make a difference in their communities in the most challenging of circumstances. I was tremendously anxious about what to say. How could I tell them anything about anything? Yes, I know UDL and have taught in challenging, inclusive classrooms, but I had never had to overcome what they have, and I felt presumptuous telling them what they needed to do.

Unfortunately, biases exist not only among non-Aboriginal educators, but also in the belief systems handed down to Aboriginal educators. Too often, as I have travelled around conducting professional development for teachers in inner-city schools and on reserve, I hear responses to my suggestions about high expectations and conceptual mastery that begin with "Well, we have to be realistic, with our kids...." Our kids? Do they mean that every First Nations child in the inner city or on reserve is incapable of understanding learning outcomes?

Extensive research demonstrates the relationship between student achievement and the expectations of teachers and parents (Rubie-Davies, Peterson, Irving, Widdowson, and Dixon 2010), particularly for marginalized populations (Jussim and Harber 2005). If we hold the bar low, and deny educational opportunity through challenging curriculum and not expecting the children to be capable, they will lower their aspirations and believe themselves to be incapable. If we hold the bar high and believe in them by providing the quality of instruction and support they need, they will reach the bar.

The problem reaches back in history. In my keynote at the Aboriginal Education conference, I spoke about creating compassionate learning communities, and the role of the teacher in building emotional resiliency in kids. I wanted the teachers to know they could make a difference. After the speech, a man quietly approached me. It was clear he had something to say, although he was having difficulty making eye contact.

"You know," he said. "I would like to do what you are talking about, but I don't know what that looks like."

I was confused. "What do you mean?" I asked.

"I never saw a compassionate teacher or a classroom in which I felt safe or nurtured, and I never had my mom and dad. I was in the residential schools. So I know I should not do what my teachers did, but I have never seen what you are talking about, and I don't know how to do that."

I was stunned. It had never occurred to me that those of us who grew up in typical public schools had a range of educational experiences. We had some teachers we liked and some we didn't, but we can conjure up an image of the teacher we did like, who made learning fun and helped us enjoy school, and model

Portage & Main Press, 2012, *Teaching to Diversity*, ISBN: 978-1-55379-353-3

ourselves after them. Many Aboriginal educators have no models to work from, no vision of what a positive school experience can be, no experience with a nurturer, and a deeply ingrained belief that they, and their students, are inferior. And so the tragedy of the residential schools continues. Clearly, we cannot undo history. However, we can be an ally and reach out our hand in friendship. If you work in a school with an Aboriginal community nearby:

- Invite their teachers to attend your next professional development day. They may not have the funds to bring in speakers for their own professional development.
- Offer to do a teacher exchange. Ask to visit a classroom where you can learn about Aboriginal culture and instructional pedagogies. Invite a teacher to visit your classroom to see universal design for learning in action—peer coaching, collaborative practices, team teaching, co-planning of units and activities.
- Create buddy classes and write to and visit each other, fostering relationships between students of Aboriginal and non-Aboriginal descent.

Connecting Block Two: Instructional Practice

Even if you have no students of Aboriginal descent in your classroom, it is imperative that all students experience content incorporating Aboriginal culture, instructional practices and perspectives. When such understanding is taught to all Canadian children, true healing can occur. There are several ways in which to achieve this.

Provincial Resources

Most provincial ministry of education websites have material—curricula, resources—and consultants that can be useful. In Manitoba, educators are expected to incorporate Aboriginal perspectives across the curricula and three resource documents are available: *Native Studies: Early Years (K–4) A Teacher's Resource Book*; *Native Studies: Middle Years (Grades 5–8): A Teacher's Resource Book Framework*; and *Native Studies: Senior Years (S1–S4): A Teacher's Resource Book Framework* are available. As well, *Integrating Aboriginal Perspectives into Curricula: A Resource for Curriculum Developers, Teachers and Administrators* has been distributed to schools. Key concepts are identified for including Aboriginal perspectives, including the medicine wheel/circle, the number four, extended family, collective decision making, cooperation, holistic approaches to life, and respect.

Ontario lists a similar, larger set of concepts including the circle, respect, treaties and more, and provides instructional resources for doing so. The majority of provinces will have this information on their websites for you to access.

Teaching to the Big Picture

Brokenleg (Brendtro et al. 1990) talks about developing "belonging" in its deepest sense as being related to all things. Similarly, helping children feel connected to a

Portage & Main Press, 2012, *Teaching to Diversity*, ISBN: 978-1-55379-353-3

global world—to the planet and all its life—is a part of what we do when we look for essential understandings, big ideas, and existential activities in the Three-Block Model of UDL.

Circular practice and curricula

In Aboriginal education, learning and concepts are repeated as many times as necessary with the goal of increasing the depth and breadth of students' learning as they move through the cycle of knowledge, understanding, wisdom and healing. This sounds complex but, in truth, it is an integral part of all teaching. As a teacher, when we assess for learning, we facilitate our learners, discover the level at which they have "looked, listened, and learned," and then either re-teach or add the next layer to their understanding. This is a spiral curriculum, and throughout the curricula of North America, this concept persists. Guess where we learned it?

Connecting Block One: Social and Emotional Learning

Creating a compassionate learning community that includes Aboriginal students, culture, and perspectives:

Modelling Respect

The families, guardians, and their children in our midst cannot be ignored or dismissed by the educators in their classrooms. In *The Common Curriculum Framework for Aboriginal Language and Culture Programs, Kindergarten to Grade 12* from the Western and Northern Canadian Protocol (WNCP) for Collaboration in Education, the following quotation from Dr. Haim Ginott describes the role of a teacher:

A Decisive Element in the Classroom

I have come to a frightening conclusion. I am the decisive element in the classroom. It is my personal approach that creates the climate. It is my daily mood that makes the weather.

As a teacher, I possess tremendous power to make a child's life miserable or joyous. I can be a tool of torture or an instrument of inspiration. I can humiliate or humour, hurt or heal.

In all situations it is my response that decides whether a crisis will be escalated or de-escalated and a child humanized or de-humanized. (WNCP 2000, p. 57)

To the question posed to me about helping children, all children, actively engage in the social and academic life in the classroom and school, I answer, "Be alert to the climate created in your classroom and to whether or not the children are 'humanized or de-humanized'" (WNCP 2000). Above all, hold high expectations for all your learners, Aboriginal and non-Aboriginal alike, with the belief that all children, all cultures, and all races have value, while teaching your own students to see the same.

Creating Places and Spaces Mindful of the Circle of Courage®

Martin Brokenleg, an Aboriginal theologian and counsellor, works with at-risk youth, using a medicine wheel as a part of his pedagogy. The medicine wheel addresses four directions and aspects of human development—mental, physical, spiritual, and emotional. In *Reclaiming Youth at Risk: Our Hope for the Future* (Brendtro et al. 1990), Brokenleg creates a circle for reclaiming at-risk youth that is based on the medicine wheel and has four central concepts:

methodical contemplation as to how we help children *belong*, develop *mastery*, foster *independence*, and become citizens of *generosity*.

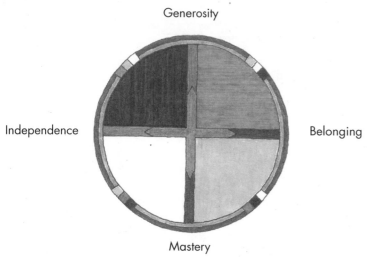

Figure 7.1 Circle of Courage (Used with Permission from Reclaiming Youth International, website: www.reclaiming.com)

Spotlight

For more information on Brokenleg's work, visit www.reclaiming.com/content/about-circle-of-courage

As we create a democratic classroom, we build student autonomy in a way that fosters independence. Mastery learning is crucial to authentic engagement and assessment for all learners. Teaching students to value diversity, work in teams, and support each other creates a generosity of spirit as children feel the joy of both giving and receiving, supporting others and being supported as members of an extended family. One can only belong to something that exists; that is, a sense of community must exist in order for an individual to feel a sense of belonging.

All the work we do each September beginning with the respecting diversity program, teaching group work, and building learning teams establishes the community to which children can attach themselves, and fits with all of the identified concepts in Manitoba curriculum, and Brokenleg's work (the medicine wheel/circle, the number four, extended family, collective decision making, cooperation, holistic approaches to life, and respect).

Teaching through Relationship, Mentoring, and Gradual Release

Brokenleg (Brendtro et al. 1990) talks about the concept of independence this way:

Independence

Power in Western culture was based on dominance, but in tribal traditions it meant respecting the right for independence. In contrast to obedience models of discipline, Native teaching was designed to build respect and teach inner discipline. From earliest childhood, children were encouraged to make decisions, solve problems, and show personal responsibility. Adults modelled, nurtured, taught values, and gave feedback, but children were given abundant opportunities to make choices without coercion.

Most First Nations cultures hold the belief that, when raising children, the ultimate consideration undertaken by the adults in their lives must be to develop the reality of each child's potential for becoming "a person of peace." The modelling and experience that the adult/teacher provides to a learner requires a developmental vision of apprenticeship that involves both the teacher and the learner in a reciprocal and mutual relationship of respect and dignity. For learners to become persons of peace, the teachers guide them through a pedagogy of learning, that involves them in looking, listening, learning, and—at the point of achieving—living what has been taught.

As teachers, then, our role is to teach in such a way that students have an opportunity to watch, to listen, to attempt with support, and to apply independently. This is gradual release at its finest, with the goal of developing a peaceful person; that is, one who walks in the world with a sense of inner peace, of self-respect, and of pride in what they have to give—one who relates to others in compassionate, peaceful, and respectful ways.

In the UDL classroom, we empower students to make choices, seek an internal locus of control, and become reflective about who they wish to be as a person and as a learner. Our role is to facilitate, model, and guide, but not to "manage." This pedagogy fits perfectly with Brokenleg's work.

Exploring "The Circle"

In Aboriginal education, instructional pedagogy is based on the concept of the circle as a sacred place and space where learning, curricula, and relationships are viewed as—and designed to be—cyclical. The concept of circles and cycles is integral to scientific concepts such as interdependence and life, weather, water cycles, historical settlement and political patterns, mathematical geometry and patterning, and plot cycles in literature. So it is easy to bring this concept into our teaching across the curriculum. But the circle goes beyond learning and curricula, to a spiritual cycle of relationship between learner and mentor, idea, belief, and all of creation. The mentorship/apprenticeship approach promotes a mutual respect between the facilitator and the learner, which will encourage an emotional response to the learning transactions. It is this response that makes this indigenous pedagogy unique to the learning circle. It is through this act of love that learners become re-engaged with schools and schooling—in other words, it is through relationship and connection.

This is a significant point. Western culture has debated the role of the teacher in this light: "To what extent are we to care, and to what extent are we to maintain 'professional' distance?" Aboriginal education clearly leans to the former and relies on this nurturing relationship to engage the learner—as do the principles of universal design for learning and the idea of building compassionate learning communities.

Portage & Main Press, 2012, *Teaching to Diversity*, ISBN: 978-1-55379-353-3

Exploring Values and Respect

It is important to focus not just on the similarities and differences of the range of Aboriginal cultures and other cultures in our classrooms, but also on the underlying values we all share. Although non-Aboriginal students need to learn about—and from—Aboriginal peoples, we all need to recognize that we have a great deal in common. One practice that Myra teaches illustrates this best, in my opinion, and allows us to work effectively with many different nations, ages, and backgrounds.

The Seven Teachings, that is, beliefs that many Aboriginal communities embrace today as foundational to living a good life, can be used with many people as a bridge to a common place of understanding and valuing one another. These teachings have been adopted as the "Principles of Aboriginal Education" in the Inner City District of Winnipeg School Division. They can also be found in children's resources, such as *Seven Sacred Teachings* by David Bouchard (2009).

Seven Teachings
Principles of Aboriginal Education

To cherish knowledge is to seek *wisdom*.
To know *love* is to find peace.
To honour all of Creation is to have *respect*.
Courage is to face life with integrity.
Honesty in facing a situation is to be brave.
Humility is to know yourself as a sacred part of creation.
Truth is to know all these things.

Spotlight

The ideas of David Bouchard and Joseph Martin as well as the Sharing Circle can be found at these websites www.davidbouchard.com/mtw/sacred.htm and www.thesharingcircle.com/sacred_teachings.htm

When working with Myra in my classroom, we took seven pieces of chart paper and laid them on the floor. Across the top, we wrote the italicized words of these seven teachings. Students moved from chart to chart, freely writing "the first words that came to their mind" associated with the word on the chart. Afterwards, we hung the charts on the wall. We then asked for seven volunteer storytellers —remember, oracy and storytelling are important. The rest of the class, "the listeners" sat in a semicircle, facing the readers, with eyes closed. One by one, the "tellers" read what was written on each chart, while the listeners were asked to experience the sounds and meanings of *wisdom, love, respect, courage, honesty, humility, and truth*. Some time was taken in silence, before a sharing of what was experienced, imagined, and felt took place in the circle. We noticed that everyone had something to say; that is, no matter what culture and life experience we came from, we all held these same values.

One can put the Seven Teachings down the left side of a rubric (Figure 7.2) and a traditional indigenous pedagogy such as the "Four L's of Learning: Look, Listen, Learn, and Live" (Laramee 2008) as the top heading. When working with students, we might use this activity for a rich conversation about what *courage* looks like and sounds like; another about where we learned about it and experiences in which we needed courage.

Portage & Main Press, 2012, *Teaching to Diversity*, ISBN: 978-1-55379-353-3

The Four L's of Learning

The Seven Teachings	Look	Listen	Learn	Live
To cherish knowledge is to seek *wisdom*.				
To know *love* is to find peace.				
To honour all of Creation is to have *respect*.				
Courage is to face life with integrity.				
Honesty in facing a situation is to be brave.				
Humility is to know yourself as a sacred part of Creation.				
Truth is to know all these things.				

Figure 7.2. Rubric of the Seven Teachings

We could do this with each of the teachings. We might choose to build a rubric with the students to determine whether these are happening in our classrooms, schools, and communities. With older students, we could look at newspaper articles and evaluate examples of the presence or lack of these teachings in our world. They can be woven into our units in science and social studies and used to self-assess group work and class climate. The possibilities are endless.

Aboriginal Perspectives on the Three-Block Model of UDL

After I spoke at "Light the Fire," an Elder called me up on stage, turned to me and said: "You have formalized the teachings of our Elders." Then she turned to the audience and said: "All of you, I want you to listen and hear the whispers of your grandmothers speaking to you." Somehow, I believe, those grandmothers must have been speaking to me all those years in the classroom because, without knowing it, I created a system that, although intended to meet the needs of diverse learners, also appears to connect in deep and profound ways with Aboriginal culture and beliefs.

Learning as ceremony is not often considered in our schools, and yet the idea of ceremony is common to many cultures, and integral to traditional Aboriginal education, where rites of passage were moments of great pride for students. In Western cultures, the bar or bat mitzvah, confirmation, and other rites of passage all have to do with a child's readiness to begin to learn, or live, a teaching as well. Graduation ceremonies persist in our schools, even for kindergarten. When we make our classrooms places of spirit and ceremony, transformation happens in our learners. Learning transcends memorization and application practice, and becomes growth worthy of celebration and relationship.

As students in my classes came to see the deeper meanings of concepts and connected them to their own lives and world events, they began to react emotionally, and passionately. They developed fundraisers for a variety of causes, and ceremonially presented a cheque to representatives of these charities or organizations. When Cory began to read, one of the other students insisted that his mother let him use his allowance to buy a bookstore gift card for Cory. We celebrated students meeting their goals, discovering new truths about themselves, and community achievements. When I have used these teachings across boundaries of faith, nationality, culture and lifestyle, the teachings have helped me bring people of diversity to recognize that there is a different movement of energy when focused on similarity, not on difference.

The Three-Block Model of UDL provides us with a bridge to effective Aboriginal education and social and academic inclusion. We can connect our themes to key teachings of the local community, invite Elders in to teach related perspectives and beliefs, allow students to operate from strengths, and take a mentoring role in their learning. By focusing first on the building of community, the valuing of our youth, and the internal characteristics we want to nurture in our children, we embody the Aboriginal values expressed in the Seven Teachings.

Myra once quoted an Elder she knew who said, "We all want the same things for our children." I think it would be a great experience for all our students, Aboriginal and non-Aboriginal alike, to see the depth of Aboriginal spirit and culture, from which we all can learn something.

Portage & Main Press, 2012, *Teaching to Diversity*, ISBN: 978-1-55379-353-3

References

Adelman, Howard S., and Linda Taylor. 1984. "Ethical concerns and identification of psychoeducational problems." *Journal of Clinical Child Psychology* 13 (1): 16–23.

Ainscow, Mel. 1999. *Understanding the development of inclusive schools.* London: Falmer Press.

Ainscow, Mel, and Abha Sandill. 2010. "Developing inclusive education systems: The role of organisational cultures and leadership." *International Journal of Inclusive Education* 14 (4): 401–416.

Anderson, Lorin W., and D. E. Krathwohl. 2001. *A taxonomy for learning, teaching, and assessing: A revision of Bloom's taxonomy of educational objectives.* New York: Addison Wesley Longman: <www.odu.edu/educ/roverbau/Bloom/blooms_taxonomy.htm>. Original publication: Bloom, B. S., M. D. Engelhart, E. J. Furst, W. H. Hill, and D. R. Krathwohl. 1956. *Taxonomy of educational objectives: The classification of educational goals; Handbook I: Cognitive Domain.* New York: Longmans, Green.

Atleo, Marlene R. 2009. "Understanding Aboriginal learning ideology through storywork with Elders." *Alberta Journal of Educational Research* 55 (4): 453–467.

Australian Principals Association: Professional Development Council. <www.apapdc.edu.au/>, <www.pai.edu.au/servlet/Web?s=157573&action=downloadResource>.

Bennett, Sheila. January 2009. "Including students with exceptionalities." Research Monograph 16: *What Works? Research into Practice*: 1–4. St. Catharines, ON: Brock University.

Bloom, Benjamin. *Taxonomy of educational objectives. See* Anderson and Krathwohl.

Bouchard, David, and Joseph Martin. 2009. *Seven sacred teachings of white buffalo calf woman.* North Vancouver, BC: MTW Publishers.

Brendtro, Larry K., Martin Brokenleg, and Steve Van Bockern. 1990. *Reclaiming youth at risk: Our hope for the future.* Bloomington, IN: Solution Tree Publishing.

Brighton, Catherine M., Holly L. Hertberg, Tonya R. Moon, Carol A. Tomlinson, and Carolyn M. Callahan. 2005. "The feasibility of high-end learning in a diverse middle school." National Research Center on the Gifted and Talented (NRCGT). Storrs, CT: University of Connecticut.

British Columbia Ministry of Education: *BC Performance Standards:* <www.bced.gov.bc.ca/perf_stands/>.

Brownlie, Faye. 2005. *Grand conversations, thoughtful responses: A unique approach to literature circles.* Winnipeg, MB: Portage & Main Press.

Burgstahler, Sheryl, and C. Chang. 2009. "Promising interventions for promoting STEM fields to students who have disabilities." *Review of disability studies: An international journal,* 5 (2), 29–47. See <www.washington.edu> for further information on Dr. Burgstahler and her work.

Caine, Renata, and Geoffrey Caine. 1990. "Understanding a brain-based approach to learning and teaching." *Educational Leadership* 48, No. 2, 66–70.

Canadian Council on Learning. 2007. "Equality in the classroom: The educational placement of children with disabilities." Ottawa: Canadian Council on Learning. <www.ccl-cca.ca/CCL/Reports/LessonsInLearning/LinL20070502_Disability_ Provincial_differences.html>.

Canadian Encyclopedia. 2012. "Aboriginal People." <www.thecanadianencyclopedia.com/index.cfm?PgNm=HomePage&Params=A1>

Center for Applied Special Technology (CAST). 2011. <www.cast.org/about/index.html>.

Cole, Cassandra M., Nancy Waldron, and M. Majd. 2004. "Academic progress of students across inclusive and traditional settings." *American Journal on Mental Retardation* 42 (2): 136–144.

Cook, Lynne, and Marilyn Friend. 1995. "Co-Teaching: Guidelines for creating effective practices." *Focus on Exceptional Children* 28 (1) 1–16.

CMEC. 2008. *Report Two: Inclusive Education in Canada: The way of the future*. Council of Ministers of Education, Canada in collaboration with the Canadian Commission for UNESCO: <www.cmec.ca/9/Publications/index.html?searchStr=&searchCat=1>.

Council of Atlantic Ministers of Education and Training: <camet-camef.ca/default.asp?mn=1.81.2>.

Crisman, Belinda W. 2008. "Inclusive programming for students with autism." *Principal*, 88, 28–32. <www.naesp.org>.

Dalai Lama. *See* Glazer.

Davidson, Richard J. 2008. "The heart-brain connection: The neuroscience of social, emotional, and academic learning." A video presented December 10, 2007, at the Collaborative for Academic, Social, and Emotional Learning (CASEL) Forum, New York. The Institute for Social and Emotional Learning, Boulder, CO: Edutopia <www.edutopia.org/richard-davidson-sel-brain-video>.

Dali, Salvador. "Persistence of Memory." Available at: <en.wikipedia.org/wiki/ The_Persistence_of_Memory>.

Deer, Frank. 2010. "Teachers' and principals' perceptions of citizenship development of Aboriginal high school students in the province of Manitoba: An exploratory study." *Canadian Journal of Educational Administration and Policy* 110: 1–33.

Delisle, James. 1986. "Death with honors: Suicide among gifted adolescents." *Journal of Counseling & Development* 64 (9): 558–60.

Dixon, David N., Jill R. Scheckel. 1996. "Gifted adolescent suicide: The empirical base." *Journal of Secondary Gifted Education* 7 (3): 386–92.

Dwyer, Brian M. 2002. "Training strategies for the twenty-first century: Using recent research on learning to enhance training." *Innovations in Education and Teaching International* 39 (1): 265–270.

Elias, Maurice J. 2004. "The connection between social-emotional learning and learning disabilities: Implications for intervention." *Learning Disability Quarterly* 27: 53–63.

Fox, Mem. 2000. *Feathers and Fools*. Illustrator: Nicholas Wilton. Boston, MA: Houghton Mifflin Harcourt.

Friend, Marilyn, and Lynne Cook. 2010. *Interactions: Collaboration skills for school professionals*, 6th ed. Toronto, ON: Higher Education, Pearson Canada.

Froese-Germain, Bernie. 1999. *Standardized testing: Undermining equity in education.* <www.ctf-fce.ca>, <www.eric.ed.gov/ERICWebPortal/contentdelivery/servlet/ERICServlet?accno=ED440107>.

Fullan, Michael. 2007. *The new meaning of educational change*, 4th ed. New York: Teachers College Press.

Gardner, Howard E. 1983. *Frames of mind: The theory of multiple intelligences.* New York: Basic Books.

Gardner, Howard E. 1995. "Multiple intelligences as a catalyst." *English Journal* 84 (8): 16–18.

Gardner, Howard E. 1999. *Intelligence reframed.* New York: Basic Books.

Gardner, Howard E. 2009. "The five minds for the future: Cultivating and integrating new ways of thinking to empower the education enterprise." *The School Administrator* 66 (2): 16–21.

Giangreco, Michael F., Susan W. Edelman, Tracy Evans Luiselli, Stephanie Z. C. MacFarland. 1997. "Helping or hovering? Effects of instructional assistant proximity on students with disabilities." *Exceptional Children* 64 (1): 7–18.

Giangreco, Michael F., and Mary Beth Doyle. 2002. "Students with disabilities and paraprofessional supports: Benefits, balance, and band-aids." *Focus on Exceptional Children* 34 (7): 1–12.

Giangreco, Michael F. 2010. "Utilization of teacher assistants in inclusive schools: Is it the kind of help that helping is all about?" *European Journal of Special Needs Education* 25 (4): 341–345.

Glazer, Steven. 1997. "The heart of learning: Spirituality in education." Presentations from the conference by Naropa Institute, CA.

Goleman, Daniel. 2006. *Social intelligence: The new science of social relationships.* New York: Bantam Books.

Government of Canada. 1982. *Canadian Charter of Rights and Freedoms.* <laws-lois.justice.gc.ca/eng/charter/page-1.html#anchorbo-ga:l_I>.

Graczyk, Patricia A., Roger P. Weissberg, John W. Payton, Maurice J. Elias, Mark T. Greenberg, and Joseph E. Zins. 2000. "Criteria for evaluating the quality of school-based social and emotional learning programs." In *The handbook of emotional intelligence: Theory, development, assessment, and application at home, school, and in the workplace*, edited by Reuven Bar-On, and James D. A. Parker, 391–410. San Francisco, CA: Jossey-Bass, A Wiley Company.

Greenberg, Mark T., Celene Domitrovich, and Brian Bumbarger. 2001. "The prevention of mental disorders in school-age children: Current state of the field." Originally published in 2000 by the former PA CASSP Training and Technical Assistance Institute. © 2008, Office of Mental Health and Substance Abuse Services: Harrisburg, PA.

Grover, Rachel L., Golda S. Ginsburg, and Nick Ialongo. 2007. "Psychosocial outcomes of anxious first graders: A seven-year follow-up." *Depression and Anxiety* 24 (6): 410–420.

Gunn, Thelma M., Guy Pomahac, Evelyn G. Striker, and Johnel Tailfeathers. 2011. "First Nations, Métis, and Inuit education: The Alberta initiative for school improvement approach to improve indigenous education in Alberta." *Journal of Educational Change* 12 (3): 323–345.

Haldane, Scott, George E. Lafond, and Caroline Krause. 2011. "Nurturing the learning spirit of First Nation students: The report of the National Panel on First Nation elementary and secondary education for students on reserve." <firstnationeducation.ca/home/>.

Hargreaves, Andrew. 2007. "The long and short of educational change." *Education Canada* 47 (3): 16–23.

Hearne, Dixon, and Suki Stone. 1995. "Multiple intelligences and underachievement: Lessons from individuals with learning disabilities." *Journal of Learning Disabilities* 28: 439–448.

Hiebert, James, Ronald Gallimore, and James W. Stigler. 2002. "A knowledge base for the teaching profession: What would it look like and how can we get one?" *Educational Researcher* 31 (5): 3–15.

Jacobson, Stephen L., Lauri Johnson, Rose Ylimaki, and Cori Giles. 2005. "Successful leadership in challenging US schools: Enabling principles, enabling schools." *Journal of Educational Administration* 43 (6): 607–618.

Jussim, Lee, and Kent D. Harber. 2005. "Teacher expectations and self-fulfilling prophecies: Knowns and unknowns, resolved and unresolved controversies."*Personality and Social Psychology Review* 9 (2): 131–155.

Katz, Jennifer, and Pat Mirenda. 2002. "Including students with developmental disabilities in general education classrooms: Educational benefits." *International Journal of Special Education* 17 (2): 14–24.

Katz, Jennifer, and Pat Mirenda. 2002. "Including students with developmental disabilities in general education classrooms: Social benefits." *International Journal of Special Education* 17 (2): 25–35.

Katz, Jennifer, and Marion Porath. 2011. "Teaching to diversity: Creating compassionate learning communities for diverse elementary school students." *International Journal of Special Education* 26 (2): 1–13.

Katz, Jennifer, Marion Porath, Charles Bendu, and Brent Epp. 2012. "Diverse voices: Middle years students' insights into life in inclusive classrooms." *Exceptionality Education International*, 22 (1): 2–16.

Kessler, Rachael. 1998/99. "Nourishing students in secular schools." *Educational Leadership* 56 (4): 49–52.

Kugelmass, J. W. 2006. "Sustaining cultures of inclusion: The value and limitation of cultural analyses." *European Journal of Psychology of Education* XXI (3): 279–292.

Laramee, Myra. 2008. "Four L's of Learning" found in "Aboriginal Education in Canadian Public Schools: A Case Study of Four Inner City Elementary Principals and Their Vision of Aboriginal Education." *First Nations Perspectives* 1 (1): 57–73.

Lawrence-Brown, D. 2004. "Differentiated instruction: Inclusive strategies for standards-based learning that benefit the whole class." *American Secondary Education* 32 (3): 34–63.

Lazear, David. 1992. *Teaching for multiple intelligences,* Fastback no. 342, 17, 18. Bloomington, IN: Phi Delta Kappa Educational Foundation.

Leithwood, Kenneth, and Carolyn Riehl. 2005. "What do we already know about educational leadership?" In *A new agenda for research in educational leadership*, edited by William A. Firestone and Carolyn Riehl, 12–27. New York: Teachers College Press.

Levine, Melvin D. 2002. *Educational care: A system for understanding and helping children with learning differences at home and in school*, 2nd ed. Cambridge, MA: Educators Publishing Service.

Little, Mary E., and Lisa A. Dieker. 2009. "Co-Teaching: Two are better than one." *Principal Leadership* 9 (8): 42–46.

Mace, Ronald L., Molly F. Story, and James L. Mueller. 1998. "A brief history of universal design." In *The universal design file: Designing for people of all ages and abilities*. Raleigh, NC: Center for Universal Design. North Carolina State University. <www.design.ncsu.edu/cud/publications/udfiletoc.htm1>.

Malecki, Christine Kerres, and Stephen N. Elliott. 2002. "Children's social behaviors as predictors of academic achievement: A longitudinal analysis." *School Psychology Quarterly* 17 (1): 1–23.

Manitoba Aboriginal and Northern Affairs. 2011. "Aboriginal people in Manitoba 2000." <www.gov.mb.ca/ana/apm2000/2/d.html>.

Manitoba Education and Literacy. 2005. *The Public Schools Act: Appropriate Educational Programming* (Regulation 155/2005) 70; Information Supporting The Public Schools Amendment Act (Appropriate Educational Programming) Regulation 155/2005. <www.edu.gov.mb.ca.edu>.

Manitoba Education and Literacy: <www.edu.gov.mb.ca/k12/index.html>.
    K–12 Curriculum: <www.edu.gov.mb.ca/k12/cur/index.html>.
    Science: <www.edu.gov.mb.ca/k12/cur/science/index.html>.
    Social Studies: <www.edu.gov.mb.ca/k12/cur/socstud/index.html>.

Manitoba First Nations Education Resource Centre: <www.mfnerc.org/>.

Marcus, Leonard S. 1998. *Dear Genius: The letters of Ursula Nordstrom*. Collected and edited by L. S. Marcus. Illustrated by Maurice Sendak. New York: HarperCollins. <www.leonardmarcus.com/biblio06.html>.

Mawdsley, Ralph D. 1995. "Does inclusion cost more? The cost of special education." *School Business Affairs* 61 (7): 27–31.

McLaughlin, Margaret J., and Sandra Hopfengardner Warren. 1994. "The costs of inclusion." *School Administrator* 51(10): 8–12, 16–19.

Mendelson, Michael. 2008. "Improving education on reserves: A First Nations Education Authority Act." Ottawa: Caledon Institute of Social Policy: <www.caledoninst.org/Publications/Search/>.

Miller, John P. 1998/1999. "Making connections through holistic learning." *Educational Leadership* 56: 46–48.

Modrcin-McCarthy, M. A., and M. M. Dalton. 1996. "Responding to healthy people 2000: Depression in our youth, common yet misunderstood." *Issues in Comprehensive Pediatric Nursing* 19 (4): 275–90.

Moyer A. E., J. Rodin, C. M. Grilo, N. Cummings, L. M. Larson, and M. Rebuffé-Scrive. 1994. "Stress-induced cortisol response and fat distribution in women." *Obesity Research* 2 (3): 255–62.

Murawski, Wendy W., and Claire E. Hughes. 2009. "Response to intervention, collaboration, and co-teaching: A logical combination for successful systemic change." *Preventing School Failure* 53 (4): 267–77.

Noddings, Nel. 1995. "Teaching themes of care." *Phi Delta Kappan* 76 (3): 675–79.

O'Boyle, Michael. 2008. "Mathematically gifted children: Developmental brain characteristics and their prognosis for well-being." *Roeper Review* 30 (3): 181–186.

Ontario Ministry of Education. 2009. *Realizing the promise of diversity: Ontario's Equity and Inclusive Education Strategy.* <edu.gov.on.ca/eng/policyfunding/equity.pdf.>

Palmer, Parker J. 1998/1999. "Evoking the spirit in public education." *Educational Leadership* 56: 6–1.

Palmer, Parker J. 2007. *The courage to teach: Exploring the inner landscape of a teacher's life.* San Francisco, CA: Jossey-Bass, a Wiley company.

Porath, Marion. 2003. "Social understanding in the first years of school." *Early Childhood Research Quarterly* 18: 468–85.

Prelutsky, Jack, and Lane Smith. 1998. *Hooray for Diffendoofer Day!* New York: RandomHouse, Knopf Books for Young Readers.

Reeve, Johnmarshall. 2006. "Teachers as facilitators: What autonomy-supportive teachers do and why their students benefit." *Elementary School Journal* 106: 225–236.

Riehl, Carolyn J. 2000. "The principal's role in creating inclusive schools for diverse students: A review of normative, empirical, and critical literature on the practice of educational administration." *Review of Educational Research* 70 (1): 55–81. <rer.sagepub.com/search/results?fulltext=Riehl%2C+C.+J&submit=yes&journal_set=sprer&src=selected&andorexactfulltext=and&x=14&y=16>.

Rose, David H., and Anne Meyer. 2002. *Teaching every student in the Digital Age: Universal Design for Learning.* Alexandria, VA. <www.cast.org/teachingeverystudent/ideas/tes/>.

Rubie-Davies, Christine M., Elizabeth Peterson, Earl Irving, Deborah Widdowson, and Robyn Dixon. 2010. "Expectations of achievement: Student, teacher and parent perceptions." *Research in Education* 83 (1): 36–53.

Ruijs, Nienke M., and Thea T. D. Peetsma. 2009. "Effects of inclusion on students with and without special educational needs reviewed." *Educational Research Review* 4 (2): 67–79.

Schonert-Reichl, Kimberley A., Veronica Smith, Anat Zaidman-Zait, and Clyde Hertzman. 2011. "Promoting children's prosocial behaviors in school: Impact of the "Roots of Empathy" program on the social and emotional competence of school-aged children." *School Mental Health* 4: 1–21. <www.rootsofempathy.org/>.

Shepard, J. S. 2004. "Multiple ways of knowing: Fostering resiliency through providing opportunities for participating in learning." *Reclaiming Children & Youth* 12: 210–17.

Silver, Debbie. 2005. *Drumming to the beat of different marchers.* Nashville, TN: Incentive Publications.

Specht, Jacqueline, and Jennifer Katz. (forthcoming). "Perspectives on teaching and diversity." In *Understanding and addressing student diversity in Canadian schools* by J. W. Andrews and J. L. Lupart, eds. Toronto, ON: Nelson Education.

Sterenberg, Gladys, and Michelle Hogue. 2011. "Reconsidering approaches to Aboriginal science and mathematics education." *Alberta Journal of Educational Research* 57 (1): 1–15.

Stonechild, Blair. 2006. *The new buffalo: The struggle for Aboriginal post-secondary education in Canada.* Winnipeg, MB: University of Manitoba Press.

Stonechild, Blair. 2012. "Fallacies in First Nations-White relationship." *CAUT Bulletin 59* (2).

Stuart, S. K., and C. Rinaldi. 2009. "A collaborative planning framework for teachers implementing tiered instruction." *Teaching Exceptional Children* 42 (2): 52–57.

Symes, W., and N. Humphrey. 2010. "Peer-group indicators of social inclusion among pupils with autistic spectrum disorders (ASD) in mainstream secondary schools: A comparative study." *School Psychology International* 31 (5): 478–94.

Timmons, V., and M. Wagner. 2008. "Inclusive education knowledge exchange initiative: An analysis of the Statistics Canada Participation and Activity Limitation Survey." Canadian Council on Learning. <www.cclcca.ca/CCL/Research/FundedResearch/201009TimmonsInclusiveEducation.html>.

UNESCO: <www.unesco.org>.

UNESCO. 1994. *Salamanca Statement and Framework for Action on Special Needs Education from the World Conference on Special Needs Education: Access and Quality.* Salamanca, Spain, 7–10 June 1994. <unesdoc.unesco.org/images/0009/000984/098427eo.pdf>.

United Nations. 1948. *Universal Declaration of Human Rights.* </www.unac.org/en/link_learn/hr_toolkit/udhr.asp>.

Valaskakis, Gail Guthrie. 2005. *Indian country: Essays on contemporary native culture.* Waterloo, ON: Wilfrid Laurier University Press. <www.wlu.ca/press/Catalog/valaskakis.shtml>.

Van De Walle, John A., and Lou Ann H. Lovin. 2006. *Teaching student-centered mathematics, grades 5–8.* Boston, MA: Allyn & Bacon/Pearson Education.

WNCP, Western and Northern Canadian Protocol: Common Curriculum Framework for Aboriginal Languages and Cultural Programs. 2000: "Aboriginal Languages Consultation Report," April 2001. <www.edu.gov.mb.ca/abedu/proactive_report.pdf>.

Wiggins, Grant, and Jay McTighe. 2001. *Understanding by design.* New Jersey: Prentice Hall Inc.

Wilhelm, Jeffrey. 2007. *Engaging readers and writers with inquiry.* New York: Scholastic.

Wilson, Shawn. 2008. *Research is ceremony: Indigenous research methods.* Winnipeg, MB: Fernwood Publishing. <fernwoodpublishing.ca/Research-Is-Ceremony-Shawn-Wilson/>.

Winnipeg School Division: *Seven Teachings.* "Principles of Aboriginal Education." <www.wsd1.org/prosupport/documents/AbEdTrusteesPresentation-June9_002.pdf>.

Wotherspoon, Terry. 2002. "Dynamics of social inclusion: Public education and Aboriginal people in Canada." *Working Paper Series on Social Inclusion.* Toronto, ON: Laidlaw Foundation. <www.laidlawfdn.org/working-paper-series-social-inclusion>.

Zins, Joseph E., Michelle R. Bloodworth, Roger P. Weissberg, and Herbert J. Walberg. 2004. "The scientific base linking social and emotional learning to school success." In *Building academic success on social and emotional learning: What does the research say?*, 3–22, by Joseph E. Zins, Roger P. Weissberg, Margaret C. Wang, and Herbert J. Walberg, eds. New York: Teachers College Press.

Appendix
Multiple Intelligences Surveys

The following pages contain blackline masters for a 4-part survey originally developed by Walter McKenzie, a teacher intrigued by Howard Gardner's outline of "multiple intelligences," who posted the survey on his website <www.surfaquarium.com> for other educators to use or adapt—and I am one educator who has adapted it (see chapter 2, beginning on page 19, and chapter 3, beginning on page 31) for use in my Respecting Diversity Program.

I made the adaptations in order to provide questions in Part 1 at three different levels (Early Years, Middle Years, and Adolescents) for students to describe their current learning profile. Students' responses to the statements in Part 1, which are grouped in Garner's nine categories of intelligences, guide them in self-awareness and provide an opportunity for students to gain a deeper understanding of each intelligence as they mark their likes and interests.

The follow-up activities in Parts 2, 3, and 4—which are the same for all three levels—guide students in summarizing and graphing the results of their work on Part 1.

To summarize: each of the three levels of Part 1 has 3 pages, but each student at all levels will also need a copy of the page containing Parts 2 and 3 and the page containing Part 4. The last page provides an example of how to prepare the bar graph in Part 4, and teachers might just provide a few copies as a model to groups of students.

Early Years Survey: Multiple Intelligences, Part 1
Middle Years Survey: Multiple Intelligences, Part 1
Adolescent and Adult Survey: Multiple Intelligences, Part 1
Part 2 and Part 3 (same for all 3 levels)
Part 4 (blank bar graph) (same for all 3 levels)
Part 4 Example (same for all 3 levels)

Early Years Survey—Multiple Intelligences

Part 1

This survey has 9 sections. Each section has 10 statements. Read each statement, and think about whether it describes you, or how you think, or how you feel most of the time. If you think the statement is true for you, write a 1 on the line beside it. Then add up the 1's, and write your total for the section.

Section 1

_____ I enjoy sorting things into groups or collecting similar things.

_____ I care about plants and trees.

_____ Hiking and camping are fun.

_____ I like taking care of plants or helping in the garden.

_____ I think we should save parks for animals and trees to live in.

_____ I like putting things in order.

_____ Animals are important in my life.

_____ I recycle cans, bottles, and paper.

_____ I like learning about animals, plants, and science.

_____ I like playing outside a lot.

_____ **TOTAL for Section 1**

Section 2

_____ I hum or sing a lot to myself without even realizing I'm doing it.

_____ I pay attention to noise and sounds.

_____ Dancing to a beat is easy for me.

_____ I am interested in playing an instrument.

_____ I like listening to poetry.

_____ I remember things by putting them in a rhyme.

_____ I like listening to music while I'm doing things.

_____ I like lots of different kinds of music.

_____ I like movies with singing and dancing in them.

_____ Remembering the words in songs is easy for me.

_____ **TOTAL for Section 2**

Section 3

_____ I keep my things neat and orderly.

_____ It helps me when people tell me how to do things one step at a time.

_____ Solving problems comes easily to me.

_____ I ask a lot of questions about how things work.

_____ I can do math quickly in my head.

_____ I like trying to figure things out.

_____ I cannot start my work until I know for sure all the things I have to do.

_____ It's easier for me to do new things when teachers or parents tell me exactly how.

Adapted from www.surfaquarium.com, ©1999 Walter McKenzie

_____ I like using the computer to do my work.

_____ If something doesn't make sense to me, I get upset.

_____ **TOTAL for Section 3**

Section 4

_____ I like helping people.

_____ I enjoy discussing questions about life.

_____ Religion is important to me, and I like going to church or temple or mosque.

_____ I like looking at paintings and sculptures.

_____ I like to relax and think about things, and I daydream a lot.

_____ I like to visit beautiful places in nature.

_____ I think about what happens to people when they die.

_____ Learning new things is easier when I know why it's important.

_____ I wonder if there are other forms of intelligent life in the universe—like aliens.

_____ Studying about what people used to do and think long ago is interesting to me.

_____ **TOTAL for Section 4**

Section 5

_____ I learn best when I work with others.

_____ I like having lots of people around.

_____ It helps me when I practise things with a partner.

_____ I like "talking" to people on the phone, or in email, or texting.

_____ I have more than 3 friends.

_____ I am a leader among my friends.

_____ I understand how other people feel, and I try to help them.

_____ I like to teach other kids.

_____ Clubs and extracurricular activities are fun for me.

_____ Lots of people ask me to play with them.

_____ **TOTAL for Section 5**

Section 6

_____ I enjoy making things with my hands.

_____ Sitting still for long periods of time is difficult for me.

_____ I like outdoor games and sports.

_____ I pay attention to the looks on people's faces when they're talking.

_____ I try to keep my body healthy.

_____ I like to take things apart and put them back together again.

_____ I like watching people dance.

_____ I like working with tools.

_____ I do a lot of sports, or I exercise a lot.

_____ I learn by doing and touching.

_____ **TOTAL for Section 6**

Adapted from www.surfaquarium.com, ©1999 Walter McKenzie

Portage & Main Press, 2012, _Teaching to Diversity_, ISBN: 978-1-55379-353-3

Section 7

_____ I enjoy reading books, magazines, and comics.

_____ I know a lot of words for someone my age.

_____ I like writing, whether letters or emails or poems or stories.

_____ It is easy for me to explain my ideas to others.

_____ I am good at spelling.

_____ I like listening to other people talk or read stories.

_____ I write for fun. OR I keep a diary.

_____ I like riddles and jokes.

_____ I find making up stories is fun.

_____ I like talking in front of the class.

_____ **TOTAL for Section 7**

Section 8

_____ I know what is appropriate to do and what is not appropriate.

_____ I learn best when I care about what I am studying.

_____ Fairness is important to me.

_____ I like playing alone or just being alone.

_____ I am very independent, and I like things that none of my friends do.

_____ I like to work alone.

_____ I need to know why I should do something before I agree to do it

_____ When I like something, I try my hardest at it.

_____ I know what I am good at.

_____ I tell people when I think something they do is not nice.

_____ **TOTAL for Section 8**

Section 9

_____ I have a good imagination.

_____ I like re-arranging my things in my room.

_____ I enjoy creating art.

_____ I use webs, mind maps, and pictures to remember things.

_____ Watching people perform (act, dance, or sing) is fun for me.

_____ I like creating or working with pictures and graphics on the computer.

_____ I like making things with Lego, K'Nex, and other building materials.

_____ I like puzzles.

_____ I can remember what things looked like months ago and even years ago.

_____ I am a good artist.

_____ **TOTAL for Section 9**

Portage & Main Press, 2012, _Teaching to Diversity_, ISBN: 978-1-55379-353-3

Middle Years Survey—Multiple Intelligences

Part 1

This survey has 9 sections. Each section has 10 statements. Read each statement, and think about whether it describes you, or how you think, or how you feel most of the time. If you think the statement is true for you, write a 1 on the line beside it. Then add up the 1's, and write your total for the section.

Section 1

_____ I enjoy sorting things into groups or collecting similar things.

_____ I care about plants and trees.

_____ Hiking and camping are fun.

_____ I like taking care of plants or helping in the garden.

_____ I care about environmental issues like logging and global warming.

_____ I like putting things in order.

_____ Animals are important in my life.

_____ I recycle cans, bottles, and paper.

_____ I like learning about animals, plants, and science.

_____ I like playing outside a lot.

_____ **TOTAL for Section 1**

Section 2

_____ I hum or sing a lot to myself without even realizing I'm doing it.

_____ I pay attention to noise and sounds.

_____ Moving to a beat is easy for me.

_____ I am interested in playing an instrument.

_____ I like listening to poetry.

_____ I remember things by putting them in a rhyme.

_____ I like listening to music while I'm studying or doing homework.

_____ I like lots of different kinds of music.

_____ I like movies with singing and dancing in them, and I like music videos.

_____ Remembering the words in songs is easy for me.

_____ **TOTAL for Section 2**

Section 3

_____ I keep my things neat and orderly.

_____ Step-by-step directions are a big help when I'm trying to do things.

_____ Solving problems comes easily to me.

_____ I ask a lot of questions about how things work.

_____ I can do math quickly in my head.

_____ Word problems and brain teasers are fun for me.

_____ I cannot start my work until I know for sure all the things I have to do.

_____ It's easier for me to do new things when teachers or parents tell me exactly how.

Portage & Main Press, 2012, *Teaching to Diversity*, ISBN: 978-1-55379-353-3

_____ I like using the computer to do my work.

_____ If something doesn't make sense to me, I get upset.

_____ **TOTAL for Section 3**

Section 4

_____ It is important to me to know how I fit in with the world or a group.

_____ I enjoy discussing questions about life.

_____ Religion is important to me, and I like going to church or temple or mosque, and praying.

_____ I like looking at paintings and sculptures.

_____ I like relaxation and meditation exercises.

_____ It is inspiring to visit beautiful places in nature.

_____ I enjoy reading about what ancient and modern people thought about the world.

_____ Learning new things is easier when I know why it's important.

_____ I wonder if there are other forms of intelligent life in the universe — like aliens.

_____ Studying about what people used to do and think long ago is interesting to me.

_____ **TOTAL for Section 4**

Section 5

_____ I learn best when I work with others.

_____ I like having lots of people around.

_____ It helps me when I practise things with a partner.

_____ I like "talking" to people on the phone, or in email, or texting.

_____ I have more than 3 friends.

_____ I am a leader among my friends.

_____ I understand how other people feel, and I try to help them.

_____ I like to teach other kids.

_____ Clubs and extracurricular activities are fun for me.

_____ Lots of people ask me to play or hang out with them.

_____ **TOTAL for Section 5**

Section 6

_____ I enjoy making things with my hands.

_____ Sitting still for long periods of time is difficult for me.

_____ I like outdoor games and sports.

_____ I pay attention to the looks on people's faces when they're talking.

_____ I try to keep my body healthy.

_____ I like to take things apart and put them back together again.

_____ I like watching people dance.

_____ I like working with tools.

_____ I do a lot of sports, or I exercise a lot.

_____ I learn by doing and touching.

_____ **TOTAL for Section 6**

Portage & Main Press, 2012, _Teaching to Diversity_, ISBN: 978-1-55379-353-3

Section 7

_____ I enjoy reading books, magazines, and comics.

_____ I know a lot of words for someone my age.

_____ I like writing or texting, whether letters or emails or poems or stories.

_____ It is easy for me to explain my ideas to others.

_____ I can spell words accurately.

_____ I like listening to other people talk or read stories.

_____ I write for fun. OR I keep a diary.

_____ I enjoy playing with words like puns, anagrams, or tongue twisters.

_____ The lyrics in a song matter to me.

_____ I like talking in front of the class.

_____ **TOTAL for Section 7**

Section 8

_____ I know what is appropriate to do and what is not appropriate.

_____ I learn best when I care about what I am studying.

_____ Fairness is important to me.

_____ I like playing alone or just being alone.

_____ I am very independent, and like doing my own thing.

_____ I like to work alone.

_____ I need to know why I should do something before I agree to do it.

_____ When I like something, I try my hardest at it.

_____ I know what I am good at.

_____ I tell people when I think something they do is not nice.

_____ **TOTAL for Section 8**

Section 9

_____ I have a good imagination.

_____ Re-arranging a room is fun for me.

_____ I enjoy creating art.

_____ I use webs, mind maps, and pictures to remember what I learn.

_____ Watching people perform (act, dance, or sing) is fun for me.

_____ I like creating or working with pictures and graphics on the computer.

_____ I like creating models and images.

_____ I daydream more than other kids.

_____ I can recall what things looked like months ago and even years ago.

_____ I am a good artist.

_____ **TOTAL for Section 9**

Adolescent and Adult Survey—Multiple Intelligences

Part 1

This survey has 9 sections. Each section has 10 statements. Read each statement, and think about whether it describes you, or how you think, or how you feel most of the time. If you think the statement is true for you, write a 1 on the line beside it. Then add up the 1's, and write your total for the section.

Section 1

_____ I enjoy categorizing things by common traits.
_____ Environmental issues are important to me.
_____ Hiking and camping are enjoyable activities.
_____ I enjoy working in a garden.
_____ I believe preserving our National Parks is important.
_____ Putting things in hierarchies makes sense to me.
_____ Animals are important in my life.
_____ My home has a recycling system in place.
_____ I enjoy studying biology, botany, or zoology.
_____ I spend a great deal of time outdoors.
_____ **TOTAL for Section 1**

Section 2

_____ I easily pick up on patterns.
_____ I focus in on noise and sounds.
_____ Moving to a beat is easy for me.
_____ I've always been interested in playing an instrument.
_____ The rhythm of poetry intrigues me.
_____ I remember things by putting them in a rhyme.
_____ Concentration is difficult while listening to a radio or television.
_____ I enjoy many kinds of music.
_____ Musicals are more interesting than dramatic plays.
_____ Remembering song lyrics is easy for me.
_____ **TOTAL for Section 2**

Section 3

_____ I keep my things neat and orderly.
_____ Step-by-step directions are a big help.
_____ Solving problems comes easily to me.
_____ I get easily frustrated with disorganized people.
_____ I can complete calculations quickly in my head.
_____ Logic puzzles are fun.
_____ I cannot begin an assignment until all my questions are answered.
_____ Structure helps me be successful.

   Adapted from www.surfaquarium.com, ©1999 Walter McKenzie

_____ I find working on a computer spreadsheet or database interesting.

_____ Things have to make sense to me, or I am dissatisfied.

_____ **TOTAL for Section 3**

Section 4

_____ It is important to me to see my role in the "big picture" of things.

_____ I enjoy discussing questions about life.

_____ Religion is important to me.

_____ I enjoy viewing art masterpieces.

_____ Relaxation and meditation exercises are rewarding.

_____ I like visiting breathtaking sites in nature.

_____ I enjoy reading ancient and modern philosophers.

_____ Learning new things is easier when I understand their value.

_____ I wonder if there are other forms of intelligent life in the universe.

_____ Studying history and ancient cultures helps give me perspective.

_____ **TOTAL for Section 4**

Section 5

_____ I learn best when interacting with others.

_____ The more people, the merrier.

_____ Study groups are very productive for me.

_____ I enjoy chat rooms.

_____ Participating in politics is important.

_____ Television and radio talk shows are enjoyable.

_____ I am a "team player."

_____ I dislike working alone.

_____ Clubs and extracurricular activities are fun for me.

_____ I pay attention to social issues and causes.

_____ **TOTAL for Section 5**

Section 6

_____ I enjoy making things with my hands.

_____ Sitting still for long periods of time is difficult for me.

_____ I enjoy outdoor games and sports.

_____ I value non-verbal communication such as sign language.

_____ I think a fit body is important.

_____ Arts and crafts are enjoyable pastimes.

_____ Expression through dance is beautiful.

_____ I like working with tools.

_____ I live an active lifestyle.

_____ I learn by doing.

_____ **TOTAL for Section 6**

Adapted from www.surfaquarium.com, ©1999 Walter McKenzie   Portage & Main Press, 2012, *Teaching to Diversity*, ISBN: 978-1-55379-353-3

Section 7

_____ I enjoy reading all kinds of materials.

_____ Taking notes helps me remember and understand what I hear or read.

_____ I keep in touch with family and friends through letters, texting, and email.

_____ It is easy for me to explain my ideas to others.

_____ I keep a journal.

_____ Word puzzles like crosswords and jumbles are fun.

_____ I write for pleasure.

_____ I enjoy playing with words like puns, anagrams, and spoonerisms.

_____ Foreign languages interest me.

_____ Debates and public speaking are activities I like to participate in.

_____ **TOTAL for Section 7**

Section 8

_____ I am keenly aware of my moral beliefs.

_____ I learn best when I have an emotional attachment to the subject.

_____ Fairness is important to me.

_____ My attitude affects how I learn.

_____ Social justice issues concern me.

_____ Working alone can be just as productive as working in a group.

_____ I need to know why I should do something before I agree to do it.

_____ When I believe in something, I will give 100% effort to it.

_____ I like to be involved in causes that help others.

_____ I am willing to protest or sign a petition to right a wrong.

_____ **TOTAL for Section 8**

Section 9

_____ I have a good imagination.

_____ Re-arranging a room is fun for me.

_____ I enjoy creating art, using varied media.

_____ I use graphic organizers to remember what I learn.

_____ Performance art can be very gratifying.

_____ Spreadsheets are great for making charts, graphs, and tables.

_____ Three-dimensional puzzles bring me much enjoyment.

_____ Music videos are very stimulating.

_____ When recalling things or events, I form mental pictures of them.

_____ I am good at reading maps and blueprints.

_____ **TOTAL for Section 9**

Portage & Main Press, 2012, *Teaching to Diversity*, ISBN: 978-1-55379-353-3

Part 2

Transfer your total points from each section to this table.

Section + M.I.	Total Points
1 Naturalistic	
2 Musical-Rhythmic	
3 Logical-Mathematical	
4 Existential	
5 Inter-personal	
6 Bodily-Kinesthetic	
7 Verbal-Linguistic	
8 Intrapersonal	
9 Visual-Spatial	

Part 3: Key to Totals

Section 1: This total reflects your Naturalistic strength.
Section 2: This total suggests your Musical-Rhythmic strength.
Section 3: This total indicates your Logical-Mathematical strength.
Section 4: This total illustrates your Existential strength.
Section 5: This total shows your Interpersonal strength.
Section 6: This total tells your Bodily-Kinesthetic strength.
Section 7: This total indicates your Verbal-Linguistic strength.
Section 8: This total reflects your Intrapersonal strength.
Section 9: This total suggests your Visual-Spatial strength.

Adapted from www.surfaquarium.com, ©1999 Walter McKenzie

Portage & Main Press, 2012, *Teaching to Diversity*, ISBN: 978-1-55379-353-3

Part 4

My Intelligence Profile

Transfer your totals for each section to this table. Then, use your ruler to create a bar graph.

	Section 1 Naturalistic	Section 2 Musical-Rhythmic	Section 3 Logical-Mathematical	Section 4 Existential	Section 5 Interpersonal	Section 6 Bodily-Kinesthetic	Section 7 Verbal-Linguistic	Section 8 Intrapersonal	Section 9 Visual-Spatial
Total 10/10									
Total 9/10									
Total 8/10									
Total 7/10									
Total 6/10									
Total 5/10									
Total 4/10									
Total 3/10									
Total 2/10									
Total 1/10									
Survey Sections	Section 1 Naturalistic	Section 2 Musical-Rhythmic	Section 3 Logical-Mathematical	Section 4 Existential	Section 5 Interpersonal	Section 6 Bodily-Kinesthetic	Section 7 Verbal-Linguistic	Section 8 Intrapersonal	Section 9 Visual-Spatial

The Totals suggest that my intelligence strengths are _____,

_____, and _____.

The Totals also suggest that I need support to strengthen my abilities and interests in _____,

_____ and _____.

Adapted from www.surfaquarium.com, ©1999 Walter McKenzie

For example:

Survey Sections	Section 1 Naturalistic	Section 2 Musical-Rhythmic	Section 3 Logical-Mathematical	Section 4 Existential	Section 5 Interpersonal	Section 6 Bodily-Kinesthetic	Section 7 Verbal-Linguistic	Section 8 Intrapersonal	Section 9 Visual-Spatial
Total 10/10									
Total 9/10							9		
Total 8/10									
Total 7/10					7				7
Total 6/10									
Total 5/10		5							
Total 4/10						4			
Total 3/10			3						
Total 2/10				2				2	
Total 1/10	1								

The Totals suggest that my intelligence strengths are _____ verbal-linguistic _____,

_____ interpersonal _____, and _____ visual-spatial _____.

The Totals also suggest that I need support to strengthen my abilities and interests in _____ naturalistic _____,

_____ existential _____, and _____ intrapersonal _____.

Portage & Main Press, 2012, Teaching to Diversity, ISBN: 978-1-55379-353-3